1993

The Bill of Rights
in Modern America

The Bill of Rights
in Modern America
After 200 Years

EDITED BY

David J. Bodenhamer

AND

James W. Ely, Jr.

Indiana University Press
Bloomington & Indianapolis

Manufactured in the United States of America

Library of Congress Cataloging-in-Publication Data

The Bill of Rights in modern America : after 200 years / edited by
David J. Bodenhamer and James W. Ely, Jr.
    p.   cm.
    Includes bibliographical references (p.   ) and index.
    ISBN 0-253-31223-X (cloth : alk. paper). — ISBN 0-253-20767-3
(paper)
    1. United States—Constitutional law—Amendments—1st-10th.
2. Civil rights—United States.   I. Bodenhamer, David J.   II. Ely,
James W., date.
KF4550.A2B49   1993
342.73'085—dc20
[347.30285]   92-15815

1   2   3   4   5   97   96   95   94   93

Contents

148, 460

PART THREE: Rights Remembered, Revised, and Extended

Introduction

James W. Ely, Jr., and David J. Bodenhamer

The bicentennial of the Bill of Rights is unquestionably an occasion for celebration. It also provides an opportunity to review the place of the Bill of Rights in American life and our constitutional order. The essays in this volume, written for a general audience, examine the significance of the Bill of Rights in modern society. Although informed by a historical perspective, the authors focus on contemporary issues and explore the current understanding of the Bill of Rights.

American thinking about rights has evolved over time. The framers of the Constitution made a conscious decision to omit a Bill of Rights. They reasoned that it was unnecessary to restrain a federal government of limited powers. The framers also believed that state bills of rights offered adequate protection to individuals. During the ratification debates, however, the Anti-Federalists used the absence of a Bill of Rights as a powerful weapon to oppose the proposed Constitution. Supporters of the Constitution found it politically necessary to promise a federal declaration of individual rights in order to win ratification. The Bill of Rights as proposed by Congress in 1791 was a legacy of the Anti-Federalist critique of the Constitution.

The Bill of Rights has not always occupied a central place in our constitutional dialogue. Consistent with the intention of the framers, the Supreme Court concluded in *Barron v. Baltimore* (1833) that the Bill of Rights applied only to the operations of the federal government. The states were restricted solely by their separate bills of rights. This did not change until the end of the nineteenth century, when the Supreme Court in *Chicago, Burlington and Quincy Railroad Company v. Chicago* (1897) concluded that the just compensation principle of the Fifth Amendment's takings clause was an inherent part of due process and thus applicable to the states through the Fourteenth Amendment. In the early twentieth century the justices began gradually to extend other provisions of the Bill of Rights to state activity. Many provisions of the Bill of Rights pertaining to the rights of criminal defendants were not applied to state proceedings until the 1960s.

Throughout much of our constitutional history the Bill of Rights played a secondary role in shaping individual liberties. Indeed, many rights that Americans assert today, such as a right to privacy, are not even mentioned in the Bill of Rights. Historically, rights were most commonly defined by legislative bodies and popular conventions. As the Bill of Rights was applied to the states, however, the Supreme Court became the major organ determining the substantive content of rights. During the Warren Court era

(1953–1969) the justices expansively interpreted freedom of speech and religion, the rights of criminal defendants, and the rights of racial minorities.

The interpretation of the Bill of Rights is again a matter of intense debate. For the first time since the New Deal the Supreme Court has a solid conservative majority. Many observers believe that the Court is poised for a significant shift of direction. The justices have recently demonstrated a willingness to trim procedural safeguards for persons accused of crime, to restrict privacy rights, and to expand the rights of property owners against legislative interference. The signs of impending change are clearly reflected in thinking about the judicial function. Liberals, long proponents of a "living constitution" that in theory evolved to meet changing circumstances, have increasingly turned to legal formalism. With so many precedents potentially in jeopardy, they now assert that the landmarks of the Warren Court era must be shielded from scrutiny and possible abandonment. Conservatives, on the other hand, have moved away from their announced preference for a deferential judiciary. Many have called for the Supreme Court to resume its historic role of actively protecting economic rights from legislative infringement.

This volume does not predict the course of future developments, nor do the essays express a common view of recent controversies. On the contrary, the editors believe it is vital to demonstrate the range and variety of attitudes that influence our thinking about rights. The essays provide a fresh and lively dialogue that probes contemporary controversies over the scope and protection of individual rights. Although the essays do not directly address the role of the Tenth Amendment, many of them touch on the important question of federalism in the context of liberties.

The volume is divided into three sections. Part One, "The Myth and Reality of Rights," broadly probes the nature of constitutionalism and its relation to individual liberties. The extent to which rights are properly confined to those set forth in written documents has long been an issue in American constitutionalism. Daniel T. Rodgers describes how historically the aspirations of different groups have done much to shape the growth of new rights. According to Rodgers, this open-ended rights consciousness could not be restricted to the specific language of the Bill of Rights. In contrast, Gary L. McDowell emphasizes the significance of a written constitution as a concrete expression of rights. He rejects natural law as a source of rights and sharply questions the appropriateness of judicially defined rights.

Part Two, "Modern Rights in Controversy," includes a series of essays that treat current issues in interpreting the Bill of Rights and related constitutional provisions. The First Amendment contains several important guarantees of personal freedom. The clauses protecting free speech and prohibiting an establishment of religion have figured prominently in recent litigation before the Supreme Court. Symbolic expression has become increasingly important in a visual age fostered by extensive television coverage of events. Paul L. Murphy examines recent Supreme Court decisions

dealing with such forms of symbolic speech as flag burning and nude dancing and so-called hate speech. The justices have also been called upon to
determine the appropriate relationship between church and state. Melvin
I. Urofsky discusses the current establishment clause jurisprudence. He
points out the distinctions between those favoring an accommodation of
church and state and those adhering to a strict separation between church
and state.

The Second Amendment has rarely been the subject of cases before the
Supreme Court, yet it looms large in current controversies surrounding the
issue of gun control. Congress and state legislatures struggle annually with
proposed legislation designed to restrict or control gun ownership, debates
always accompanied by intense lobbying and highly emotional rhetoric.
Robert J. Cottrol and Raymond T. Diamond examine the intent of the framers and discuss the relevance of the amendment to the right of contemporary Americans to own and bear firearms.

James Madison's decision to place guarantees of property in the Fifth
Amendment next to criminal justice protections underscores the close association of property rights with personal liberty in the mind of the framers
of the Constitution. Following the constitutional revolution of 1937, however, the Supreme Court largely abandoned its historic role as a champion
of the rights of property owners. James W. Ely, Jr., assesses the uncertain
place of property in modern constitutional thought, giving particular attention to the takings clause of the Fifth Amendment. He considers the likelihood that the justices will strengthen the property clauses of the Constitution.

The Fourth and Fifth Amendments contain significant provisions to safeguard individuals from abuse of the criminal process and deprivation of
property. Since the 1960s the control of crime and Supreme Court decisions
interpreting the scope of criminal due process have become heated political
issues. Against the background of earlier Court decisions, David J. Bodenhamer examines the due process revolution engineered by the Warren
Court and suggests that the Rehnquist Court is poised to reverse many of
the landmark decisions of the 1960s. Laurence A. Benner and Michal R.
Belknap also focus on rights of the accused, especially the changing judicial
understanding of the Fourth Amendment's prohibition against "unreasonable searches and seizures." They then analyze the Fifth Amendment's
privilege against self-incrimination and the controversial *Miranda* rule.

Throughout most of American history the Eighth Amendment's ban on
cruel and unusual punishments was of slight consequence. Yet in recent
decades the Eighth Amendment has figured prominently in challenges to
the death penalty. Joseph L. Hoffmann treats the Supreme Court's attempts to fashion a principled interpretation of this provision. He suggests
that the Court may ultimately follow its traditional path of permitting those
punishments sanctioned by majority sentiment.

Although the Fourteenth Amendment was adopted much later than the

Bill of Rights, the equal protection clause elevated equality into a cardinal principle of American constitutionalism and profoundly shaped interpretation of the first ten amendments. As demonstrated by decades of legally imposed racial segregation, it proved difficult to achieve the ideal of equality. Herman Belz explores the contemporary meaning of equality in the context of employment and affirmative action policy. Stressing the inherent tension between the traditional conception of individual rights and the more recent notion of collective equality among racial groups, he notes the lack of consensus about the meaning of equal rights.

Part Three, "Rights Remembered, Revised, and Extended," considers the prospect of protecting individual liberties through neglected constitutional provisions. The Ninth Amendment has long occupied an enigmatic place in our constitutional history. The Supreme Court has consistently ignored the Ninth Amendment as a basis for adjudicating individual rights. Tracing the natural law background of the Ninth Amendment, Randy E. Barnett seeks to demonstrate the constitutional function of this overlooked provision. He concludes that the amendment creates a presumption of liberty that requires the government to justify any actions that restrict rightful conduct.

As the Supreme Court moves in a more conservative direction, some commentators have urged greater reliance on state constitutional law to safeguard individual rights. Kermit L. Hall probes the neglected role of state constitutions in our federal system and assesses the prospect for libertarian decisions based on state bills of rights. He discusses judicial enforcement of state bills of rights in the nineteenth century and cautions that there are important limits on inventive assertions of state constitutional law.

Today Americans are engaged in a far-ranging debate about the role of the Supreme Court in society. Central to this dialogue is the need to balance the fundamental premise of majority rule with the protection of core values expressed in the Bill of Rights. The following essays speak to this debate and illustrate the wide diversity of opinion that characterizes current constitutional thinking. By design, the essays are annotated sparingly. We wish to invite discussion, not overwhelm readers with footnotes. The sources relied upon by the authors, as well as suggestions for further reading, may be found in the bibliographic essay for each chapter.

Finally, we wish to acknowledge the help of Marcia Pilon and Martha Waggoner in preparing this volume. Their careful attention to detail and deadlines was exceeded only by their patience. Without them, these essays would still be submerged on the editors' desks.

PART ONE

The Myth and Reality of Rights

Rights Consciousness
in American History

Daniel T. Rodgers

"The Words We Live By" ran the Burger Commission's motto during the bicentennial celebration of the Constitution. As advertising slogan, the phrase was brilliantly chosen. As history, of course, it was wrong. Wrong not only in the literal sense that, aside from the opening "We, the people," few of the phrases of the Constitution have ever become part of common American speech. But wrong, more fundamentally, in its implication that the Constitution has served Americans as a collective affirmation, an effortlessly worn legal skin, containing and accommodating the organic growth of American life itself. From the closely fought struggle over the Constitution's ratification, through the bloody constitutional explosion over section and slavery, to the most recent scandal of presidential privilege, the past has been far messier and less convenient than the phrase allowed. In truth, the Constitution has given Americans not only words to live by but words to contest and, in a pinch, to fight over.

Scarcely less is true of the Bill of Rights. From its construction to the present day, the rights of Americans have never been out of the teeth of controversy. The progressive frame Americans have been prone to impose upon their history would have it otherwise. In our mythic history, the place of privilege goes to the framers, whose tersely compressed wisdom has slowly unfolded its latent promise. The rhetoric of constitutional adjudication, whereby judges can legitimately imply new rights only by appearing to extract them from the amendments' compact and abstract phrases, sustains the illusion of organic growth. Yet any realistic view of rights has it otherwise. The rights of Americans have not simply grown; they have been invented and repudiated, expanded and violated, striven for and struggled over. The current, angry clamor over abortion rights is no aberration; it is one of the basic noises of our history.

Only a fraction of the historic contest over rights has taken place within the confines of courts and law books. Here too the image of the framers' justice, at quiet remove from the push and pull of democratic politics, misleads Americans. As in the current struggle over abortion policy, rights talk is the talk of the streets, churches, newspapers, family quarrels, and electoral huckstering. It has been the characteristic language of popular politics, dominant enough to transform policy issues into talk of rights. In moments of crisis the upshot has been angry collisions of competing rights, as the rights of women have smashed up against the rights of the unborn, the breadline standee's right to a job against the rights of free enterprise, the rights of slaves against the property rights of slaveholders. Popular politics in America has been the site not only of rights assertion but ugly rights violations, perpetrated in the name of justice, security, race—even in the name of rights themselves. Yet it is from this ongoing, passionate, democratic debate over rights, often far from the *dicta* of courts, that the expansion of rights has drawn its primary historic energy.

Rights consciousness has been a fixture of American politics, but it has not been static. There are four key phases to its history. Moments of heightened rights consciousness, they were, by consequence, moments of fertile, even audacious rights invention. The first of these, extending from the beginning of the struggle against English colonial policy through 1791, witnessed an explosion of popular rights claims, the habit of thinking about rights with "natural" as the key term, a passion for rights declarations—and a nervous reaction against them—out of which, scarred and truncated, came the federal Bill of Rights. The period from the 1820s through the Civil War saw a second eruption of rights claims, more radical in its focus on the social rights of workers, women, and slaves. A quite different dynamic governed the third phase, from the mid-1870s through the mid-1930s, as the movement of the courts into the creation of rights, through a wholesale construction of new property and entrepreneurial rights, triggered a sharp reaction among many of those who were the normal constituents of a rights-based politics. Then out of the changed mental landscape of the Second World War and the dynamics of race came yet a fourth era of rights invention—this time, for a moment, with the courts and the outsiders in common cause—whose reverberations still dominate the politics of post-Reagan America.

Waves of massive rights invention, most of them from outside the structures of law and power, passionate contest, partial incorporation, and retreat—these have been the primary dynamics of rights in America. A messier history than Bill of Rights mythology permits, it is not without its own heroism and inspiration.

I

"Certain inalienable rights." The least surprising part of Jefferson's phrase in 1776 was its last term. In a different historical context, the Americans' grievances over taxes and trade might have coalesced around other claims: justice, for example, or tradition, or (as some of the phrases of the 1770s had it) the people's "happiness."[1] In the late eighteenth century, however, a multitude of factors conspired to press the fears and outrage of the colo-

nists into declarations of rights. One was the precedent of 1688–89, the Glorious Revolution in which Parliament had deposed a king and forced the Declaration of Rights down the throat of his successor. Afterward, with each expansion of Parliament's powers the colonial assemblies had been quick to assert equivalent "rights" for themselves. Some of the colonies had won bodies of liberties and privileges from their governors, charters that the Americans had begun to imagine as local variations on the great English *Carta*. Not the least influential was the common law, important not only for its specific bounty of legal rights but for binding the notion of a body of traditional rights to the very concept of English citizenship.

Not surprisingly, then, when resistance heated up to the heavy-handed imperial reforms, its leaders were quick to denounce the new measures as violations of their "most essential rights and liberties."[2] From the Stamp Act Resolutions of 1765 through the Continental Congress's declaration of rights in 1774 and beyond, the patriot leaders drummed home the point that the new measures endangered their chartered and constitutional rights, the historic rights due to every British subject.

What was less predictable in Jefferson's phrase was the adjective, "inalienable." There was little in the Anglo-American past to predict that the leaders of the rebellion would desert the safe ground of history and precedent for rights that were merely imaginary: natural, inalienable rights, antecedent to law, indeed to history itself. "The sacred rights of mankind are not to be rummaged for among old parchments or musty records," Alexander Hamilton declared in 1775. "They are written, as with a sunbeam, in the whole *volume* of human nature. . . ." John Adams had made the point a decade earlier: there were rights not to be found in any particular constitution but "in the constitution of the intellectual and moral world," and hence could not be alienated without alienating liberty itself.[3]

The danger of rights talk of this sort, the danger of departing from legally established rights to rights grounded in the laws and original design of nature, was not lost on the patriot leaders. Not the least danger was allowing the definition of rights to escape the control of lawyers and throwing it open to any colonist with a philosophic bent. To the end there were those who resisted the open-ended adjectives. The exigencies of argument pressed hard in the other direction, however, as escalating cycles of protest, repression, and outrage pushed the patriot demands beyond the sure foundation of precedent and constitution. Compounding these pressures was a mounting utopianism from below, constructed partly of nightmares of unrestrained official power, partly of hope that in the revolutionary moment the Americans might pin down rights no other people had successfully secured against the corruptions of history.

Rights grounded in nature were rights that legitimately bound every government, even the emergency committees of safety that had begun to move into the revolutionary power vacuum by 1774–75. Like all revolutions, the American Revolution suppressed a good many rights, as loyalists whose property was seized, or buildings burned, or who were harried out of their villages, experienced. There is "no *Loss of Liberty*, that court-minions can complain of, when they are silenced," a South Carolina newspaper insisted; "no man has a right to say a word, which may lame the liberties of his country."[4] Yet coming on the heels of a decade of petitions and declarations, the same revolutionary fervor that made liberty seem so fragile that rights had to be smashed to preserve it impelled the patriots to put rights on paper. And, in the now deeply politicized process, risk a flood of new ones.

The first declaration of rights to bind a patriot government was Virginia's, debated at length in May and June 1776. The resulting declaration was an untidy mix of individual rights (freedom of the press, for example, and the "free exercise" of religion), legal and procedural rights (trial by jury and protection from excessive bail and punishments), collective rights (the right to a popular militia and the revolutionary right to abolish any government faithless to the "publick weal"), together with general statements of political principle and pious statements of morality. Most important was the Virginians' gesture in putting the Declaration of Rights at the head of their revolutionary constitution, as their new government's "basis and foundation."[5]

During the first years of independence, less than half the states followed Virginia's example. How deeply talk of rights had lodged in popular politics, however, became clear as early as 1778 when the Massachusetts town meetings rejected a constitution drafted without a bill of rights. Nowhere in late-eighteenth-century America can one find so close a reading of public opinion as in the returns of the town meetings that discussed the constitution's failings. Some of them bear the marks of bookish lawyers; others have the spelling of little-schooled farmers. What is striking is the breathtaking inventiveness with which persons were now talking about rights: the inalienable right to following the dictates of one's conscience (though it meant disestablishment of the clergy); the right to absolute property in oneself (though it meant the death of slavery); the right of even poor or black men to vote; the right to make public officials stand for annual election; the right "engraved in human nature" to a fairly apportioned legislature; the "unalienable right" of popular ratification of a constitution.[6] Unhinged from history and formal law, loosed from the monopoly of learned men, the business of imagining rights had grown from an argumentative strategy to a volatile popular movement.

Rights talk of this sort was still alive when the Constitutional Convention met in 1787, and it is in this context that its failure to propose a federal bill of rights must be understood. Prudence, to be sure, was against the project, given how fiercely the clauses of the state bills of rights had been debated and with what diverse results. So was the exhaustion of the delegates by the time George Mason, author of the Virginia Declaration, raised the issue in Philadelphia. The deeper instinct, however, was more conservative than this. The drafters had already carefully deleted every instance of the term "rights" from the Constitution in favor of a more cautious reference to "immunities" and "privileges." As the *Federalist*'s lame and belated treatment of the issue made clear, the Constitution's drafters were anxious to evade altogether the unpredictable talk of popular rights and focus debate instead on constitutional mechanics and national pride.

When the Constitution came before the state ratifying conventions, it quickly became evident that the framers had miscalculated popular sentiment. The Anti-Federalists' objections to the Constitution only began with the omission of a bill of rights. The sticking point was the power, scope, and elasticity of the proposed national government. By the time the ratification debate reached Virginia, however, the Anti-Federalists had made enactment of a bill of rights, prefixed to the Constitution, a condition of their acquiescence.

It fell to Madison in the first Congress to fulfill the bargain, though he was himself no partisan of bills of rights. When Jefferson wrote from France, "a bill of rights is what the people are entitled to against every government on earth," a skeptical Madison responded that "parchment barriers" like Virginia's rarely made much difference. In his opening remarks to an impatient Congress he stressed that consideration of a bill of rights was "highly politic, for the tranquillity of the public mind, and the stability of the Government."[7]

Indeed, finding that point of tranquillity was Madison's project, which he achieved through strategic compromise and equally strategic omission. Had he had his way, the guarantees of the first ten amendments would not have stood out as a separate bill of rights but would have been woven unobtrusively through the body of the Constitution. Several of the rights most strongly agitated for in the ratifying conventions Madison dropped from his proposal altogether: the right of the people to "instruct" their representatives, a prohibition on chartered monopolies, and a constitutional limitation on peacetime armies. Other demands of the ratifying conventions succumbed to the caution of Madison's colleagues. In response to the demand that the Constitution begin with a clear statement of constitutional principle, Madison proposed prefixing a clause acknowledging the people's constituent right to reform (though not abolish) their governments; but the proposal did not get past the House. Following the language of the ratifying conventions, Madison proposed three substantial paragraphs elaborating the rights of free speech, assembly, and conscience. The House compacted them into two abbreviated clauses; the Senate bundled the personal rights into a sentence. The House would have preserved those rights against both state and federal governments; the Senate restricted the First Amendment's scope to acts of Congress.

It was no wonder that leaders of the bill of rights movement like William Grayson complained that their amendments had been "so mutilated and gutted that in fact they are good for nothing."[8] Disappointment exaggerated the failure. In time the amendments were to become, as Madison grudgingly admitted they might, "a good ground for an appeal to the sense of the community."[9] Unlike the Constitution, drafted in secret convention, the Bill of Rights was born as a demand from below. Politically, however, its enactment had been a holding action. It was not a speaking of the framers' mind, as the current partisans of "original intent" have imagined, but a document born in debate, dissension, compromise, and politics—in short, out of the usual processes of democracy. The amendments proposed no new rights. They gathered up, rather, the fervor of rights invention that the struggle with Britain had loosed and filtered out only a cautious sliver of it.

II

Rights consciousness in the late eighteenth century focused on official oppression: the tyranny of priests and kings, rapacious tax collectors, corrupt judges, and overbearing office holders. Despite the efforts of a Thomas Paine or a Mary Wollstonecraft, domination rooted in property, class, race, or patriarchy proved harder to oppose with the existing language of rights. The primary domain of the first bills of rights were rights *vis-à-vis* the state; power whose source lay in social custom and convention fell largely outside their purview. When in the middle years of the nineteenth century Americans on the margins began to think seriously about socially constructed forms of power, a second eruption of rights invention ensued.

The first hints of the new uses of rights appeared in the artisans' and workingmen's associations of the 1820s and 1830s. Urban artisans had been central to the struggle against Britain; it was their spokesmen who, in the debates over the Pennsylvania bill of rights of 1776, had tried to incorporate a declaration "That an enormous Proportion of Property vested in a few Individuals is dangerous to the Rights, and destructive of the Common Happiness of Mankind."[10] As new forms of wage labor and capital organization began to erode the traditional props of artisan life and aspiration, workingmen's groups revived, recasting the Revolutionary language of rights to meet changed class relations.

These new rights were not already fixed in the law. As in the eighteenth century, the dynamic in rights talk lay in the concept of natural rights—the invitation to imagine those rights that, at the birth of a just society, must have preceded law, custom, and social convention. This was Locke's imaginative game, with labor and property at its center. People in radically different social and economic circumstances seized Locke's idea and recast it as a labor theory of property built on novel claims of rights: the "natural and unalienable right" of "all who toil . . . to reap the fruits of their own industry," as the Philadelphia journeymen mechanics put it in 1828; the right to "just remuneration" for their toil; and the "natural right" to dispose of their own time as they saw fit.[11] Everywhere in the Atlantic economy that the new class relations took hold, workers reached into the dominant language of politics for terms to express their sense of injustice. In mid-nineteenth-century America, the result was not only to revive but sharply expand the domain of rights.

If the language of rights could be turned from claims against government to claims against private oppression, there were other potential users. By the 1830s, a burgeoning antislavery movement was spinning off incendiary claims to inalienable rights, among them the slavery-defying right of "every man . . . to his own body [and] to the produce of his own labor."[12] A decade later a new women's rights movement was alive with equally radical rights claims: to property separate from a woman's husband; to a "sphere of action" as broad as her conscience demanded; to the vote; to all the rights "integral" to her moral being.[13] Although antislavery lawyers pressed the constitutionality issue before the courts, it was not the language of the state and federal bills of rights that dominated the radical challenges of the mid-nineteenth century. More contagious were the abstract phrases of the Declaration of Independence. The workingmen's petitions were saturated with Jeffersonian borrowings. The women's rights convention at Seneca Falls in 1848 put its case into an elaborate paraphrase of the Declaration. Four years earlier the antislavery Liberty Party had shoehorned Jefferson's "certain inalienable rights" passage into its platform, as the Republicans would do again in 1860.

The rights innovators of the mid-nineteenth century formed no common movement. The abolitionist and women's rights advocates, though historically allied, were not without mutual tension. In both movements, many preferred talk of duties and Christian obligations to the Revolution-descended claims of rights. As for the workingmen's movement, in an era of ugly mob attacks on free Northern blacks and their white allies, it was shot through with the surrounding racism. Many of the same political figures who championed the rights of white free labor succeeded in cutting down the civil freedoms of Northern black citizens and forcing them from the voting rolls. What joined the inventors of new rights was no common cause but a tactical and ideological contagion—a sense, passed from outgroup to outgroup, that the rhetorical legacy of the Revolution was ripe for reemployment, this time not against the grand tyranny of kings and despots but against the customary, everyday tyrannies of capital, bosses, slavemasters, and husbands.

The response at the political center to the new wave of rights demands was, as before, mixed and ambivalent. In the Virginia debate over slavery in 1829, some of slavery's defenders tried to scotch the idea that governments rested on any fundamental rights at all. Others tried to elaborate a politics grounded in loyalty and obligation. But as long as white Southerners clung to the ultimate right of secession; as long as owners felt the need to call their property something other than a social convention; as long as husbands and slaveholders clung to their right to manage their own "do-mestic institutions" without interference; as long as all this remained, do-ing without a language of rights was unthinkable. The result was not re-pudiation but circumlocutions, silences, compromises, and strident reassertions, until—in a spectacular collision of competing rights—the na-tion broke into pieces in 1861.

The second wave of rights invention came to a more mixed end than the first. The death of slavery was its boldest, most sweeping achievement. With the defeat of the Confederacy, Northern Republicans went south to force into the Reconstruction constitutions phrases from Northern bills of rights, including clauses guaranteeing persons the right to the "fruits of their own labor," which they hoped would prevent slavery from rising up, phoenix-like, under any other name. By 1868 the right of black men to vote had been temporarily forced on the South—not as a natural right, as the ex-slaves demanded, but as a reward for character and loyalty. The Civil Rights Act of 1875 drew, for a moment, accommodations in private the-aters, inns, railroad cars, and steamboats into the realm of rights. The right of women to vote, on the other hand, was abruptly set aside. The labor movement, raising the call for the eight-hour day as a basic right in the late 1860s, saw the antislavery Republicans flee the cause. On the margins of power, a new array of social rights had been elaborated and thrust against the center, a handful of them successfully.

<h1 style="text-align:center">III</h1>

For the first century of independence, the strongest talk of rights was to be found outside the courts. Had Madison succeeded in binding the states to the First Amendment, had the Supreme Court not abjectly evaded the slav-ery issue, the pattern might have been different. For a time the courts had played with the principles of natural justice, usually to reaffirm property rights against invasion. But state and federal court judges quickly found their accustomed ground in the written words of statute and constitution. Balancing rights was the natural work of judges; inventing rights, during the first century after independence, had other, more popular sources.

Reconstruction marked, in this sense, a sharp and unprecedented turn. From the 1870s through the early 1930s—first in a trickle of dissenting opinions, then a stream of majority decisions, and finally in a flood—the courts began to invent rights on their own. The first of these, pressed by Justice Steven J. Field in 1873, was a direct offshoot of the Reconstruction debates over rights: the "sacred and imprescriptible" right to choose one's occupation freely. In a different historical setting, Field's "right of free la-bor" might have focused on the plight of the ex-slaves. By the late 1880s and 1890s, however, in an atmosphere acrid as never before with labor dis-putes and the smell of class warfare, the old antislavery slogan was reformulated as the "right of free contract" and thrust aggressively into labor law. With it state and federal courts overturned laws forbidding company stores and scrip payment, laws setting maximum working hours, laws regulating the weighing of miners' coal output, laws preventing employers from firing union workers—all in the name of lifting "paternal" and "tutelary" burdens from wage earners and setting them free to make whatever employment contracts they had the will and "manhood" to make. Freedom of contract adjudication reached its high-water mark in 1923, when the United States Supreme Court invalidated a District of Columbia statute setting a minimum wage for women on the grounds that the "individual freedom of action contemplated by the Constitution" mandated an unrestrained market of prices, the price of labor included.[14]

The urgency of the courts in elaborating these newly invented rights can be sensed in the extraordinary expansion of cases of judicial review. Before the Civil War, the U.S. Supreme Court had, on the average, struck down a single state law each year. In the period 1865–1898, the figure jumped to five a year; in the 1920s, it leaped to fourteen. State courts followed the same sharp upward slope in declaring state laws unconstitutional, as did general legal consciousness of the courts' new role as legislative censor. Judicial review, the president of the American Bar Association urged in 1892, was "the loftiest function and the most sacred duty of the judiciary"; it was "the only breakwater against the haste and the passions of the people— against the tumultuous ocean of democracy."[15]

Rights talk, to be sure, was only one of the devices of the new judicial activism. The courts mixed precisionistic Constitutional construction, elastic readings of the Reconstruction amendments, and appeal to the "fundamental rights of liberty" in general and the "sacred rights of property" in particular—all with a high eclecticism. For the judges, more than for most of the rights inventors who had preceded them, the natural-rights line of argument carried liabilities, and they picked their way through the eighteenth-century phrases with considerable care. The mental game of thinking out of time—either retrospectively to a vanished state of nature or prospectively to human nature in its fulfillment—was not their project.

Cite though they did the bills of rights formula that "acquiring, possessing, and protecting property" was a natural right, judges were not interested in probing property's origins, much less the workingmen's claims to property rights in their labor. Rights that might have been construed as kinds of property, or essential to property's protection, they let the legislatures annul. The 1875 Civil Rights Act's sections dealing with invasion of rights by private firms and persons was set aside as beyond the Constitution's reach. Also uncontested were the disfranchisement measures that swept black voters off the Southern electoral rolls at the turn of the century. In an era of lynch mobs, red scares, and violently suppressed and violent strikes, the courts evinced little interest in what are now called personal liberties. The preoccupation of the courts was not with the basic ground of

rights, or even property in general, but the defense of aggressive, entrepreneurial property. Theirs was a rights revival from above, defining, de-
limiting, and shoring up the ascendant power of their day.

Although the court system was too complex to be viewed through a single lens, the general drift of the era was clear. During the period of high
industrial capitalism, massive immigration, business consolidation, and
bitter and continuous labor conflict, the courts threw themselves into politics as never before. Legislatures—sometimes crudely, sometimes with
care and sophistication—tried to forestall the worst exploitations of industrial capitalism, citing the principles of protection, public health and safety,
and the common good. The courts, with a rhetoric of rights, resisted.

Others remained free to make what they could of the language of rights.
The Socialist Labor Party in the 1890s went to the polls with a platform ap-
pealing to inalienable rights. So did the advocates of women's suffrage until shortly after the turn of the century. The pacifists, socialists, and labor
sympathizers who founded the American Civil Liberties Union in reaction
to the strident patriotism of World War I included fervent Bill of Rights believers. But the more striking phenomenon of the late nineteenth and early
twentieth centuries was the abandonment of rights talk by many progressive Americans.

Some of the desertion stemmed from a changed intellectual climate,
dominated as never before by a sense of evolution and history. In that context, the concept of timeless, abstract rights seemed a throwback to ahis-
toric eighteenth-century reasoning. This was the ground on which Woodrow Wilson, at Princeton in the 1890s, dismissed Jefferson's natural rights
philosophizing as "false," "abstract," and "un-American." Despite their
"last despairing flicker in the courts of the United States," Wilson's Harvard counterpart agreed, the concept of natural rights had been "abandoned by almost every scholar in England and America."[16] If the intellec-
tuals' new consciousness of social evolution worked against the rights
tradition, so did a general eagerness to extinguish the line of argument that
had lured the South (and might lure others) into revolutionary misadven-
ture. "The right of revolution does not exist in America," the state of Indiana instructed its schoolchildren in 1921. "One of the many meanings of
democracy is that it is a form of government in which the right of revolution has been lost."[17]

Most powerful, however, was a sense that rights consciousness was
shackled to an archaic individualism, blind to historical circumstances and
oblivious to the larger good. "The doctrine of natural rights really furnishes
no guide to the problems of our time," Charles Beard insisted in this vein
in 1908. One might talk like Theodore Roosevelt of the national "will," like
Woodrow Wilson of "the best practicable adjustment between the power of
the government and the privilege of the individual," or like the New Dealers of the "common good" and "the public interest." In every case the progressives' consciousness of society combined with their deepening quarrel

with the courts to spur them away from the rights language of the judges. Rights talk was obfuscating talk. "More than anything else," Roscoe Pound summed up the realists' critique of the new adjudication in 1923, "the theory of natural rights and its consequence, the nineteenth century theory of legal rights, served to cover up what the legal order really was and what court and lawmaker and judge really were doing."[18]

Progressives and New Dealers struggled for alternatives. The Progressive Party in 1912, discarding every reference to rights from its platform, went to the people with a case for "social and industrial justice" and the "public welfare." The Democratic Party platform of 1936, ringing with "self-evident truths," turned Jefferson's phrases into pledges to preserve the people's "safety," "happiness," and economic "democracy."[19] The language of the Revolution had been coopted by the defenders of entrepreneurial "liberty." To those struggling to bring industrial capitalism under public control, the eighteenth- century heritage was an impediment, an archaic word game, a set of "exploded" concepts.

The progressive and New Deal eras present no monolithic face in this regard. Rights consciousness remained a protean and unpredictable force in American political culture. But at no other time has rights talk been as polarized or, in democratic circles, as deeply out of favor.

IV

Then came the Second World War and in its wake a return to the more familiar pattern: a vigorous, rights-based popular movement beating against a more cautious center. The precipitating event was the rise of fascism— the ascendancy of political systems in which all rights seemed to have been swallowed up into a monstrously swollen state. In the late 1930s the dominant theme of Franklin Roosevelt's speeches had been "democracy"; by 1940 his speech writers were reaching back to eighteenth-century traditions to talk of "fundamental" and "essential human freedoms," whose fate now hung in the balance. The New Dealers' war-accelerated rediscovery of rights culminated in Roosevelt's promulgation of a "second Bill of Rights" in 1944. A translation of the New Deal into claims progressives had once spurned, it pledged the nation to an "economic bill of rights": the right to a useful job, adequate earnings, a decent home, adequate medical care, and protection from the economic fears of sickness, old age, accident, and unemployment.[20] The language of rights, joined to New Deal liberalism, had become protean and unpredictable once more.

The Supreme Court, beaten in its confrontation with the New Deal, took an even more decisive turn in the late 1930s and 1940s. Rejecting the political and economic program of their predecessors, the new appointees shifted their attention from property rights to the issues brought to a head by the specter of fascism: the rights of free expression, the guarantees of fair criminal process against overbearing state power, and the festering double standards of race. The Court did not arrive at its new program of "preferred rights" without its share of backtracking during the revived Red Scare of the 1950s, but its new course in the shadow of the European dictatorships was clear.

Dismantling the elaborate edifice built on freedom of contract with the damning observation that the phrase was nowhere in the Constitution, the Supreme Court had reason to keep its distance from its predecessors' abstract reasoning about rights. Hugo Black was among those urging the course, plumping for a literalist Bill of Rights-based constitutionalism. But the resources of the political culture, the needs of the moment, and the revived talk of political fundamentals all pressed toward appropriation, rather than rejection, of the older lines of argument. By the 1940s the Supreme Court was beginning to pick its way through rights again, establishing some of the sections of the Bill of Rights as so "basic" and "fundamental" as to be incorporated into state law through the Fourteenth Amendment. Before the decade was out the Court was again beginning to spin off inventions: rights nowhere specified in the Constitution but so "fundamental" ("natural" by another name) that they were morally and logically entailed in the Bill of Rights itself. Sometimes through simple assertion, sometimes through ingenious argument, the rights of marriage and procreation, travel, association, the vote, education, and privacy had all been framed as "fundamental" by the end of the 1960s and laid beside the Bill of Rights as its modern addendum.

So centrally involved in policymaking did the new Court (like its predecessor) become that the rights revolution of the postwar years has often been misconstrued as a revolution from the top down. But this time, as before in the late eighteenth and early nineteenth centuries, the fuel came from below. Most important was the civil rights movement. Unlike white progressives, black progressives had clung to the language of rights through the early twentieth century. In keeping with the mood of the times, the "Declaration of Principles," from which the NAACP had emerged in the first decade of the century, ended with a list of the Negro-Americans' "duties," but these duties were only ancillary to claims of rights.[21] Rights mediated between the talk of "freedom" running deep in African-American political culture and the broken promises of Reconstruction. Given urgency by the comparison with Nazi racism, a civil rights movement remobilized during the war, supplying the courts with arguments and pushing them down the path that would lead to *Brown v. Board of Education* (1954) and, in the face of massive resistance to that decision, to the intensified judicial activism of the 1960s.

Equally significant was the contagious effect of the civil rights movement on other outsiders. Through imitation, reaction, or rivalry the tactics and rights claims of the black protest movement spread, slowly in the 1950s, then with snowballing effect in the 1960s and early 1970s. The women's rights movement was reborn in a consciousness-intensifying intersection with the civil rights protest. The American Civil Liberties Union mushroomed to its modern size in the 1960s, forming for the burgeoning liberation movements a powerful lobby for rights litigation. By the early 1970s, dozens of such movements had sprung up, holding deeply entrenched customs to the test of fundamental rights: movements for the rights of gay Americans, Native Americans, Chicanos, or Asian Americans; movements for the rights of the young, the aged, the handicapped, or the homeless; neighborhood rights defense committees and committees for international human rights; movements for welfare rights and movements for taxpayer rights; an abortion rights movement and a movement for the rights of the unborn. Heightened by television and by the historic conjuncture of an activist judiciary willing to give a hearing to the rights claims roiling up from below, rights talk spread with unprecedented speed from outgroup to outgroup—creating outgroups, at its peak, where group consciousness had not had a public language before.

This eruption of rights claims and rights-claiming organizations went hand in hand with resistance and angry backlash, some of it between the rival rights movements themselves. As in the early nineteenth century, rights consciousness was not cut out of a common ideological piece. What made rights claims contagious was their ability to concentrate so diverse an array of grievances and aspirations into a language with historical, political, and (for the moment) legal legitimacy. Almost no one talked now of "natural rights." The game of imagining the original state of nature tempted few players. But couched in more modern terms, the inventive power in rights consciousness remained its invitation to think at cross-purposes to history, custom, and massively entrenched convention and to measure them against original principles of justice. The sheer volume of rights invention in the generation after *Brown* has no historic parallel. But the dynamics were familiar.

Also familiar, by the end of the 1970s, was the resistance at the center. "The rights of Americans" was too inviting a phrase, too deeply fixed in the Reaganites' own constituency, to make rights celebration anything other than an asset. But rights invention was another matter. Among the Reagan federal court appointees there was no mistaking the desire to curb the unpredictable, protean side of rights talk, to roll back the concept of "fundamental" rights, to get the courts out of the business of abstract and fundamental reasoning altogether.

V

"None of the supposed rights of man," Marx objected in 1843, " . . . go beyond the egoistic man, man as . . . an individual separated from the community, withdrawn into himself, wholly preoccupied with his private interest and acting in accordance with his private caprice."[22] The point, born in the conservative reaction to the French Revolution and a common coin of early twentieth-century progressive thought, cannot be dismissed. Rights claims are claims *against* other persons. Rights do not exist outside a situation of real or potential antagonism. Claims of humanity, community, or the common good emphasize likenesses. The logic of rights claims necessitates divisions. From the beginning of American history, to talk of rights has been to specify tyrannies and hold them up to the bar of justice — the practical justice of the courts, when justice is to be found there, or the principles of justice itself, when the courts are blind. Like the Anglo-American legal system itself, rights claims invite sharp distinctions between self and others. It is hardly an accident that a political culture repeatedly flooded by popular claims of rights has no easy time talking directly about common possessions, common interests, or entangled and interdependent destinies.

But rights consciousness in America has never been a simple vehicle for possessive individualism. From the Virginia Bill of Rights through the New Deal's declaration of economic rights and beyond, strong rights claims have gathered individual and collective rights into a common fold. Some rights in the American polity are held by persons, others by groups, by the "community" (as the Pennsylvania bill of rights of 1776 had it), or the "people" as a whole. The rights of contemporary Americans include rights of possession and privacy; but they also include the right to assemble, organize, worship, vote, and strike—all collective rights, capable of being held only by communities of persons.

That rights claims carry both public and private potential, that a rights-based justification of social democracy can be constructed out of the language that once buttressed laissez-faire, is not due to the capriciousness of language. Rights consciousness contains its own peculiar collective dynamic. Translating pain and injury—a policeman's beating, a "no Jews wanted" sign, or a compulsory religious oath—into claims of rights not only transfers personal wounds into the realm of justice, but it simultaneously translates private experience into a public category, a general claim, and potentially universalizing language. This is the collective dynamic intrinsic to rights movements, many of which have been as deeply steeped in consciousness of solidarity and common power as in rights. This is likewise the dynamic of rights contagion, as universally stated rights slip past the adjectives (white, male, Christian, native-born, and the rest) constructed to hedge them in.

Above all, what is most striking about the history of rights consciousness in America is its democratic character. That has not precluded Americans from trampling massively on rights, not the least in the slavery that bore so hard on the Constitution's drafters' minds. But the utopian strain in rights consciousness remains a powerful, unpredictable lever of change. Since the Revolution, rights consciousness in America has never been fully separable from inquiry into rights as they ought to be, or might be, or must once have been. The result has been a widely diffused, often destabilizing, inventive popular debate about fundamental rights and the fundamentals of a just society.

The members of the first Congress who served as arbiters of the Bill of Rights' final language had far more narrow, immediate goals than this. Their project was to consolidate rights. As nervous as all centrists about the instability of rights arguments, they pruned the open-ended natural rights abstractions out of their document with the rigor of men determined to lock up that line of argument against the future and the external democratic clamor. The failure of that effort is one of American history's fortunes.

The Explosion and Erosion of Rights

Gary L. McDowell

The history of America is, by and large, the history of the idea of individual liberty and rights. As a nation we were, as Abraham Lincoln reminded his morally torn generation, "conceived in liberty and dedicated to the proposition that all men are created equal." When Thomas Jefferson and the other patriots of 1776 declared their independence from England and proclaimed their rightful place among the powers of the Earth, they believed that the rightness of their cause impelled them to the separation—an act never before undertaken as a moral matter. To that generation, there was no doubt that men are created equal; that they are endowed by their Creator with certain inalienable rights; and that governments, to be legitimate, must derive their just powers from the consent of the governed. The laws of nature and of nature's God demanded nothing less.

Those lessons of the American Founding have been well learned by every subsequent generation of Americans; it is not too much to say that the philosophic language of our founding echoes still in our daily politics. The bedrock principles of the American republic continue to inspire and direct public discussion over law and policy, from judicial nominations to legislative efforts to enact civil rights laws to acrimonious disputes over whether the First Amendment demands governmental funding for "art" as that may be defined by each and every artist. As a people, we Americans take our rights very seriously, indeed.

During the twentieth century this American devotion to rights has grown even stronger. Especially since World War II there has been an ever-increasing public consciousness about rights and liberties. And with that has come a subtle transformation in the way we think about rights.

The Rhetoric of Rights

Rights have come to be associated in the public mind almost exclusively with the courts of law and with the Supreme Court of the United States in particular. Where earlier generations thought rights were to be protected by the constitutional system as a whole—including the states in their sovereign capacities—we have come to think of rights primarily as the result of judicial review at the national level. Sooner or later, it seems, every political question is reduced to a question of rights, and the definition of those rights left to the courts.

As a result, ours is the age of rights—or at the very least, the age of rights rhetoric. Nothing dresses up a political cause like the rhetorical garb of rights; and neither the political Right nor the political Left is able to resist the seductive allure the rhetoric of rights presents. Thus the contemporary debate over the nature and extent of rights exposes at once what is best and worst in American politics and, thereby, in American law.

We see our best side—what Abraham Lincoln once called "the better angels of our nature"—in the continuing commitment to the notion that all are created equal and are endowed by their Creator with certain inalienable rights. On the whole, we continue to believe, as did Jefferson and the others of his age, that governments are instituted in order to secure those rights that nature gives but leaves insecure. Our noblest impulse moves us to seek ways to render those abstract philosophic principles into concrete political reality.

But this worthy side cannot conceal what all too often is really going on. For the very power of fundamental principles to inspire carries with it a terrible temptation. If one can couch policy preferences in the evocative and provocative language of civil rights, those preferences will have a far greater chance of success in the political battles that must be fought. It is simply unseemly to argue against, or even to appear to argue against, what is proffered as a further step toward the American goal of securing rights for all.

The problem is that such temptation is not without its costs: it cheapens the very idea of rights. Calling an ordinary policy preference a fundamental right does not, because it cannot, make that preference a right in any meaningful, philosophical sense. It only confounds the idea of rights with the power of clever rhetoric.

There is yet a deeper problem: the new logic of rights wreaks havoc on the idea of a written constitution. By and large, the textual provisions for rights in the original Constitution and in the Bill of Rights are relatively few in number and are rather precisely crafted. To fit ever more innovative claims of rights within those original provisions requires more than a little stretching of the text. Take, for example, the question of whether a person has the "right" to burn the American flag.

The First Amendment is splendidly unambiguous on the protection it affords free speech: "Congress shall make no law abridging the freedom of speech." But what about the states? What if a person chooses to express his political views not in words but in actions—as one Joey Johnson did when he burned the flag outside the Republican National Convention in 1984. Does the First Amendment cover such circumstances? The Supreme Court in *Texas v. Johnson* (1989) ruled that it did indeed. But the Court could not base its decision on the text of the First Amendment; nor could it base it on the original intentions of those who framed and ratified that amendment. Rather the Court had to rest its decision only on prior decisions of its own, decisions that had departed in very serious—and arguably illegitimate— ways from text and original intention.

To reach its decision in *Texas v. Johnson*, the Court had to accept its prior holdings that the First Amendment applies not just to Congress but to the states; this was achieved by the doctrine that the due process clause of the Fourteenth Amendment "incorporates" certain provisions of the Bill of Rights and obliges the states to be bound by them. Second, burning the flag may be many things, but strictly speaking, it is not speech. Thus the Court had to point to yet another earlier decision wherein a majority of the justices had agreed that there is, within the protections afforded speech by the First Amendment, a special category called "symbolic speech." Protests such as flag burning, the Court held, are properly understood as symbolic speech.

However one might view the results reached in the *Texas v. Johnson* case, this much is indisputable: the holding had nothing to do with the original understanding of the First Amendment. It could only be reached by a Court willing to stretch the document to fit a new situation that was looked down upon by a majority of the Court as it is presently constituted. The "right" thus protected depended not upon the Bill of Rights in any strict sense, but only upon how the Court has been persuaded to view the Bill of Rights.

The claim raised in *Texas v. Johnson* at least began by raising the question of what the text of the First Amendment means. In yet another world of rights, special protections as fundamental rights are claimed for an assortment of human endeavors, even though they are founded on no explicit provision of the Constitution or any of its amendments. Rather, these claims rest on the assumption that there is an "unwritten constitution" of unenumerated rights that both antedates and transcends the written Constitution and all of its amendments. By this logic, the textual constitution contains metaphysical portals such as the due process clause and the Ninth Amendment through which judges may import new rights that are not mentioned in the existing texts. This jurisprudential view was granted the legitimating imprimatur of the Supreme Court in the 1965 birth control case of *Griswold v. Connecticut*. The impact has been profound. Indeed, *Griswold* has ceased to be merely a case in constitutional law and has become a metaphor for the new politics of rights.

The Privacy Metaphor

The Court in *Griswold* declared unconstitutional a Connecticut law restricting the use of contraceptives even by married couples in the privacy of their own home. The majority held that, despite the Constitution's failure to mention it explicitly, the document contained an implicit "right to privacy." It emerged, said Justice William O. Douglas, as a penumbra formed by emanations of particular rights that were explicit—rights such as being free from unreasonable searches and seizures in one's home. Thus this unenumerated right, once discerned and decreed by the Court, became equal in power to those rights that are enumerated.

By definition, such a broad and unenumerated right must depend for its form on judicial decree. What is included and excluded by the right to privacy must remain a matter of judicial discretion on a case-by-case basis. This is why Judge Robert Bork has called this right "the loose canon of constitutional law." Its lines and limits depend not upon any clear textual provision but only upon judicial predilection. This judicially created right is best known as the foundation for *Roe v. Wade* (1973) and the idea of a woman's right to have an abortion. But it is far more than simply that. It is simply pregnant with possibilities for new rights.

There are new notions of privacy that go far beyond the questions of contraception and abortion in *Griswold* and *Roe*. They are currently churning their way from professors' theories to lawyers' briefs to judges' opinions. Indeed, they go far beyond such questions as homosexual sodomy and the right to die, two other privacy issues recently addressed by the Court in *Bowers v. Hardwick* (1986) and *Cruzan v. Missouri* (1990).

Articles defending the private use of hard-core pornography (and thus, by extension, its production and availability), arguing for the abolition of laws prohibiting incest, and urging freedom for drug use as a matter of "psychic freedom" have begun to appear with regularity in the major law reviews. The authors are not a group of fringe theorists; they constitute the new "mainstream" of legal education.

Kenneth Karst of the UCLA law school, for example, has suggested that laws against adultery and bigamy are "debatable on principle." Harvard's Laurence Tribe finds it questionable whether the public interest can justify "a *per se* prohibition on extramarital sexual contacts" while yet another theorist has argued that "all legal distinctions between children and adults [should] be abolished." Further, Professor David A. J. Richards of New York University law school has challenged the constitutionality of laws prohibiting prostitution, maintained that "decisions to use drugs are embraced by the constitutional right to privacy," and argued that there is "no convincing moral justification for the refusal to constitutionalize the right to certain basic services" such as education and welfare. These theories will inevitably come to form the basis of litigation; as a result, they will influence public policy questions of nearly every sort.

Before *Griswold* enshrined the idea of a fundamental right to privacy it was understood that in such areas in which the Constitution was silent, the power to deal with those issues touching privacy resided with the states where the opinions of the people as to what was moral or immoral, acceptable or unacceptable, would fashion laws reflective of the moral sense of the community. After *Griswold* such laws cannot reflect the moral sense of the community unless the judge or justice in question happens to agree.

The judicial arbitrariness inherent in the idea of a fundamental right to privacy is what raises serious questions about its legitimacy—and, by extension, about the legitimacy of the whole notion of unenumerated rights for which privacy stands. The public morality of the community is supplanted by the private morality of the judge. By the logic of *Griswold* and its constitutional progeny, the individual becomes everything, the community nothing. And thereby an older and more stable understanding of rights is abandoned. To understand where we are, it is helpful to remember where we began.

The Foundation of Community

To those who framed and ratified the Constitution and the Bill of Rights the primary concern was not simply rights in an abstract and absolute sense. For that generation, rights were properly understood only within the context of a scheme of government that served to define and protect those rights. While they surely appreciated and accepted the idea that there were rights bestowed upon mankind by nature and nature's God, they also knew that without governments being instituted among men, those rights nature gave were left in a most precarious position.

The founding generation drew its philosophic bearings from the great philosophers of modern politics, those who fashioned the theory of the social contract. Of particular importance were such writers as Thomas Hobbes and John Locke. In such works as Hobbes's *Leviathan* and Locke's *Two Treatises of Government*, the entire body of traditional thinking about politics and human nature was called into question—and supplanted. Where earlier generations had taught of natural right to which all mankind was beholden, Hobbes and Locke taught the language of natural rights. Whereas their predecessors located the order in the universe in places external to man—either nature in an Aristotelian sense or the word of God—Hobbes and Locke centered all things in man himself.

By the reckoning of Hobbes and Locke, knowledge began not with philosophy or Scripture but with the senses. Mankind drew conclusions about the world as the result of experiencing the world and fashioning notions to explain its otherwise impenetrable phenomena. The senses set reason in motion, and reason gave rise to ideas that allowed man to make sense of the world. The basic teaching of Hobbes's and Locke's new theory of politics was that men are born free and equal and are radically independent actors, each with a mind of his own. Nature makes no distinction as to the important question who is to rule; man's own reasoning could decide what sort of government would best serve his interests. By nature's command that all men are equal, no one is obliged to submit to another's opinion against his will. The only legitimate means of imposing order on the chaos of nature's bounty was the social contract, an agreement entered into freely by all; this device alone could legitimately transform isolated human beings into citizens.

Central to this theory of politics was the idea of the state of nature, man's pristine and primitive condition before law and society and civilization. The purpose of the state of nature theory was not to argue that there had ever been such a place (although both Hobbes and Locke wondered about America) but to strip mankind down to its bare essentials in order to see human nature most clearly. In that hypothetical original state all men were, in the truest sense, equal. Nature endowed each person with certain inalienable rights, rights that did not spring from governments but were antecedent to all government. The most basic of rights was, of course, life itself, mere preservation; beyond that was man's liberty to live unencumbered by the commands of another.

The problem of this state of nature was that in practice each man's natural equality meant that each man had the power to enforce his natural rights as he saw fit. But nature was not so generous as to allow everyone to see the world the same way; man's natural impulses led inevitably to conflict rather than consensus. As a result of their natural reasoning men would fashion notions of what was right or just—for themselves. Self-interest was the most that one could expect from men in such a state. The result, as Hobbes so famously put it, was that life in the state of nature was "solitary, poor, nasty, brutish and short."

The great and abiding virtue of man's ability to reason was that he would come to see that, whatever the virtues of the state of nature, its vices were overwhelming. There was no security for life or property for anyone. Thus moved by their innate desire for self-preservation and commodious living, the bleak prospects of life in the state of nature would prompt men to come to see the logic of entering a mutual covenant. By this fundamental agreement—the social contract—men could join together to put an end to "the warre of all against all" that plagued them.

By terms of the social contract men would move from the barbarous state of nature to the more convivial climes of civil society. In the process, their natural rights would be transformed into civil rights. The advantage was that civil rights within the context of civil society would come backed by the sanction of law. Because the social contract and the creation of the sovereign commonwealth was the result of a voluntary covenant of each with all, when man obeyed those laws to which he had consented he was, in effect, only obeying himself.

This was the philosophic backdrop of the founding of the American republic that began with the Declaration of Independence in 1776. When Thomas Jefferson set out the reasons for the rebellion of the colonies against the pretensions of Great Britain, he did not merely make the case for the Americans' rights as Englishmen. By 1776 events had caused the

Americans to deepen their appeal; they now justified the revolution by re-course to the laws of nature and nature's God. As a result, in Abraham Lincoln's praise, Jefferson

> in the concrete pressure of a struggle for national independence by a single people, had the coolness, forecast, and capacity to introduce into a merely revolutionary document, an abstract truth, applicable to all men and all times, and so to embalm it there, that today and in all coming days, it shall be a rebuke and a stumbling block to the very harbingers of re-appearing tyranny and oppression.

Jefferson's well-known prologue to the Declaration of Independence merits repeating:

> We hold these truths to be self evident, that all men are created equal, that they are endowed by their Creator with certain inalienable rights, that among these are Life, Liberty, and the Pursuit of Happiness—That to secure these rights, Governments are instituted among men, deriving their just powers from the consent of the governed. —That whenever any form of Government becomes destructive of these ends, it is the Right of the people to alter or abolish it, and to institute new Government, laying its foundation on such principles, and organizing its powers in such forms, as to them shall seem most likely to effect their Safety and Happiness.

Central to Jefferson's catalog of those truths deemed self-evident is that governments have but one legitimate purpose—"to secure these rights"—and only one legitimate foundation—the consent of the governed. Any other purpose or any other foundation would be utterly and profoundly illegitimate.

But the political focus of the philosophic purpose of establishing a civil society was never simply on the individual as an individual, but as part of society. The focus was always upon the "right of the people." The very idea of the consent of the governed is one that is communitarian at its deepest level. Consent, then, is more than merely the sum of the parts; yet it is characterized precisely as consisting in those parts, those individuals whose consent is necessary as individuals. In a sense, this theory of consent is analogous to a chemical compound; oxygen and hydrogen, for example, combine to form water yet never cease to be hydrogen and oxygen.

The mechanics of popular consent hinge on the idea that each man's private conscience can somehow be transformed into something more than itself yet not lose its essential characteristic as *private* conscience. The core of the process lay in the notion that such a transformation can only occur as a result of voluntary consent; consent and coercion are antithetical. Man's private conscience will arrive at the conclusion that what is right is to enter into the social compact. Rights without sanctions to protect them are not, in any meaningful sense, rights at all. It is in the interest of each to enter into such an agreement and to create a government "from reflection and choice." As John Jay rather eloquently put it in *The Federalist*: "Nothing is more certain than the indispensable necessity of Government, and it is equally undeniable, that whenever and however it is instituted, the people must cede to it some of their natural rights, in order to vest it with requisite powers."[1]

The essential right ceded to the government is the right to make and enforce laws in order to protect the safety and happiness of each individual who has consented to live under that sovereign authority. The people, in their collective capacity, shall judge whether or not the government is keeping its end of the bargain. If the government is found wanting in this essential regard, the people, as Jefferson put it in the Declaration, properly retain the right to alter or abolish the government and to institute a new government as they see fit. Thus there is no preordained form of government; it remains the choice of the governed.

The question then arises as to how this consent can be given some expression that will elevate it merely above the private opinions of those who will come to hold power. The answer the American founders gave, following Hobbes and Locke, was to get it in writing. The idea of a written constitution, Jefferson would later say, was America's "peculiar security." To his great rival, Chief Justice John Marshall—with whom Jefferson rarely agreed on anything else—a written constitution was the "greatest of improvements on political institutions."

By the device of a written constitution duly ratified by those to live under it, the consent of the governed would be given concrete expression. Such a written constitution, said Alexander Hamilton, would be seen by all, and especially the judges, as "a fundamental law."[2] The Constitution was to be understood as embodying "the intention of the people"; as such it would serve as the basic check against the pretensions of power. It was to be preferred to the "intentions of [the people's] agents" of any branch of the government.

The Constitution reflected the structure of the government to which the people consented; further, and perhaps more important, it reflected the wishes of the people as to the lines and limits of the powers granted to the government. In particular, as Hamilton noted, a "limited constitution . . . [is] one which contains certain specified exceptions to the legislative authority; such for instance as that it shall pass no bills of attainder, no *ex post facto* laws, and the like." As a result of such "specified exceptions," Hamilton could argue that "the constitution is itself in every rational sense, and to every useful purpose, a BILL OF RIGHTS."[3]

Thus were rights originally seen as a matter of community judgment as to what the limits to governmental power ought to be. Within the text of the Constitution itself the framers, as Hamilton indicated, put things off limits. They undertook to protect rights precisely, by clear and common definitions of what was, and what was not, to be tolerated. When the demand for a Bill of Rights led to the first ten amendments to the original Constitution, they opted again for precision. In particular, they added the Bill of Rights at the behest of the Anti-Federalists, who feared that an over-reaching national government would in time "devour" the states. Thus there was no ambiguity as to the applicability of the Bill of Rights: it did not extend as a restriction on the powers of the several states.

This issue, which in fact lies at the heart of the rise of the privacy meta-phor and the decline of community, was first addressed by Chief Justice John Marshall in his last constitutional decision, *Barron v. Baltimore* (1833), in which it was argued that the Fifth Amendment was a brake not merely on national power but on the powers of states and localities as well. In dis-missing this argument, Marshall went to the very heart of the notion of constitutionalism that informed the American founding:

> The constitution was ordained and established by the people of the United States for themselves, for their government, and not for the government of the individual states. [A]nd, in that constitution, provided such limitations and restrictions on the powers of its particular government as its judgment dictated. The people of the United States framed such a government for the United States as they supposed best adapted to their situation, and best cal-culated to promote their interests. The power they conferred on this govern-ment was to be exercised by itself; and the limitations on power, if expressed in general terms, are naturally, and, we think, necessarily applicable to the government created by the instrument. They are limitations of power granted in the instrument itself; not of distinct governments, framed by different per-sons and for different purposes.

Thus, Marshall concluded:

> Had the Framers of these amendments intended them to be limitations on the powers of the state governments, they would have imitated the Framers of the original constitution, and have expressed that intention. These amend-ments contain no expression indicating an intention to apply them to the state governments. This Court cannot so apply them.[4]

Implicit in Marshall's opinion in *Barron* are two fundamental principles. First, rights are rights by virtue of having been given certain concrete ex-pression in a constitutional text; they represent the intentions of the people as to the form of their government. They are not natural but civil in their origin and practical extent. While there may arguably be a constellation of natural rights or common law rights, they do not become constitutional rights until explicitly adopted in the manner prescribed by the Constitution itself.

Marshall's second point is equally significant: rights are fashioned as re-straints on government antecedent to the government itself. Thus they are not subject to creation or recreation by the powers of that government. The courts are no more empowered to exercise their will independent of the people in their original collective capacity than is the legislature or the executive. The opinions of the judges stand in the same relation as the laws of the legislature to the original will and consent of the people. Neither is superior to the other nor to the people themselves. Indeed, as Hamilton said, "the power of the people is superior to both."[5]

The Transformation of Rights and the Decline of Community

This view of rights generally held sway until the middle of the nineteenth century. There were fits and starts by the Court to go down the largely unmarked path of natural law and unwritten rights—Samuel Chase in *Calder v. Bull* (1798) and John Marshall in *Fletcher v. Peck* (1810), for example—but such philosophic flutters never gave way to a complete jurisprudential flight on the part of the Court. Rights continued to be viewed as deriving in the first instance from the *written* Constitution of which, of course, the first ten amendments were as integral a part as the other provisions. The reason, as Justice James Iredell put it in his opinion in *Calder*, was simple and powerful: "The ideas of natural justice," he explained, "are regulated by no fixed standard: the ablest and the purest men have differed on the subject." And, as Justice Iredell said elsewhere, "fixed principles of law cannot be grounded on the airy imagination of man."

In 1857 the first fissure in this foundation appeared. It came in the opinion of Chief Justice Roger B. Taney in the slavery case *Dred Scott v. Sandford*, a case aptly described at one level as a "self-inflicted wound." In seeking to calm the political waters so roiled by slavery, Taney set out to deny that Congress had the power to prohibit slavery in the territories lining up to enter the Union. In the end, of course, he decreed that the Missouri Compromise was unconstitutional; it was the first time since *Marbury v. Madison* (1803) that the Court had struck down a federal law by judicial review.

In the course of his opinion, however, Taney did more than merely declare an act of Congress invalid; he introduced into a seemingly ordinary, if vexatious, case a truly revolutionary principle. "[A]n act of Congress," the Chief Justice wrote, "which deprives a citizen of the United States of his liberty or property in a particular Territory of the United States, and who has committed no offence against the laws, could hardly be dignified with the name of due process of law." By linking the idea of vested interests to the due process clause of the Fifth Amendment, and using it to protect the property of slaveholders—in this case, Dred Scott—Taney imported into the Constitution the notion that rights were protected even though unenumerated. In the name of protecting the citizens such as John Sandford from the zeal of government, Taney radically expanded the objects to which the judicial power was originally thought to extend.

Taney's logic hardly went unnoticed. But before Lincoln and Stephen

Douglas took to the byways of Illinois in their battle for the Senate in 1857, and before the decision threw fuel on the already smoldering political fire of slavery, Justice Benjamin Curtis dissented vigorously from the holding in *Dred Scott*. "When a strict interpretation of the Constitution, according to the fixed rules which govern the interpretation of the laws, is abandoned," Curtis warned, "and the theoretical opinions of individuals are allowed to control its meaning, we have no longer a Constitution; we are under the government of individual men, who for the time being have the power to declare what the Constitution is, according to their own views of what it ought to mean." At a minimum, the decision of the Court was an unwarranted "assumption of authority" to the detriment of the more representative institutions of government.

By invalidating the Missouri Compromise, *Dred Scott* undermined the political legitimacy of the legislature to address the seemingly intractable dilemma slavery posed. In the name of unspecified transcendent rights and liberties, the Court denied the people the political liberty to deal with their greatest political problem according to the powers clearly given the Congress by the Constitution itself. But ultimately it was not *Dred Scott* that would most contribute to the demise of community and the transformation of the meaning of rights under the Constitution: that distinction, ironically, was reserved for that device meant to rid the republic of the more noxious elements of *Dred Scott*, the Fourteenth Amendment ratified in 1868.

The Fourteenth Amendment sought to clear the constitutional waters muddied by *Dred Scott* by guaranteeing each citizen that the privileges and immunities of their national citizenship would not be abridged by any state; that they would not be deprived of "life, liberty, or property without due process of law"; and that no state would be able to "deny to any person within its jurisdiction the equal protection of the laws." (The Thirteenth Amendment, of course, had laid the foundation: it had prohibited slavery and involuntary servitude.) These noble goals were all to be achieved by the true power of the Fourteenth Amendment, which in its final section empowered Congress "to enforce, by appropriate legislation, the provisions of this article." The original federal design of the Constitution had been altered in a very fundamental way; henceforth, Congress would be able to intrude into the domestic affairs of the theretofore sovereign states in the name of privileges and immunities, due process of law, and equal protection.

But the most significant transformation of the federal principle would come not from the laws of Congress but from the decrees of the Court. Within a very short time the Fourteenth Amendment would be put to uses never imagined by those who framed and ratified it—and not uses for which it had been intended. While the Court would deny the applicability of the amendment to racial discrimination in *The Civil Rights Cases* (1883) and *Plessy v. Ferguson* (1896), the justices would infuse it with new meaning by its creation of the idea of "liberty of contract," a doctrine whereby the

Court stretched the meaning of "liberty" in the due process clauses of both the Fifth and the Fourteenth Amendments to protect economic interests against governmental regulation.

This reached its high-water mark in *Lochner v. New York* (1905), when the Court struck down New York law that regulated (in the name of health and safety) the hours bakers could work. Such a regulation, the Court decreed, denied the employer and the employees their fundamental right freely to enter into a contract. Such regulations violated due process of law insofar as they were, in the view of a majority of the Court, "unreasonable."

Lochner and its descendants would rule the juridical roost until 1937 when the Court, bearing the marks of Franklin D. Roosevelt's appointments, handed down its decision in *West Coast Hotel v. Parrish* allowing a state wage law to stand. In the process of overruling the earlier case of *Adkins v. Children's Hospital* (1923), the Court argued that under the Constitution, the "community may direct its law-making power to correct the abuse which springs from [unconscionable employers'] selfish disregard of the public interest." Yet all was not well: while the Court gave with one hand, it took away with the other. That same year the Court handed down one of its truly landmark cases, *Palko v. Connecticut*, in which the justices sought to defend the idea that the Fourteenth Amendment "incorporated" at least certain if not all of the provisions of the Bill of Rights.[6]

Palko was not the first time the Court had argued that a particular limitation in the Bill of Rights applied with equal force to the states. That honor goes to *Gitlow v. New York* (1925), a First Amendment case. In *Gitlow*, the Court had not bothered to defend its radical move by anything approaching a reasoned argument; the majority simply asserted that the First Amendment applied to the states.[7] And between 1925 and 1937 the Court had "incorporated" yet other provisions of the first ten amendments. But in *Palko* the Court sought finally to offer a defense of its encroaching power.

The essence of the *Palko* decision by Justice Benjamin Cardozo lies in his notion that not all rights are equal; some few are properly deemed "superior," he argued, in that they are distinguished from those without which "justice . . . would not perish." Certain rights, Cardozo went on, are "implicit in the concept of ordered liberty [and] so rooted in the traditions and conscience of our people as to be ranked fundamental." While procedural rights such as the prohibition against "double jeopardy" (the issue in *Palko*) were not to be held as fundamental, such rights as the "freedom of thought and speech" were. The reason, Justice Cardozo concluded, is that they form the "matrix, the indispensable condition of nearly every other form of freedom."[8]

The significance of *Palko* for understanding our current confusions over the nature and extent of rights can be reduced to Cardozo's two essential premises. First, incorporation of the rights spelled out in the Bill of Rights was not to be wholesale but rather on a case-by-case basis. Second, and most important, because all rights are not equal in their applicability, it is up to the Court—or, in truth, to a majority of the justices—to determine on that case-by-case basis which rights are superior or fundamental and which are not. The implication of the opinion in *Palko* was stunning: rights depend only upon the Court not only for their application but for their definition.

A big year in the development of the theory of rights that still dominates contemporary politics was 1937. A few months after the Court handed down *Palko*, the justices decided *United States v. Carolene Products*.[9] The opinion itself pales in comparison to the subsequent use made of only one of its footnotes—"footnote four," as it is known in the trade. For by the reasoning buried beneath the text of the opinion, Justice Harlan Fiske Stone carved out a new standard for judicial consideration of rights. There was a need, Stone wrote, for a "more searching judicial inquiry" when laws seemed to cut especially harshly against "discrete and insular minorities." Thus rights claims were no longer to be simply a matter of individuals; henceforth they would be viewed with increasing frequency in light of group definition. This would not be limited to racial minorities but expanded to minorities of every sort—ethnic, religious, ideological, and so on.

The deepest strand of thinking in the *Carolene Products* footnote, an idea that would be fully fleshed out during the Warren Court, was that majority rule is somehow inherently suspect. But more troubling was the idea that the collective sense of the community, as expressed in its laws, was to be easily trumped by nearly any minority claim of rights. In time this logic would be so expanded as to lead the late Alexander M. Bickel to mourn the passing of the idea that under majority rule minorities may sometimes lose—legitimately. Taken together with the implications of *Palko*, *Gitlow*, and other innovative rights rulings, *Carolene Products* would help usher in the increasingly politicized world of rights within which our courts still operate.

There is a paradox to the legacy spawned by these early cases. As their underlying logic has been allowed to expand in case after case, two seemingly contradictory principles have emerged as dominant. On the one hand, rights have come to be seen as increasingly absolute; on the other, rights are seen as amorphous and ill-defined things, dependent on judicial definition. Taken together, these two strands of legal logic have formed the fabric of contemporary judicial activism, what has aptly been labeled government by judiciary.[10]

This new thinking about the nature and extent of rights was not limited simply to applying the Bill of Rights. For some, as Justice William O. Douglas once put it, the Bill of Rights was not enough.[11] There was a need to free judges from the misconception, in this view, that the only rights to be enforced in the courts were rights to be found in the Constitution and its subsequent amendments. There, it was argued, a universe of rights was simply waiting to be divined and decreed by the courts; these were "unwritten but still binding principles of higher law."[12] Appropriately, it was Justice Douglas who took the lead in creating the doctrine of unenumerated rights that finally captured a majority of the Court in *Griswold v. Connecticut*.

There is a splendid irony to the notion of unenumerated rights that has taken for its general rubric the "right to privacy." Its roots are to be found in the constitutional soil tilled by the economic libertarians, those justices who on nearly every other count are anathema to today's liberal defenders of expanding rights. The first trace of what would become the heart of *Griswold* appeared in two liberty of contract cases, *Meyers v. Nebraska*[13] and *Pierce v. Society of Sisters*.[14] In both of these cases, Justice James Clark McReynolds developed the idea that liberty in the due process clause, as he put it in *Meyers*,

> denotes not merely freedom from bodily restraint but also the right of the individual to contract, to engage in any of the common occupations of life, to acquire useful knowledge, to marry, to establish a home and bring up children, to worship God according to the dictates of his own conscience, and generally to enjoy those privileges long recognized at common law as essential to the orderly pursuit of happiness by free men.[15]

The law in question, prohibiting the teaching of foreign languages, the Court concluded, was "arbitrary" and without "a reasonable relation to some purpose within the competency of the State to effect."[16] Thus seen as unreasonable by their measure, the justices struck down the law as unconstitutional.

In *Pierce v. Society of Sisters*, a case involving the Oregon Compulsory Education Act that with few exceptions mandated children be sent to public schools, McReynolds returned to the issue. The law would have had the effect, if allowed to stand, of putting the private schools operated by the Society of Sisters out of business. But the Court faced a dilemma. As McReynolds put it, because the plaintiffs were corporations, they could not "claim for themselves the liberty which the Fourteenth Amendment guarantees."[17] Yet there was a way out. What the plaintiffs in fact sought, McReynolds noted, was "protection against arbitrary, unreasonable and unlawful interference with their patrons and the consequent destruction of their business and property."[18] Thus the Court concluded: "Under the doctrine of *Meyers v. Nebraska* we think it entirely plain that the Act . . . unreasonably interferes with the liberty of parents and guardians to direct the upbringing and education of children under their control."[19] What is significant in both *Meyers* and *Pierce* is that in neither case did the Court presume to craft a general and unenumerated "right to privacy" in the sense in which that is now understood. To the Court at the time, both cases were merely new links in the doctrinal chain of economic liberties.

In 1942 the Court first addressed the underlying issue of unwritten civil rights beyond the Constitution's explicit provisions in *Skinner v. Oklahoma*, a case involving an Oklahoma law mandating the sterilization of certain classes of prisoners. In this case, Justice Douglas first expressed his belief that the Court had the legitimate power to protect "the basic civil rights of man" even though not clearly articulated in the constitutional text. It would prove to be a preface to his opinion twenty-three years later in *Griswold*.

Douglas noted in *Skinner* that the case "touches a sensitive and important area of human rights . . . the right to have offspring."[20] Picking up the theme McReynolds had begun in *Meyers*, Douglas struck down the law in question not as a violation of the due process clause but as a violation of the equal protection clause. Two concurring opinions, one by Chief Justice Harlan Fiske Stone and one by Justice Robert H. Jackson, seemed willing to go further. Stone argued that what constitutes due process of law is "a matter of judicial cognizance" and that in his view the law at issue was simply "lacking in the first principles of due process."[21] In Jackson's view the issue was similarly clear: "There are limits to the extent to which a legislatively represented majority may conduct biological experiments at the expense of the dignity and personality and natural powers of a minority."[22] What is most interesting in *Skinner* is that there is still no expression of a fundamental constitutionally protected right to privacy.

The Court's major step toward creating such a general right to privacy came in 1961, in a case that involved the same Connecticut birth control statute that would finally be struck down in *Griswold*. Yet, in *Poe v. Ullman*, the Court refused to reach the constitutional questions because the cases were brought in such a way as to "raise serious questions of nonjusticiability of [the] appellants' claims."[23] This the Court did over the dissents of Justices Douglas, Black, Harlan, and Stewart. The dissent of Justice Douglas is of special interest.

"Though I believe that 'due process' as used in the Fourteenth Amendment includes all of the first eight amendments," Douglas confessed, "I do not think it is restricted and confined to them." On the basis of McReynolds's reasoning in *Meyers*, Douglas went even further. " 'Liberty,' " he said, "is a conception that sometimes gains content from the emanations of other specific guarantees . . . or from experience with the requirements of a free society." Reflecting Cardozo's logic in *Palko*, Douglas argued that there are certain rights so fundamental as to be deemed "implicit in a free society." The right to privacy in the marital relationship is one of those fundamental rights. "This notion of privacy," he concluded, "is not drawn from the blue. It emanates from the totality of the constitutional scheme under which we live." Douglas's dissent in *Poe* would prove to be the bridge between his opinion in *Skinner* and his opinion in *Griswold*.

By the time the Connecticut law that had been skirted in *Poe* came back to the Court in *Griswold* four years later, Douglas at last reached the juridical destination pointed to in *Skinner*. As he famously put it: "specific guarantees in the Bill of Rights have penumbras, formed by emanations from those guarantees that help give them life and substance. . . . Various guarantees create zones of privacy. . . . The present case, then, concerns a relationship lying within the zone of privacy created by several fundamental constitutional guarantees." Douglas reached his conclusion by reasoning from particular rights to a general spirit. Those who framed and ratified the Bill of Rights itself had reasoned from a general principle to specifics they thought worthy of special treatment by singling them out for special and explicit protection. Douglas thus left the reasoning characteristic of the judge and engaged in the reasoning of a framer.

This was precisely the point of Justice Hugo Black's spirited dissent. Black did not disagree because he thought the law in question prudent or appropriate as a matter of policy; indeed, he dissented precisely because he thought it was none of the Court's business whether the law was wise or not. The power of the Court to weigh constitutionality did not extend that far. What Douglas had undertaken to do in the majority opinion, Black said, was to "keep the Constitution in tune with the times." And that the Court did not have the power to do; that was left to the cumbersome but safe process of formal amendment.

As Black saw it, the majority was "merely using different words" to claim the same power an earlier Court had claimed to strike down other sorts of laws the Court had then deemed to be "irrational, unreasonable or offensive." Whether the test embraced was that of "fairness and justice," "rational purpose," or the "traditions and conscience of our people," they all boiled down to one thing—judicial review based on what the Court claimed was "natural justice." As Black put it, echoing Justice Curtis's dissent in *Dred Scott*:

> If any broad, unlimited power to hold laws unconstitutional because they offend what this Court conceives to be the "[collective] conscience of the people" is vested in this Court by the Ninth Amendment, the Fourteenth Amendment, or any other provision of the Constitution, it was not given by the Framers, but rather has been bestowed on the Court by the Court.

Further, he argued, reliance

> on the Due Process Clause or the Ninth Amendment or any mysterious and uncertain natural law concept as reason for striking down . . . state law . . . is no less dangerous when used to enforce this Court's views about personal rights than those about economic rights.

The problem with the majority opinion in *Griswold*, Black was arguing, was that such an assumption of power not rooted in the text of the Constitution was enough to turn the Court into a continuing constitutional convention. There was no doubt in Black's mind that times might demand changes in the Constitution. The question was whether that power to alter the fundamental law was given to the Court. Black thought not. In his disagreement with the reasoning of the Court, he stood with such constitutionalists as Iredell, Marshall, and Joseph Story. Black believed in the idea of constitutional change as Story had summed it up in his *Commentaries on the Constitution of the United States*. If any part of the Constitution be deemed "inconvenient, impolitic, or even mischievous," Story argued,

> the power of redressing the evil lies with the people by an exercise of the power of amendment. . . . [A] departure from the true import and sense of [the words of the Constitution] is, *pro tanto*, the establishment of a new constitution. It is doing for the people what they have not chosen to do for themselves. It is usurping the functions of a legislator, and deserting those of an expounder of the law.

This is precisely the dilemma posed by the logic of judicially defined unenumerated rights that was established in *Griswold v. Connecticut*. In the name of rights governmental power is enhanced without recalling that it is such power that most threatens rights properly understood.

The Erosion of Rights

As the nation celebrates in earnest the bicentennial of the Bill of Rights, it is a good time to pause and think about precisely what rights are—and what rights are not.

Modern constitutionalism contains at its core a philosophic paradox: a stable political order depends upon the successful reconciliation of the undeniable fact of men's individuality and natural independence with their absolute need for community and rule in light of the common good. The only means likely to transform radically isolated individuals into citizens is a system of majority rule in a constitutional order derived from the consent of the governed.

The framers understood very well the dangers posed to individual liberty by majority rule; indeed, the Constitution was framed expressly to deal with the problem of majority tyranny. However, the framers did not abandon the idea of majority rule but only strove to reconcile, as James Madison said, the "rights of individuals" and "the permanent and aggregate interests of the community." This the framers sought to do by so contriving the interior structure of the Constitution that its balanced and checked institutions would combine "the requisite stability and energy in government, with the inviolable attention due to liberty, and to the republican form."

In the framers' view, rights were too important to leave dependent upon any institution of government; no governmental power could ever be so trusted. The contemporary view of rights forgets that judicial power exercised by the Supreme Court is still governmental power and hence not to be trusted to create new rights as the ideological mood may strike a majority of justices. The true roots of our rights are worth remembering if our rights are to be truly preserved.

PART TWO

Modern Rights in Controversy

Symbolic Speech and
the First Amendment

Paul L. Murphy

The modern Supreme Court has evolved an intriguing body of law dealing with symbolic expression. The question of the permissible limits of such expression has been raised by a panoply of modern issues. These range from flag desecration and flag burning to cross burning; from controversial and ideological art to performance art; from entering forbidden property to nude dancing; and from proscribing hair and dress styles to sanctioning statements coming out of counterculture.

What is symbolic expression and when did it become associated with First Amendment protection? How does it relate, if at all, to the framers' understanding of speech and the government's role in relation to that speech? Similarly, is it to be seen as an individual right or a societal right? And if the latter, are there limits to its function of projecting expression, through often controversial behavior, into the marketplace of ideas? One current example, recently decided by the Supreme Court, demonstrates the centrality of such issues and the danger of assuming there are easy answers to the First Amendment dilemmas here raised.

In 1989, St. Paul, Minnesota, like a number of other cities, passed an ordinance against various forms of expression based on bias or hatred. "We were seeing more racially motivated and religion oriented crimes," explained the city council president, and the city wanted to send a message that "we would not tolerate crimes against people because of their race or religion."[1] Several months later, in June 1990, a teenager was arrested under the ordinance and charged with burning a cross at the home of the only black family in a neighborhood of St. Paul. A county district judge initially held the ordinance unconstitutional as a violation of the First Amendment. The Minnesota Supreme Court, however, overturned this decision and upheld the ordinance, maintaining that it could be narrowly interpreted to ban acts of bigotry that arouse anger in others and still protect free speech. "Burning a cross in the yard of an African American family's home is deplorable conduct that the city of St. Paul may without question prohibit. The burning of a cross is itself an unmistakable symbol of violence and hatred based on virulent notions of racial supremacy,"[2] the state court said.

The case was subsequently appealed to the United States Supreme Court.

Community reaction to these developments was strong. Officials of the National Association for the Advancement of Colored People (NAACP) and the Anti-Defamation League supported the ordinance and filed briefs with the Supreme Court. "The St. Paul ordinance is not a model hate crime law," stated the attorney for the Anti-Defamation League, "but neither is it misdirected in limiting clearly bigoted conduct that goes beyond constitutional protection. Our position is not one of warmly embracing the ordinance in its entirety, but rather that the burning of a cross in the yard of a black family is quintessentially a hate crime. We believe that the ordinance, insofar as it banned that activity, was banning criminal conduct, and not speech."[3]

Attorneys for the Minnesota Civil Liberties Union prepared a brief urging the Court to strike down the ordinance: "We think it overbroad and vague, and one of the worst ordinances we have seen. Even if it could be narrowly construed, it would require extensive litigation to define the boundaries of protected speech."[4] This stance reinforced the city attorney's argument that the key issue in the case is whether a content-based hate crime law—that is, one seeking to prohibit certain kinds of speech—can be narrowed by court interpretation to avoid trampling on First Amendment rights.

In taking this case, the Supreme Court was responding to a flurry of recent state and city laws against various forms of expression based on bias or hatred. Constitutional experts were themselves split. First Amendment absolutists (no law abridging free speech means no law) ruled out any thought of making such action as cross burning a crime, contending that the right to sue for civil damages, plus the right to speak out in opposition, should curtail troublesome conduct. First Amendment relativists disagreed. They argued that there is a danger in following the amendment blindly, discounting the pain that deliberately harmful expression can inflict. Even some liberal commentators raised a caution in this area, contending that an evenhanded determination to protect all expression can degenerate from an abiding faith in the First Amendment to an obsession with the alluring abstractions of neutral principles.

The Court, surprising some commentators, unanimously agreed that the ordinance was unconstitutional. Justice Scalia delivered the opinion of the Court. He accepted the Minnesota court's narrowing of the ordinance to apply only to so-called fighting words, which Scalia termed constitutionally proscribable, but even so, he found the ordinance to be unconstitutional on its face because "it prohibits otherwise permitted speech solely on the basis of the subjects the speech addresses."[5] Cross burning and other reprehensible acts, Scalia argued, could be prosecuted under a variety of existing statutes. These means were sufficient for St. Paul to prevent such behavior "without adding the First Amendment to the fire."[6] Four other Justices—White, Stevens, O'Connor, and Blackmun—agreed with the result but not Scalia's reasoning. Their three separate opinions suggested that future cases regarding similar categories of speech might find a sharply divided Court.

What is the constitutional tradition regarding symbolic expression that this case raises so dramatically? A look at the record is in order.

Symbolic expression is as old as humankind. It has played a vital role in political, and certainly in religious, life for centuries. The colonial cause in the American Revolution was expressed symbolically at many turns, the Boston Tea Party being a prime example. The idea of making such expression constitutional and wrapping it with the protection of the First Amendment, however, was not a concept that occurred to nineteenth-century Americans. Demonstrating, picketing, and striking as a way of protesting slavery or exploitative working conditions was not a form of permissible speech protected by Bill of Rights guarantees. Rather, the government well into World War I operated on a contrasting premise that the property rights being assaulted deserved constitutional protection under the Fourteenth Amendment. Government used symbolism to rally patriotism to the defense of the nation and the status quo in the face of external and internal assault and criticism. And it used the Espionage and Sedition Acts, passed by Congress in 1917 and 1918, to prosecute individuals who criticized the war overtly or symbolically, whether in speech or print.

Under such circumstances, sensitive advocates of truly free speech evolved the notion of a "marketplace of ideas." Speech, they contended, had a social value. Government actions to deny differing points of view, even distasteful or unpopular opinions, deprived a democratic society from drawing upon a range of ideas that might serve the interest of the people more effectively.

This argument did not persuade conservative patriots. When the federal wartime laws expired, they induced the states to pass similarly repressive laws to keep dangerous ideas out of that marketplace. This movement confirmed the perceptive observation of lawyer and later Supreme Court Justice Louis D. Brandeis that "the main repressive forces in American society have been either private power or state government acting at the behest of private power."[7] The peacetime sedition laws, criminal syndicalism laws, and red-flag statutes passed by the various states were devices for preventing malcontented elements from preaching the values of industrial democracy and social justice through actual and symbolic expression. In this regard, the 1931 *Stromberg* case became an important landmark.

Yetta Stromberg was a member of the Young Communist League, in charge of a California summer camp for a group of young people. As a part of the daily camp ritual there was a flag raising ceremony that entailed saluting the communist red flag and pledging support for the struggle of the working class. After a citizens' arrest, following vigilante action on the part of local American Legionnaires, Stromberg was indicted and convicted under a California state law that inherently recognized the communicative elements of a flag as a symbol by making it a felony to, among other things, "display a red flag and banner in a public place and in a meeting place as a sign, symbol, or emblem of opposition to organized government."[8] The Supreme Court found this language unconstitutionally vague. Although the opinion did not address symbolic expression directly, the Court did explain that the law, due to its vagueness, might be construed to prohibit peaceful and orderly opposition to government by legal means. It thus curtailed the opportunity for the free exchange of ideas. In this regard the flag was recognized as a symbol that could function as a part of the "political discussion of a free society."[9]

Years later, in 1978, when a group of American Nazis sought to march through Skokie, Illinois, a heavily Jewish suburb of Chicago, the federal district court cited *Stromberg* to strike down as unconstitutional a local ordinance against the wearing of military-type uniforms and regalia in marches and demonstrations. Even the hated symbols of the Nazis, the court held, were forms of symbolic political speech protected by the First Amendment.[10]

In the years between *Stromberg* and Skokie, the Supreme Court dealt with symbolic expression on a number of different occasions. Particularly pertinent were the flag-salute cases of 1940 and 1943. In *Minersville School District v. Gobitis* (1940), the majority sanctioned a compulsory flag salute for public school children, imposed by the state. It then had second thoughts in 1943 and reversed itself in *West Virginia Board of Education v. Barnette.* Writing for the Court in *Gobitis,* Justice Felix Frankfurter waxed patriotic in stressing that national unity is the basis of national security and that unity is "fostered by the symbols we live by." These symbols included first and foremost the flag, which "transcended all internal differences, no matter how large, within the framework of the constitution."[11] Frankfurter drew his reverence for symbols from the famous jurist Oliver Wendell Holmes, yet, as critics pointed out at the time, Holmes had been circumspect here. "We live by symbols," Holmes had once stated, but then he added, "what shall be symbolized by any image of the sight depends upon the mind of him who sees it."[12] On the other hand, Holmes had addressed the symbolic speech issue. When he spoke of "free trade in ideas," he made clear this may not be reduced to mere trade in words. It was the freedom to express ideas and feelings, not merely the freedom to engage in verbal locutions, that had to be protected if the First Amendment's central values were to be realized.

Justice Harlan Fiske Stone, in the lone dissent, demonstrated the truth of such a position. In his opinion, the flag-salute requirement suppressed freedom of speech and free exercise of religion, coercing children "to express a sentiment violative of their deepest religious convictions." To him, the coercing of these children of Jehovah's Witnesses was unacceptable; the Court had a special obligation to protect the freedom of helpless minorities, even if it supplanted legislative judgments in doing so.

In the 1943 *Barnette* case, the Court again focused on the element of communication inherent in nonverbal symbols when it declared unconstitutional the compulsory flag salute of the schools of West Virginia. Justice Robert Jackson, for the Court, stressed in his opinion that "there is no doubt that, in connection with the pledges, the flag-salute is a form of utterance. Symbolism is a primitive but effective way of communicating ideas. The use of emblem or flag to symbolize some system, idea, institution, or personality, is a short cut from mind to mind. Causes and nations, political parties, lodges and ecclesiastical groups seek to knit the loyalty of their followings to a flag or banner. Symbols of State often convey political ideas just as religious symbols come to convey theological ones." But, he added, "A person gets from a symbol the meaning he puts into it, and what is one man's comfort and inspiration is another's jest and scorn. . . . The flag has a spectrum of meanings which should be respected."[13] The majority speaking through Jackson did more than merely affirm the possibility of nonverbal speech. For the first time, the Court recognized that government could not enforce participation in a symbolic act. The case rested clearly on speech grounds, with an element of freedom of conscience. "No official," Jackson wrote in his most quoted phrase, "can prescribe what shall be orthodox in politics, nationalism, religion, or other matters of opinion, or force citizens to confess by word or act their faith therein."[14]

The same principle, that government may not force unwilling individuals to become couriers of an ideology, was reaffirmed thirty-four years later when the Court ruled in 1977 that the state of New Hampshire could not constitutionally enforce criminal sanctions against persons who covered the state motto, "Live free or die," on passenger vehicle license plates because that motto was repugnant to their moral and religious beliefs. "Where the state's interest is to disseminate an ideology, no matter how acceptable to some," wrote Chief Justice Warren Burger, "such interest cannot outweigh an individual's First Amendment right to avoid becoming a courier for such message."[15]

Free speech issues of the 1950s, '60s, and early '70s, however, turned far more on protest against government and governmental policy. These were the civil rights and Vietnam War years. Outrage at Southern white intransigence and a misguided foreign policy led to vehement public expression and to actions to dramatize such protest, what came to be referred to as "speech plus," a term employed by First Amendment specialists to describe the distinction made by the courts between "pure speech"—verbal expression, for example, in a traditional public speech or a newspaper editorial—and speech combined with conduct such as marches, pickets, and sit-ins. More concretely, the conduct, which was the "plus," was often symbolic conduct—flag desecration, draft card burning, pouring human blood upon the files of a local draft board. Thus "speech plus" was shorthand for speech interwoven with action, and it raised a question as to whether that action or conduct should receive the same level of First Amendment protection as did pure speech.

At one point in a 1965 civil rights demonstration case, *Cox v. Louisiana*,[16] Justice Arthur Goldberg sought to clarify that distinction, arguing for less protection for conduct. But critics felt the dichotomy too arbitrary and destructive of legitimate First Amendment rights, since it provided no functional basis for deciding what is pure speech and what is other conduct or for differentiating between the kind of protection that should be extended to one but not the other. One symbolic speech case demonstrated the complexity of the problem.

In the late 1960s, David O'Brien and three companions were convicted in federal district court of burning their draft registration certificates on the steps of the South Boston Courthouse before a large crowd in violation of a 1965 federal provision making it illegal to forge, alter, knowingly destroy, or knowingly mutilate such a document. Although the federal court of appeals reversed the conviction on First Amendment grounds, accepting O'Brien's argument that his act was symbolic expression protected by the Constitution, the Supreme Court disagreed and, with only Justice William O. Douglas in dissent, reinstated the conviction. The Court, speaking through Chief Justice Earl Warren, weighed the "speech" element of O'Brien's action against the conduct element of burning the card in violation of federal law and came down on the side of protecting government documents from deliberate destruction. "We cannot accept the view," Warren wrote, "that an apparently limitless variety of conduct can be labeled speech, whenever the person engaging in the conduct intends thereby to express an idea."[17]

Acknowledging that there was a communicative element in O'Brien's conduct, the Chief Justice argued that it was not sufficient to bring into play the First Amendment. Here governmental interest in regulating the nonspeech element justified incidental limitations on First Amendment freedoms. There was no protection for this symbolic conduct. From the case, then, emerged a test subsequently used for determining the constitutionality of governmental regulation of excessive conduct: "governmental regulation is sufficiently justified if it is within the constitutional power of the government; if it furthers an important and substantial governmental interest; if the governmental interest is unrelated to the suppression of free expression; and if the incidental restriction of alleged First Amendment freedoms is not greater than is essential to the furtherance of that interest."[18]

Symbolic protest of the Vietnam conflict in other forms received more sympathy from the justices the following year in *Tinker v. Des Moines School District* (1969). School principals in the Iowa city had forbidden high school students from wearing armbands to classes in protest against the war. Several students defied the principals' edict and were suspended. Their families sought an injunction from a federal district court prohibiting the principals and the school district from disciplining the children for their symbolic protest. The parents lost in the district court, with the decision affirmed by an equally divided court of appeals. The parents appealed to the Supreme Court. Justice Abe Fortas delivered the opinion of the Court.

Fortas began by noting that the district court recognized the wearing of an armband for the purpose of expressing certain views as "the type of symbolic act that is within the Free Speech Clause of the First Amendment."[19] He further noted that the wearing of armbands in the circumstances of this case was entirely divorced from actual or potentially disruptive conduct by those participating in it. It was closely akin to the "pure speech" entitled to comprehensive protection under the First Amendment. The problem posed by the present case, Fortas argued, did not relate to regulation of the length of skirts or the type of clothing, hair style, or deportment. It did not concern aggressive, disruptive action or even group demonstrations. The problem involved direct, primary First Amendment rights. Also, he argued, the case did not concern speech or action that intruded on the work of the schools or the rights of other students. There was no finding that engaging in the forbidden conduct would materially interfere with the requirements of appropriate school discipline. Tellingly, he pointed out that school authorities did not prohibit other symbols from being worn. Students got in no trouble when they were wearing the Iron Cross, traditionally a symbol of Nazism. Instead, the rule prohibited only a certain symbol—black armbands worn to exhibit opposition to the nation's involvement in Vietnam. Clearly, he argued, the prohibition of expression of one particular opinion was not constitutionally permissible.

Justice Byron White concurred, but he made clear that the Court continued to recognize a distinction between communicating by words and communicating by acts or conduct that sufficiently impinged on some valid state interest. But Justice Hugo Black, to the surprise of many, dissented sharply. Questioning whether the students and teachers may use the schools at their whim as a platform for the exercise of free speech— "symbolic" or "pure"—and whether the courts will allocate to themselves the function of deciding how the pupils' school day will be spent, he saw the behavior as disruptive and defended the authority of school administrators to make reasonable restrictions on symbolic expression of this kind. Perhaps piqued by student demonstrators at the time, he ended: "I wish wholly to disclaim any purpose on my part to hold that the Federal Constitution compels the teachers, parents, and elected school officials to surrender control of the American public school system to public school students."[20]

The 1971 case of *Cohen v. California*, while peripherally involving symbolic expression, also raised other kinds of First Amendment issues in terms of nonverbal communication. The case involved a young man arrested in the Los Angeles County Court House for knowingly wearing a jacket on which the words "Fuck the Draft" were plainly visible. Sentenced to thirty days imprisonment for violating a state law against maliciously and willfully disturbing the peace of any neighborhood or person by offensive conduct, he explained that the message on his jacket expressed his opposition to the war in Vietnam. There was no evidence that he had spoken any words in the courthouse prior to his arrest. The facts also showed that Cohen was not loud or threatening when he did speak and that no person threatened him because of the message on his garment.

An appellate court sustained the conviction. The California Supreme Court refused review, and Cohen appealed to the U.S. Supreme Court. There a majority of five reversed his conviction and in doing so addressed at length the First Amendment issue raised by the case: was it permissible to punish shocking words by classifying them as conduct, even though the language in question was legally neither obscene nor composed of fighting words?

Justice John Marshall Harlan delivered the opinion, making clear that the conviction rested upon the asserted offensiveness of the words Cohen used to convey his message to the public. The only "conduct" that the state sought to punish, Harlan pointed out, was the fact of communication. The conviction rested solely upon "speech," not upon any separately identifiable conduct, even though the state argued that the words alone did not necessarily convey any message and hence could be regulated without effectively limiting Cohen's ability to express himself.[21]

Harlan then set forth three main reasons for reversing the conviction: there was no clear principle by which certain words would be allowed and others disallowed; language such as that used by Cohen has important emotive content; and forbidding certain words created a serious risk that protected ideas will be suppressed. Implicit in the opinion were broader arguments: that the Constitution protected expression of this sort, since it was not possible to articulate a rule by which citizens can distinguish permissible from impermissible words; that provocative language served to communicate ideas and emotion; and that when the state attempted to prohibit certain words, it inevitably created a substantial risk of suppressing ideas.

The Court's concern for the emotive dimension of the words particularly interested free speech commentators. The idea that the expression of emotion is as entitled to First Amendment protection as is its content was intriguing. So was the idea that emotive expression can be fully as important as intellectual or cognitive content in the competition of ideas for acceptance in the marketplace. Of course, most communications encompass both cognitive and emotive content. But even if a communication was substantially devoid of all intellectual content, its emotive content arguably lay within the First Amendment's scope.

Harlan granted the unpopularity of this view and acknowledged that verbal tumult, discord, and offensive utterance often appeared to be the immediate consequence of such free expression. But these side effects, he argued, were merely consequences of the open debate that permitted the emergence of broader, more enduring values. Surely, he contended, the state had no right to cleanse public debate to the point where it was grammatically palatable to the most squeamish. No readily ascertainable general principle existed for stopping short of that result. One man's vulgarity is another man's lyric. Indeed, he concluded, it is largely because governmental officials cannot make principled distinction in this area that the Constitution leaves matters of taste and style largely to the individual.

Three justices—Blackmun, Burger, and Black—disagreed, asserting that Cohen's absurd and immature antic was mainly conduct and contained little speech. The majority's agonizing First Amendment values seemed misplaced and unnecessary, they contended. But the dearth of cases involving symbolic speech muted the dissents. With the exception of flag desecration cases, the remainder of the 1970s produced little clarifying case law on the question. The 1980s, by contrast, saw several unique circumstances raising the issue again.

In *Clark v. Community for Creative Non-Violence* (1984), the majority, speaking through Justice White, sustained a District of Columbia ordinance that banned sleeping in public parks. The issue was complex. A group advocating increased public assistance for the homeless, intent upon dramatizing the plight of the needy, had received from the National Park Service a renewable seven-day permit to conduct an around-the-clock demonstration on the Mall and in LaFayette Park in Washington, D.C., beginning the first day of winter. The permit allowed the demonstrators to maintain two symbolic campsites at these locations, the first with 100 participants and 40 tents and the second with half that number of people and tents. Although the Park Service permitted continuous operation of the symbolic campsites, it denied permission for the demonstrators to sleep there because revised regulations strictly limited camping in national park areas not identified as conventional campsites. The Park Service defined camping to include sleeping as well as other activities normally associated with areas designated for living accommodations.

The primary purpose for making sleep an integral part of the demonstration was "to reenact the central reality of homelessness" and to dramatically impress upon public consciousness that homelessness, a widespread but often ignored problem, confronted its victims with life-threatening conditions. As one of the homeless men seeking to demonstrate explained: "Sleeping in LaFayette Park or on the Mall, for me, is to show people that conditions are so poor for the homeless and poor in this city that we would actually sleep outside in the winter to get the point across."[22] Thus the demonstrators contended that in requesting the right to sleep, they were exercising their rights to engage in symbolic speech as protected by the First Amendment. More specifically, they argued, the Park Service's ban on sleeping at the symbolic campsites abridged the First Amendment guarantee of free speech. The prohibition on sleeping struck at the central message the demonstrators sought to convey, namely, that homeless people have no permanent place to sleep.

Justice White, for the majority, cast the issue in the terms posed by the demonstrators: did the National Park Service regulation prohibiting camping in certain parks violate the First Amendment when applied in connection with a demonstration intended to call attention to the plight of the homeless? No, he concluded, in reversing a contrary judgment by the Court of Appeals. Expressive conduct, he conceded, was to some extent protected by the First Amendment, but it was also subject to reasonable government regulation. He then applied the 1940 rule of *Cantwell v. Connecticut*[23] that the government could regulate "the time, place and manner" of expression as long as its administration was neutral as to the content of the message the demonstrators wished to convey. In this instance, White maintained, regulation narrowly focused on the government's substantial interest in maintaining attractive parks in the nation's capitol, readily available to the millions of people who wish to see and enjoy them.

Thurgood Marshall dissented, joined by Justice William Brennan. He stressed that LaFayette Park and the Mall have served as the site for some of the most rousing political demonstrations in the nation's history and that they constituted a fitting and powerful forum for political protest. Although Marshall agreed with the standard enunciated by the majority and conceded that the government interest in maintaining the parks was significant, he did not agree that prohibiting sleeping would substantially further that interest. In his view, the First Amendment required the government to justify every abridgment of its rights, even if the Constitution did not compel the government to permit the expression in the first place.

The *O'Brien* precedent also drew some application in the 1980s. Unlike some "content-neutral" restrictions, such as laws prohibiting the distribution of leaflets in certain places or times, the regulation against burning a draft card was not directed at expressive activity. Its effect on free speech was merely incidental. Thus, *O'Brien* raised an important question: should it matter whether a content-neutral law was designed specifically to restrict expression or designed to restrict a broader range of activities, with only an incidental effect on free speech? Two cases are pertinent.

In *Wayte v. United States* (1985),[24] the Court upheld as an "incidental" restriction on free speech the government's policy of enforcing the selective service registration requirement only against those men who had advised the government that they had failed to register or who were reported by others as having failed to register. The facts were clear. After the reinstitution of draft registration in 1980, Wayte, an eighteen-year-old, wrote several letters to the president and other government officials, saying that he had no intention of complying. Wayte's letters were added to a file of similar letters written by other nonregistrants. The selective service then embarked on a policy of investigating and prosecuting only those nonregistrants whose letters were contained in the file. Wayte argued that this constituted selective prosecution and violated the First Amendment because of his vocal opposition to draft registration. The federal district court agreed. The federal appeals court reversed this judgment. It acknowledged that Wayte and the other twelve men who had been indicted (out of an estimated 674,000 people who failed to register) were vocal opponents of draft registration, but it held that Wayte failed to show that he was being prosecuted because of his protest activities.

The Supreme Court affirmed the judgment of the court of appeals. Justice Powell, for the Court, acknowledged that prosecutorial discretion, while broad, is not unfettered. Selective enforcement of a law is barred where the decision to prosecute is based upon unjustifiable standards, such as race, religion, or some other arbitrary classification, or where it is motivated by an attempt to impede the exercise of protected statutory or constitutional rights. There was no such impediment in this case; the restriction upon Wayte was only incidental.

In *United States v. Albertini*,[25] later the same term, the Court upheld as an "incidental" restriction on free speech a federal statute prohibiting any person from reentering a military base after being ordered not to do so, as applied to an individual who sought entrance for purposes of free speech. The circumstances were unusual. In 1982, Albertini and a companion had entered Hickam Air Force Base in Hawaii, ostensibly to present a letter to the commanding officer. Instead, they obtained access to secret Air Force documents and destroyed them by pouring animal blood on them. For these acts they were convicted of conspiracy to injure government property. Albertini also received a "bar letter" from the base commander, informing him that he was forbidden to enter the confines of this installation without the written permission of the commander. Yet during the annual open house for armed forces day, Albertini entered Hickam again and engaged in a peaceful demonstration criticizing the nuclear arms race. This time he only took photographs of the displays at the open house and did not disrupt any activities. Albertini was subsequently convicted in federal district court for his defiance of the ban and for his conduct. The court of appeals reversed, holding that he had a First Amendment right to enter Hickam during the open house because the base had been transformed into a temporary public forum.

Justice Sandra Day O'Connor, for the Supreme Court, ruled that the court of appeals erred in holding that the First Amendment barred Albertini's conviction for violating the law by his reentry during the open house. A military base generally is not a public forum and did not become one merely because the base was used to communicate ideas or information during the open house, she argued. Regardless of whether Hickam was considered an open forum on that day, the action to exclude Albertini did not violate his First Amendment rights. The fact that he had received a valid "bar letter" distinguished him from the general public and provided a reasonable ground for excluding him from the base, she contended. Further, the exclusion was not greater than was essential to protect the government's interest in the security of military installations. Nothing in the First Amendment, she maintained, required military commanders to wait until persons subject to a valid "bar order" have entered a military base to see if they will conduct themselves properly during an open house.

The question of flag desecration and flag burning that produced national controversy and congressional action in the late 1980s and early 1990s had roots in the 1960s and 1970s. Involved were changing popular views of symbolic speech, in this case focusing upon the nation's most familiar and emotionally laden symbol, the Stars and Stripes. In 1969, a young black man, Sidney Street, heard over the radio that civil rights activist James Meredith had been wounded by a sniper's bullet during a protest walk in Mississippi. In disgust, he took his American flag outside, walked to a nearby intersection in Brooklyn, New York, set it afire, and tossed it on the pavement. To a small crowd that had gathered he stated: "we don't need no damned flag" and "if they let that happen to Meredith, we don't need an American flag." The crowd's behavior was not menacing, nor did people block the street or sidewalk. Street was convicted in state court for violating a New York statute making it illegal "to publicly mutilate, deface, defile, or defy, trample upon or cast contempt upon, either by words or act" any flag of the United States.

Justice Harlan, who had dissented in *Tinker*, wrote the majority opinion reversing Street's conviction on the grounds that either his speech or his burning the flag or both might have provided the basis for his conviction and his speech was constitutionally protected. Here the Court combined speech and action, contending Street's conviction could not stand because "the right to differ as to things that touch the heart of the existing order" encompasses a "freedom to express publicly one's opinions about our flag, including those actions which are defiant or contemptuous."[26] Having thus reversed the conviction, the Court found it unnecessary to consider other issues raised by the case. The understanding from *Street* then was that the Constitution protected an individual's right to abuse the flag verbally, but that it was uncertain whether it protected his right to burn the flag as an expression of political protest.

Although the ACLU's attorney had argued for Street that flag burning was a form of symbolic expression protected by the First Amendment, the majority in *Street* never reached that issue. But the four dissenters did, arguing that laws against flag desecration were constitutional and that Street's conviction should have been sustained. Chief Justice Warren was particularly categorical in stating that the states and the federal government do have the power to protect the flag from acts of desecration and disgrace. A follow-up case, *Cowgill v. California* (1974),[27] which involved the wearing of a vest made from a cut-up American flag, provided no further resolution, since the Court again failed to address the issue of symbolic speech.

Variants of this issue took numerous and, at times, off-beat forms in the 1970s. The Supreme Court divided evenly in *Radich v. New York* (1971),[28] a case involving the display of several works of art. An artist, Marc Morrell, had created thirteen constructions from various flags, including the American, including a gun caisson wrapped in a flag, a flag in the form of a human hanging from a noose, and an erect penis shape wrapped in a flag. A policeman who saw the exhibit arrested the gallery operator, who was tried and convicted under New York's flag desecration act. The Supreme Court let the conviction stand, but a federal district court, agreeing with Radich that the tie vote had not settled the matter, subsequently acquitted him on First Amendment grounds.

Valarie Goguen wore a small cloth version of the American flag on the seat of his pants and was convicted of violating the Massachusetts flag desecration statute, which provided that whoever publicly mutilated, trampled upon, defaced, or treated the American flag contemptuously had violated the law. The federal district court reversed the conviction on the grounds that the law was too vague; that is, the statute's terms were so unclear as to give no warning about the kind of conduct outlawed. The Supreme Court, on appeal, agreed.[29] Justice Powell spoke for the Court and emphasized that Goguen was charged not with any act of physical desecration but with publicly treating the flag of the United States with contempt. This aspect of the statute was inherently vague and hence violated due process. Reflecting his sense of the times, Powell pointed out that it was not clear, in a day of "relaxed clothing styles," that wearing the flag was necessarily an act of contempt. Thus, the Court's decision generally ignored the question of symbolic expression.

In *Spence v. Washington* (1974),[30] a college student, using removable black tape, affixed a peace symbol to each side of his American flag and then hung it upside down from a window in his apartment as a way of protesting the Vietnam War and the shooting of students by national guardsmen at Kent State University. For this he was convicted of violating a state law forbidding improper use of the flag. The statute prohibited the exhibition of the national flag to which is attached or superimposed "any word, figure, mark, design, drawing or advertisement." But the Court held that this Washington law impermissibly infringed upon free expression, at least when applied to Spence's activity. In the course of the *per curiam* opinion, the Court agreed that Spence was indeed expressing an opinion by displaying the flag as he did and that there was in this instance no overriding state interest in preventing him from so using the flag. The Court went on to justify the reversal on four more explicit grounds: that the flag was privately owned; that Spence displayed the flag on private property; that there was no breach of the peace; and that Spence did engage in a form of communication, namely, he wanted others to know of his belief that America stood for peace. Finally, he displayed it in a way closely analogous to the manner in which flags have always been used to convey ideas. His message was direct, likely to be understood, and thereby within the contours of the First Amendment.

This antiwar spirit and apparent need to make public statements against the war in symbolic fashion produced one interesting "dress" case. Three performers in an antiwar "street theater" skit in front of the Armed Forces Induction Center in Houston, Texas, wore army uniforms as costumes to symbolize the presence of the U.S. military in Vietnam. The leader, Schacht, was convicted for violating federal laws against the unauthorized wearing of a military uniform and the use of a uniform in a theatrical production that tended to discredit the armed forces. The Supreme Court unanimously reversed the conviction, ruling that the Constitution protected street theater and that skits and plays critical of the armed forces were fully protected by the First Amendment.[31] Justice Black delivered the opinion of the Court and made clear that the restrictive law that left Americans free to praise the war in Vietnam through symbolic action could hardly be used to send Schacht to prison for opposing it.

No further dress or hair-length cases reached the Supreme Court, despite their plethora at the lower-court levels through this period. The Supreme Court seemed reluctant to decide for the nation as a whole whether elements of freedom of expression were involved in the way public school or college students wore their hair or their clothing.

Ironically, the Reagan years, with its wave of conservative patriotism fired by the White House and an increasingly conservative Supreme Court, witnessed a decision that declared flag burning to be protected by the First Amendment. The circumstances that produced the key case[32] were revealing. During the Republican National Convention in Dallas in 1984, Gregory Johnson participated in a demonstration dubbed the "Republican War Chest Tour," to protest the policies of the Reagan administration and of certain Dallas-based corporations. The demonstrators marched through the streets, chanting slogans and staging "die-ins" outside various corporate locations to dramatize the consequences of nuclear war. The demonstration ended in front of the Dallas City Hall, where Johnson unfurled an American flag (given to him by a fellow demonstrator who had taken it from outside a building along the route), doused it with kerosene, and set it on fire. While the flag burned the protestors chanted, "America, the red, white, and blue, we spit on you." Johnson was subsequently convicted for violating a Texas law prohibiting "the desecration of venerated objects," including the national flag. The law defined "desecrate" as "deface, damage, or otherwise physically mistreat in a way that the actor knows will seriously offend one or more persons likely to observe or discover his action."

The opinion, derived from the *O'Brien* test, was delivered by Justice Brennan, with the state of Texas conceding, for purposes of its oral argument, that Johnson's conduct was expressive conduct. Under these circumstances, Johnson's burning of the flag was conduct "sufficiently imbued with elements of communication" to implicate the First Amendment. "If there is a bedrock principle underlying the First Amendment," Brennan wrote, "it is that the Government may not prohibit the expression of an idea simply because society finds the idea itself offensive or disagreeable." Citing the *Street* case and even going back to the 1943 *Barnette* decision, Brennan contended that nothing in the Court's precedents suggested that the state may foster its own view of the flag by prohibiting expressive conduct relating to it:

> It is not the state's ends, but its means to which we object. It cannot be gainsaid that there is a special place reserved for the flag in this Nation and thus we do not doubt that the government has a legitimate interest in making efforts to preserve the national flag as an unalloyed symbol of our country. But to say that the government has an interest in the proper treatment of the flag is not to say that it may criminally punish a person for burning a flag as a means of political protest. National unity as an end which officials may foster by persuasion and example is not in question. The problem is whether under our Constitution compulsion as here employed is a permissible means for its achievement.[33]

Justice Anthony Kennedy concurred. The ruling, Kennedy stated, was simply "a pure command of the Constitution. . . . [I]t is poignant and fundamental that the flag protects those who hold it in contempt."[34]

Four Justices, speaking through Chief Justice William Rehnquist, dissented. Rehnquist wrote a highly emotional opinion stressing that millions of Americans have a "mystical reverence" for the flag and deriding the majority for "bundling off" under the rubric of "designated symbols" the "uniquely deep awe and respect for our flag felt by virtually all of us."[35]

Reaction to the ruling was strong and highly negative. Veterans groups denounced the Court's action across the country. President George Bush deplored it. A *Newsweek* poll found that 65 percent of Americans disagreed with it. By a vote of 97 to 3, the U.S. Senate passed a resolution expressing "profound disappointment" with the ruling. Members of Congress called for constitutional action overruling the Court, namely, proposing an amendment to the First Amendment to exclude flag burning from its protection and to deny that flag burning was free speech.

Many civil libertarians were appalled at this reaction, and the American Bar Association (ABA), at its annual meeting in August 1989, went on record as urging Congress and the American public to preserve freedom of speech under the First Amendment and oppose a constitutional amendment concerning desecration of the American flag. The organization also voiced its opposition to federal legislation that would seek to criminalize desecration of the American flag as a political protest, while it deplored any desecration of the flag and declared its full support for the proposition that the flag is a revered national symbol that ought to be treated with great respect by all citizens of the United States. The ABA resolution made clear that the body believed that attempts to amend the Constitution were "an unwarranted infringement on freedom of speech and expression and a dangerous precedent for the future" and that attempts at federal legislation were "not only futile but irresponsible."[36]

Nonetheless, federal legislation did pass, in the form of a Flag Protection Act, in October 1989. After much patriotic rhetoric, the House voted 317 to 43 to complete congressional action on the bill. The measure required up to a year in jail and a $1,000 fine for anyone who "knowingly mutilates, defaces, physically defiles, burns, maintains on the floor or ground, or tramples upon any flag of the United States," except for conduct related to the disposal of a "worn or soiled flag."[37] President Bush allowed the measure to become law without his signature, indicating it was not the ultimate answer and that he would continue to push for a constitutional amendment. Congressional Democrats, however, declared that a constitutional amendment should be used only as a last resort and argued that their bill was so carefully worded that it probably could survive a Court challenge. "It is the act of harming the physical integrity of the flag, rather than any action that the message might convey, that is to be punished," said House Judiciary Chairman Jack Brooks of Texas. He went on to argue that the idea was to make flag defacement illegal regardless of whether it had anything to do with political protest and to make the statute content-neutral. House minority leader Robert Michels scoffed at that notion, however, arguing there was no way to draw up such a bill. "To those who believe we can overturn a Supreme Court decision by statute I can only repeat the immortal words of the farmer, who, when asked directions, said 'You can't get there from here.' "[38]

But while the bill became law, it did not survive long. On June 11, 1990, the Supreme Court declared the statute unconstitutional as an unwarranted qualification on symbolic expression and hence on the First Amendment. It thus ruled the federal statute unconstitutional. Justice Brennan again spoke for the Court. The cases *United States v. Eichman* and *United States v. Haggerty*[39] were consolidated in his opinion. In the former the government had prosecuted men who had knowingly set fire to several American flags on the steps of the capitol while protesting various aspects of the government's domestic and foreign policy. In the latter, it had prosecuted four individuals who knowingly set fire to a flag while protesting the Flag Protection Act's passage. In each case the respective appellants moved to dismiss the flag-burning charge on the ground that the act, both on its face and as applied, violated the First Amendment. Brennan's opinion pointed out that, in this case, the government conceded that the flag burning constituted "expressive conduct." Even so, it urged the Court to reconsider the claim of the *Johnson* case that flag burning was a mode of expression, like obscenity or "fighting words," and therefore did not enjoy the full protection of the First Amendment.

Brennan declined to take this approach. The only remaining question, he maintained, was whether the Flag Protection Act was sufficiently distinctive from the Texas statute that it may constitutionally be applied to proscribe the appellees' expressive conduct. He acknowledged that the federal act, unlike the Texas law, contained no explicit content-based limitation on the scope of prohibited conduct. It was nevertheless clear that the government's asserted interest was related to the suppression of free expression. Its concern for protecting the physical integrity of a privately owned flag rested upon a perceived need to preserve the flag's status as a symbol of the nation and certain national ideals. "But the mere destruction or disfigurement of a particular manifestation of the symbol, without more, does not diminish or otherwise affect the symbol itself in any way."

Although Congress cast the Flag Protection Act in somewhat broader terms than the Texas statute at issue in *Johnson*, the act still suffered from the same fundamental flaw, Brennan claimed. It suppressed expression out of concern for its likely communicative impact. "Despite the Act's wider scope, its restriction on expression cannot be justified without reference to the content of the regulated speech."[40] He also acknowledged that the government can create national symbols, promote them, and encourage their respectful treatment. But the Flag Protection Act went well beyond this by criminally proscribing expressive conduct because of its likely communicative impact. Punishing desecration of the flag, Brennan concluded, diluted the very freedom that makes this emblem so revered.

Justice Stevens, as he did in *Johnson*, dissented, with Rehnquist, White, and O'Connor joining him. Contending that the federal act protected the symbolic value of the flag, without regard to the specific content of the flag-burner's speech, he argued for its preservation, stating that "what makes this case particularly difficult for me is what I regard as the damage to the symbol that has already occurred as a result of this Court's decision to place its stamp of approval on the act of flag burning."[41] Nonetheless, this position was that of a minority. Public reaction was much more muted than before, many politicians seeing little more advantage to be gained from further flag-waving patriotism, and the issue largely disappeared as a source of controversy.

It seems ironic that the Supreme Court, in the 1990–91 term, took up the question of nude dancing as a principal symbolic speech case. While easily lampooned, the case nonetheless raised interesting First Amendment questions, while also reflecting ongoing splits among the justices regarding the control of public morality.

As national permissiveness grew in the 1970s and '80s, a number of states and cities moved to ban totally nude erotic dancing. The essence of the 1991 ruling, *Barnes v. Glen Theatre*, was that, by 5 to 4, the justices held that requiring dancers to wear at least pasties and a G-string did not violate their freedom of speech. It thus gave local prosecutors a new option to restrict totally nude entertainment in their communities. Civil liberties lawyers, who had feared that the Court might apply a sweeping analysis that could call into question constitutional protection for many forms of artistic expression, said they were relieved by the Court's relatively narrow approach.

The test case involved nude dancers in the Kitty Kat Lounge in South Bend, Indiana, arrested for violating the state's public indecency law. A federal appeals court in Chicago had ruled that the dancing was inherently expressive, communicating an emotional message of eroticism and sensuality, and that the ban therefore violated the First Amendment. Five justices voted to reverse, but they could not agree on a single reason.

Chief Justice Rehnquist for the majority made clear that nude dancing enjoyed some marginal First Amendment protection. But, due to the state's interest in promoting order and morality, it could be prohibited, just as can other forms of public nudity. He observed that the pasties and G-string requirement was a modest imposition and "the bare minimum necessary to achieve the state's purpose."[42] Justice David Souter felt that the law was constitutional because nude dancing was associated with such other evils as prostitution and sexual assault, while Justice Antonin Scalia argued that the First Amendment does not protect such conduct at all, contending the state had a legitimate interest in stopping public nudity generally. Justice White, in dissent, disagreed, believing that the state was repressing the dancers erotic message, which was constitutionally protected. He was joined by Marshall, Blackmun, and Stevens.

National response was predictable. The conservative American Family Association gloated that "after today, states can totally regulate nude dancing without fear of violating the First Amendment." The liberal advocacy group People for the American Way was relieved that the ruling was narrower than it could have been, even though its brief had argued strongly against the law's constitutionality.

Thus, the current interpretation of the permissible limits of symbolic speech remained in flux. The 1992 St. Paul hate-speech case casts in doubt the acceptability of speech codes on scores of college campuses and elsewhere. But by and large the distinctions drawn in case law since the 1960s has created sufficient ambiguity so that further finetuning in this field is inevitable. It will come from an increasingly conservative and activist Court.

Church and State
The Religion Clauses

Melvin I. Urofsky

The First Amendment to the Constitution contains two clauses concerning religion: "Congress shall make no law respecting an establishment of religion, or prohibiting the free exercise thereof." For most of the first 150 years following the adoption of the Bill of Rights Congress obeyed this injunction, and not until 1947 did the Court rule that the religion clauses applied to the states as well as to the national government. Justice Hugo Black, in his majority ruling in *Everson v. Board of Education*, expounded at length on the historical development of religious freedom in the United States, and concluded:

> The "establishment of religion" clause of the First Amendment means at least this: Neither a state nor the Federal Government can set up a church. Neither can pass laws which aid one religion, aid all religions, or prefer one religion over another. Neither can force nor influence a person to go to or remain away from church against his will or force him to profess a belief or disbelief in any religion. No person can be punished for entertaining or professing religious beliefs or disbeliefs, for church attendance or non-attendance. No tax in any amount, large or small, can be levied to support any religious activities or institutions, whatever they may be called, or whatever form they may adopt to teach or practice religion. Neither a state nor the Federal Government can openly or secretly, participate in the affairs of any religious organization or groups and vice versa. In the words of [Thomas] Jefferson, the clause against establishment of religion by law was intended to erect "a wall of separation between church and State."[1]

This paragraph contains the root rationale for nearly every religion case decided by the Court in the last forty years, whether it involves the establishment clause (in which the government promotes a religious function) or the free exercise clause (in which the government restricts an individual from adhering to some practice).

Yet the *Everson* decision provided an interesting twist. A New Jersey statute authorized school districts to make rules providing transportation for students, "including the transportation of school children to and from school other than a public school, except such school as is operated for profit." One local board allowed reimbursement to parents of parochial school students for fares paid by their children on public buses when going to and from school, and a taxpayer in the district challenged the payments as a form of establishment.

After his lengthy review of the history of the clauses, and language that implied that no form of aid—direct or indirect—could be tolerated under the establishment clause, Justice Black concluded that the reimbursement plan did not violate the First Amendment, which only requires that "the state be a neutral in its relations with groups of religious believers and non-believers; it does not require the state to be their adversary. . . . [The] legislation, as applied, does no more than provide a general program to help parents get their children, regardless of their religion, safely and expeditiously to and from accredited schools."[2]

The opinion evoked dissents from four members of the Court, and Justice Robert H. Jackson noted that Black, after marshaling every argument in favor of a total separation of church from state, weakly allowed that no breach of the wall had occurred. "The case which irresistibly comes to mind as the most fitting precedent is that of Julia who, according to Byron's reports, 'whispering "I will ne'er consent,"—consented.' "[3] Justice Wiley B. Rutledge took the logic of Black's historical argument and reached the inevitable conclusion that if "the test remains undiluted as Jefferson and Madison made it, [then] money taken by taxation from one is not to be used or given to support another's religious training or belief, or indeed one's own. [T]he prohibition is absolute."[4]

In fact, by the time the Court heard its next religion cases, Justice Black had moved to the position Rutledge had suggested, that the prohibition had to be absolute. In a 1948 decision, *McCollum v. Board of Education*, the Court struck down a so-called released time program in Illinois, in which classrooms in the public schools were turned over for one hour each week for religious instruction. Local churches and synagogues could send in instructors to teach the tenets of their religion to students whose families approved. To Justice Black, writing for the 8–1 majority, the issue could not have been clearer. "Not only are the state's tax-supported public school buildings used for the dissemination of religious doctrines, the State also affords sectarian groups an invaluable aid in that it helps to provide pupils . . . through use of the state's compulsory public school machinery."[5]

Four years after *McCollum*, the Court issued what might be called its first "accommodationist" ruling on the establishment clause. To continue the released time program, a number of states had moved the religious instruction off school property, but taxpayers challenged the program on grounds that it still involved the state in promoting religion. The authority of the school supported participation in the program; public school teachers policed attendance; and normal classroom activities came to a halt so students in the program would not miss their secular instruction.

Justice William O. Douglas's opinion for the six-member majority indicated that the Court had heard the public outcry over the *McCollum* decision, and he went out of his way to assert that the Court was not antagonistic to religion. "We are," he intoned, "a religious people whose institutions presuppose a Supreme Being."[6] Although the First Amendment prohibition against an establishment of religion was "absolute," this did not mean that "in every and all respects there shall be a separation of Church and State." He went on to argue that historically the Amendment had been interpreted in a "commonsense" manner, because a strict and literal view would lead to unacceptable conclusions; "municipalities would not be permitted to render police or fire protection to religious groups. Policemen who helped parishioners into their places of worship would violate the Constitution." Such a view would make the state hostile to religion, a condition also forbidden by the First Amendment.

The conflicting opinions in *Everson*, *McCollum*, and *Zorach* left very little clear, other than that the religion clauses now applied to the states as well as to the federal government. In all three cases the majority as well as the dissenters had seemingly subscribed to the "wall of separation" metaphor and to the absolute nature of the First Amendment prohibitions but disagreed on how "absolute" the separation had to be. During the 1960s it appeared that the separation would be very absolute, as exemplified in the prayer and Bible cases; since the early 1970s, however, the pendulum has swung back and forth between strict separation and accommodation, and the issue remains undecided.

The school prayer decision is a good example of absolutism, and it also indicates the strong feelings that Court decisions touching upon religion arouse. In New York, the statewide Board of Regents had prepared a "nondenominational" prayer for use in the public schools. After one district had directed that the prayer be recited each day, a group of parents challenged the edict as "contrary to the beliefs, religions, or religious practices of both themselves and their children." The New York Court of Appeals, the state's highest tribunal, upheld the school board, providing that it did not force any student to join in the prayer over a parent's objection. The Supreme Court reversed in *Engel v. Vitale*.[7]

In his opinion for the 6–1 majority, Justice Black (who had taught Sunday school for more than twenty years) held the entire idea of a state-mandated prayer, no matter how religiously neutral, as "wholly inconsistent with the Establishment Clause." A prayer, by any definition, constituted a religious activity, and the First Amendment "must at least mean that [it] is no part of the business of government to compose official prayers for any group of the American people to recite as part of a religious program carried on by government." Black saw the nature of prayer itself as essentially religious, and, by promoting prayer, the state violated the establishment clause by fostering a religious activity that it determined and sponsored.

The *Engel* decision unleashed a firestorm of conservative criticism against the Court that, while abating from time to time, has never died out. In the eyes of many the Court had struck at a traditional practice that served important social purposes, even if it occasionally penalized a few nonconformists or eccentrics. This sense that, as one newspaper screamed, "COURT OUTLAWS GOD" seemed to be reinforced one year later when the Court extended its reasoning in *Abington School District v. Schempp*[8] to invalidate a Pennsylvania law requiring the daily reading of ten verses of the Bible and the recitation of the Lord's Prayer.

Justice Tom Clark, normally considered a conservative, spoke for the 8–1 majority in striking down the required Bible reading. He built upon Black's comments in *Engel* that the neutrality commanded by the Constitution stemmed from the bitter lessons of history, which recognized that a fusion of church and state inevitably led to persecution of all but those who adhered to the official orthodoxy. Recognizing that the Court would be confronted with additional establishment clause cases in the future, Clark attempted to set out rules by which lower courts could determine when the constitutional barrier had been breached. The test, he said, may be stated as follows:

> What are the purpose and the primary effect of the enactment? If either is the advancement or inhibition of religion then the enactment exceeds the scope of legislative power as circumscribed by the Constitution. That is to say that to withstand the strictures of the Establishment Clause there must be a secular legislative purpose and a primary effect that neither advances nor inhibits religion.[9]

In this last sentence, Clark set out the first two prongs of what would later be known as the *Lemon* tripartite test, which the Court has used to evaluate all establishment clause challenges. The legislation (1) had to have a secular purpose and (2) could neither advance nor inhibit religion.

One can describe the school prayer and Bible cases as instances in which a benign majority unthinkingly imposed its views, unaware that the results restricted the religious freedom of a minority. In the third major establishment clause case of the Warren Court, however, a local majority deliberately attempted to establish its views as official dogma in defiance of what the rest of the country believed.

One of the most famous battlegrounds of the 1920s between the forces of tradition and modernism had been the Scopes "Monkey Trial" in Dayton, Tennessee, in which a young teacher named John Scopes had been convicted for teaching the theory of evolution. The Tennessee Supreme Court reversed the conviction on a technicality, but the law remained on the Tennessee statute books, and similar laws could be found in other "Bible Belt" states. Following the Dayton uproar, however, they remained essentially dead letters, unenforced and in many cases nearly forgotten.

In Arkansas, the statute forbade teachers in state schools from teaching the "theory or doctrine that mankind ascended or descended from a lower order of animals." An Arkansas biology teacher, Susan Epperson, sought a declaratory judgment on the constitutionality of the statute. The Arkansas Supreme Court, aware of antievolution sentiment within the state, evaded the constitutional issue entirely. But the U.S. Supreme Court, without a dissenting vote, voided the Arkansas statute as a violation of the establishment clause.[10] Justice Abe Fortas concluded that the Arkansas law "selects from the body of knowledge a particular segment which it proscribes for the sole reason that it is deemed to conflict with a particular religious doctrine, that is, with a particular interpretation of the Book of Genesis by a particular religious group."

Antievolutionists in Arkansas and elsewhere sought to bypass the *Epperson* ruling a generation later. Instead of removing biology and the evolutionary theory from the schools, they added so-called creation science, which advocated the Biblical narrative as supported by allegedly scientific evidence and required that any school teaching evolution had to give "equal time" in the classroom to "creation science."

The Louisiana Balanced Treatment Act of 1982 reached the Supreme Court in 1987, and Justice Brennan spoke for a 7–2 majority in striking down the statute as a violation of the establishment clause.[11] The Court denounced the stated purpose of the law, to advance academic freedom, as a sham, since the sponsors of the bill had made it quite clear during the legislative debate that they wanted to inject religious teachings into the public schools. It is unlikely that the issue will go away; like prayer and Bible reading, the true believers will keep seeking some way to get their views grafted onto the school curriculum.

In some ways, but only some, free exercise cases are easier than establishment problems, because they involve the state restricting an individual's religious practices. There is, of course, much overlap between the two clauses, and often a governmental program that tries to help religion in general may in fact restrict the freedoms of individuals. The school prayer and Bible readings offended the Court not just on establishment grounds but because they also limited the free exercise of those who disagreed with the prayer or worshipped from another Bible.

Free exercise claims also overlap with claims to freedom of expression; several important cases prior to 1953 involved Jehovah's Witnesses, who claimed a right to proselytize, without state regulation, as essential to the free exercise of their beliefs. In these cases, the Court's analysis concentrated almost solely on the criteria used to safeguard speech.[12] In addition, there are some issues unique to free exercise claims.

First is the belief/action dichotomy first enunciated by Chief Justice Morrison Waite in a Mormon bigamy case.[13] While the First Amendment absolutely prohibits government efforts to restrict beliefs, it does not prevent the state from forbidding practices that threaten public order or safety. In the example Waite used, if a sect believed in human sacrifice, the government could do nothing to restrict that belief; but it could, without violating the free expression clause, bar the actual sacrifice. The Court soon recognized, however, that one could not divide belief and action so easily, and in 1940 it modified Waite's rule; while action remained subject to regulation, it deserved some protection under free exercise claims.[14]

A second problem involves limits placed by the establishment clause on the free exercise clause. The two clauses overlap in their protection, but there are also instances where they conflict. A state's efforts to accommodate certain groups by exempting or immunizing them from general laws may also be seen as providing a preference to one sect.

The flag-salute cases of the 1940s indicated how closely free exercise and freedom of expression are intertwined; the Sunday laws show the interconnectedness of the two religion clauses. A number of states had, and many still do have, laws requiring the majority of businesses to close on Sunday. In 1961 the Court heard four cases challenging these laws as violation of the First Amendment, and in three of them the Court refused to consider free exercise claims. In *McGowan v. Maryland*,[15] Chief Justice Earl Warren conceded that "the original laws which dealt with Sunday labor were motivated by religious forces." He rejected, however, the argument that this constituted an establishment of religion, because in modern times the laws represented an effort by the state to enforce one day's rest in seven.

In the companion case of *Braunfeld v. Brown*,[16] orthodox Jewish merchants attacked the Sunday laws on free exercise grounds. Their religious beliefs required them to close on Saturdays, and having their shops closed two days a week would seriously undermine their ability to earn a livelihood. Chief Justice Warren recited the accepted distinction between belief and action and noted that nothing in the law forced the appellants to modify or deny their beliefs; at worst, they might have to change occupations or incur some economic disadvantages.

There is a striking insensitivity, almost callousness, in Warren's opinion to the problem raised by the Jewish merchants, especially when one considers the great sensitivity he showed to the plights of other minority groups. Justice William Brennan in his dissent pointed the way toward future First Amendment jurisprudence. He had no doubt but that the Sunday law imposed a great burden on the Jewish merchants, forcing them to choose between their business and their religion, and this, he believed, violated the free exercise clause. To impose such a burden, the state had to prove some compelling state interest to justify this restriction on freedom of religion, and the "mere convenience" of having everybody rest on the same day did not, in his eyes, constitute a compelling state interest.

Did Pennsylvania have any options by which the state's interest in fostering one day's rest in seven would not conflict with the appellants' religious freedom? Of course it did. Of the thirty-four states with Sunday closing laws, twenty-one granted exemptions to those who in good faith observed another day of rest. The Court, he charged, had "exalted administrative convenience to a constitutional level high enough to justify making one religion economically disadvantageous."[17]

Brennan not only pointed out that a commonsense solution existed, but his opinion showed greater sensitivity to the problems economic hardship would cause religious freedom, and the Brennan view triumphed fairly quickly. Two years after the Sunday closing law cases, the Court heard a case in which a Seventh-day Adventist in South Carolina had been discharged from her job because she would not work on Saturday. Her refusal to work on her Sabbath prevented her from finding other employment, and then the state denied her unemployment compensation payments. South Carolina law barred benefits to workers who refused, without "good cause," to accept suitable work when offered.[18]

In what we would now term the "modern" approach to First Amendment issues, Justice Brennan posed the same question he had in *Braunfeld*: Did the state have a compelling interest sufficient to warrant an abridgment of a constitutionally protected right? This is, of course, the same question the Court asks in regard to speech restrictions, because the analytical process in speech and free exercise claims are similar.

The *Sherbert* case, as well as that involving the Amish in Wisconsin (*Wisconsin v. Yoder*), raises the question of whether the Constitution can be read as totally "religion-neutral" or "religion-blind." Professor Philip B. Kurland has suggested that one can find a unifying principle in the two religion clauses and that they ought to be "read as a single precept that government cannot utilize religion as a standard for action or inaction, because these clauses prohibit classification in terms of religion either to control a benefit or impose a burden."[19] The argument parallels the suggestion made by the first Justice Harlan that the Constitution is "color-blind,"[20] and, like that argument, it is manifestly incorrect.

Neutrality in religious matters is more of an ideal than a reality in constitutional adjudication, and for the same reason. Very few issues that reach the Court can be resolved in simple ways; if the cases had been easy, the Court would not have heard them. Religion, like race, is a tangled skein, and not amenable to simplistic solutions. The Court has recognized this, and from the absolutist decisions of the early Warren era, the Court has moved steadily toward a jurisprudence of balancing various considerations. It is this balancing that marked the Court's approach to church-state issues since the early 1970s.

The Warren Court dealt with the religion clauses almost as if they were a blank slate; as a result, its landmark cases on school prayer, Bible reading, evolution, and Sabbath observance captured public attention and struck many Americans, especially those who believed that religion belonged in schools, as wrong. Political and religious conservatives expected, indeed demanded, that the Burger Court reject these earlier rulings. Some members of the Court appeared quite willing to do so and espoused an accommodationist view based on what came to be known as a jurisprudence of original intent. Especially in the latter years of Warren Burger's tenure, debate over original intent, and what the religion clauses actually meant, occupied a central place in both popular and academic debate over the Court.

Justice Black, in his majority ruling in *Everson v. Board of Education*, had expounded at length on the historical development of the establishment clause and had concluded that "in the words of [Thomas] Jefferson, the clause against establishment of religion by law was intended to erect 'a wall of separation between church and State.' "[21] Black's opinion had set the basis for all establishment clause cases for the next forty years; it also opened the door to a flourishing debate over the original intent of the framers in drafting not only the First Amendment but the Constitution as a whole and over how justices today ought to interpret that document. The debate—in the courts, in law schools, and in public—has gone under several names, "judicial restraint" vs. "activism" and "interpretivism" vs. "noninterpretivism," but the core issue is whether judges, in deciding constitutional issues, should confine themselves to norms that are either stated or clearly implicit in the written document (restraint and interpretivism), or whether they can go beyond the four corners of the written Constitution to discover evolving or implied standards (activism and noninterpretivism).

Edwin Meese, who served as Attorney General in the second Reagan administration, led the attack for a strict adherence to what he called a "jurisprudence of original intention," in which the courts would determine exactly what the framers had meant and interpret the Constitution accordingly:

> Where the language of the Constitution is specific, it must be obeyed. Where there is a demonstrable consensus among the framers and ratifiers as to a principle stated or implied by the Constitution, it should be followed. Where there is ambiguity as to the precise meaning or reach of a constitutional provision, it should be interpreted and applied in a manner so as to at least not contradict the text of the Constitution itself.[22]

But what exactly did the framers and ratifiers of the First Amendment religion clauses intend? Did they mean, as Justice Black argued, that the statement "Congress shall make *no* law" meant just that, that Congress (and through the Fourteenth Amendment the states) could not in any way, shape, or form do anything that might breach the "wall of separation"? Or did they mean that while government could not prefer one sect over another, it might provide aid to all religions on an equal basis? Is the historical record quite as clear as Meese and others would have us believe, or is it somewhat murky, so that the "original intent" of the framers is either not available or irrelevant to contemporary jurisprudence? Many scholars believe that the historic record is, at best, often confused and contradictory.

At the core of the problem is one's view of the Constitution and its role in

American government. Advocates of original intent believe that the vision of the framers is as good today as 200 years ago, and any deviation from that view is an abandonment of the ideals that have made this country free and great. Judges, they argue, should hew strictly to what the framers intended, and if revisions are to be made, it must be through the amendment process.

Defenders of judicial activism agree that courts ought not to amend the Constitution, but they believe that for the document to remain true to the intent of the framers, it must be interpreted in the light of two lamps: the spirit of the framers and the realities of modern society. They believe that the founding generation never intended to put a straitjacket on succeeding generations; rather, they set out a series of ideals, expressed through powers and limitations, and deliberately left details vague so that those who came after could apply those ideals to the world they lived in.

In regard to the establishment clause, for example, advocates of original intent argue that the founders never intended a complete prohibition of aid to religion or to establish an impregnable wall. Rather, they meant no single sect would be elevated above the others, and government could aid religious agencies provided it did so on a nondiscriminatory basis. Therefore, state aid to parochial schools, nondenominational prayers, and public involvement in religious activities are not forbidden provided no particular religion is favored above the others.

The noninterpretationist response is that while this may or may not have been true in 1787, conditions have changed dramatically in the intervening two centuries; in fact, conditions were changing even in the latter part of the eighteenth century. The framers sought language in the First Amendment that would reflect not so much their distaste for a single established church (that model was already passing from the scene), but their fears of church-state entanglement in general. That accounts for the absolute prohibitions expressed in the First Amendment, and courts should, therefore, decide establishment clause cases to preserve inviolate a wall of separation between religion and the state.

The conflict between these two schools of thought can easily be seen in the decisions on state aid to parochial education. Beginning with the Elementary and Secondary Education Act of 1965, both Congress and the states made determined efforts to establish programs that benefited parochial and private schools as well as public systems. Proponents of a strict wall between church and state soon flooded the courts with challenges to the constitutionality of such aid.

The Court heard the first of these cases in 1968, an attack against a 1965 New York law mandating local school boards to furnish textbooks from a state-approved list to nonprofit private schools within their jurisdictions. Technically, the boards merely "loaned" the books and retained title to them; in fact, the books would remain in possession of the private schools until the school boards wrote them off for wear and tear. In *Board of Edu-*

cation v. Allen[23] the Court upheld the law on what is known as the pupil benefit theory, which derived directly from Justice Black's opinion in *Everson*. The loan of the texts, according to Justice Byron White, did not aid religion but benefited the individual student, whether at a public or parochial school, and that, he claimed, had been the primary intent of the legislature. Given these facts, the Court found no violation of the establishment clause.

Under the pupil benefit rule, the Court had now upheld bus transportation and the loan of textbooks; might not this philosophy be extended to cover the actual costs of instruction in history, mathematics, or science? The launching of Sputnik in 1957 triggered an enormous public clamor for better education, and many parents, dissatisfied with the public schools, saw religious schools as an attractive alternative. Why should not tax monies be used to support school systems that provided good education to children? The students, and not religious doctrine, would benefit. This argument commanded the support of a number of justices, and in some cases it found a majority.

The Warren Court had handed down two tests in establishment clause cases—legislation had to have a secular purpose and neither advance nor inhibit religion. In *Walz v. Tax Commission* (1970),[24] the Court added a third, a prohibition against "an excessive government entanglement with religion." One year later, Chief Justice Burger articulated the three-pronged test that has governed all subsequent establishment clause cases, the so-called *Lemon* test: "First, the statute must have a secular legislative purpose; second, its principal or primary effect must be one that neither advances nor inhibits religion; finally the statute must not foster an excessive government entanglement with religion."[25]

In articulating the three-pronged test, the Chief Justice seemed to be sending several messages. First, proponents of the pupil benefit theory should not rely on the limited application of that doctrine in *Everson* and *Allen* to justify further support. Second, he wanted to provide lower courts with a clear and easily applied constitutional rule that could be used in an anticipated flood of litigation resulting from literally hundreds of state and federal programs.

The Court now had its rule, and it was one that could be used either to prohibit or approve state aid to religious schools. In cases over the next fifteen years, nearly every majority and minority opinion invoked the *Lemon* rule, often with strikingly opposite conclusions. Some of this unpredictability stemmed from shifting alignments among the justices, but by the early 1980s, the jurisprudential differences between the separationists and the accommodationists had become quite pronounced.

Following the *Lemon* decision, state governments tried a variety of measures either to meet the three-part test or to get around it. This drive increased with the resurgence of fundamentalist religious groups as part of the conservative coalition that carried Ronald Reagan into the White House in the 1980 election. But despite the presence of an articulate accommodationist bloc, the Court's rulings from the time Warren Burger took the center chair in 1969 and throughout the 1970s had reinforced rather than repudiated the separationist doctrine that had been expounded during the Warren years. The government could not support religious practices or institutions; government had to be neutral in its dealings with religions; and in those secular programs that benefited pupils in religious schools, the government had to avoid excessive entanglement in the management or activities of those schools.

The accommodationists, however, seemed to have gained the upper hand for a while in the mid-eighties. Chief Justice Burger, in *Marsh v. Chambers* (1983),[26] spoke for a 6–3 Court in holding that paid legislative chaplains and prayers at the start of each session of the Nebraska legislature did not violate the establishment clause. Just as Justice Black had elaborated a long historical analysis to justify his view of a wall of separation, so now Burger went back to show that the framers of the First Amendment had been aware of such practices and had not objected to them and that opening prayers had been a staple of national, state, and local government since the founding of the republic.

The following term the Court, by a 5–4 vote, upheld placing a crèche — the Christmas nativity scene — at public expense in front of the city hall in Pawtucket, Rhode Island. For many people, no matter what their faith or view on the First Amendment, there could hardly be a more religious symbol than a crèche. Nor could one imagine any activity more likely to run counter to all the values enunciated by the Court in regard to the establishment clause since 1947, or more likely to flunk all of the criteria of Burger's own *Lemon* test — it was not a secular activity, it advanced religious ideas, and it entangled the government in religion. Moreover, even if one took all of the arguments used by the accommodationists to justify previous decisions — free speech, secular benefits, historical exceptions — none of them applied to this case. Public monies were being expended to support an openly religious display.[27]

The majority opinion in *Lynch v. Donnelly* (1984)[28] must be recognized as the most extreme accommodationist position taken by the Burger Court, but also one that upset and dismayed legal scholars and laypersons alike. Burger's opinion stood more than three decades of establishment clause jurisprudence on its head when he claimed that the Constitution "affirmatively mandates" accommodation. He referred to his earlier decision in *Marsh v. Chambers* to prove that the framers had intended there to be public support for some activities religious in nature, although he did not make clear the connection between a chaplain opening Congress with a prayer and the display of a crèche.

The crèche decision carried a message that it is doubtful had been intended by the Chief Justice, namely, that those who did not subscribe to such "national" symbols, such as atheists, Muslims, Hindus, or Jews, did not belong to the community. Many Christians who, like Justice Brennan, recognized the deep spiritual significance of the crèche objected to the majority's debasing of the religious aspects of Christmas. A spokesperson for the National Council of Churches complained that the Court had put Christ "on the same level as Santa Claus and Rudolph the Red-Nosed Reindeer,"[29] and soon many cars sported bumper stickers to "Keep Christ in Christmas." For scholars, the decision seemed to constitute a major breach in the wall of separation, one that might not be repairable. Reports of the wall's demise, however, proved premature, and the Court began to reaffirm its commitment to a wall of separation.

The first case involved the highly emotional issue of school prayer. Fundamentalist groups had never accepted the Court's 1962 *Engel* ruling, and the resurgence of the religious right in the 1970s led to a number of efforts to overturn the decision by constitutional amendment or to bypass it statutorily. In Alabama, the legislature passed a law in 1978 requiring elementary school classes to observe a period of silence "for meditation" at the beginning of the school day. Three years later it amended the law and called upon the teacher to announce "that a period of silence not to exceed one minute in duration shall be observed for meditation or voluntary prayer." The following year saw another change, this time authorizing any teacher or professor in any of the state's public educational institutions to lead "willing students" in a prescribed prayer that recognized "Almighty God" as the "Creator and Supreme Judge of the World."[30]

Speaking for a 6–3 majority, Justice Stevens struck down the Alabama statute in *Wallace v. Jaffree* (1985) and reaffirmed, at least in part, the vitality of the *Lemon* test. Perhaps most important, a majority of the Court rejected a basic challenge to post-*Everson* jurisprudence. Judge W. Brevard Hand in his district court opinion had held that the Constitution imposed no obstacle to Alabama's establishment of a state religion. Had this view been articulated in 1947, it would have been considered correct; to say it in the 1980s, however, struck most observers as a mental and judicial aberration. The incorporation of the protections guaranteed in the Bill of Rights and their application to the states had been going on for more than six decades and, with very few exceptions, had been accepted throughout the judicial, academic, and political communities. No one on the Court supported this view, and Stevens provided the strongest opinion in support of the traditional jurisprudence that the Court had issued in a number of years.

At the very end of the 1984 term, the Court handed down two important school aid cases that apparently signaled a return to the stricter standards that had prevailed in the 1970s. In *Grand Rapids School District v. Ball*,[31] the Court voided the "shared time" program, in which the city's public school teachers offered remedial and enrichment reading and mathematics, as well as some art, music, and physical education courses, in religious schools. *Aguilar v. Felton*[32] dealt with a federally funded New York program similar to the Grand Rapids "shared time" scheme.

The Court invalidated both shared-time programs by narrow 5–4 votes, the Grand Rapids plan because in effect it advanced religion, and the New York scheme because of excessive government entanglement. The Court produced no new doctrine in these cases, but the return to the basic principles of *Lemon*, *Nyquist*, and earlier cases produced great relief among separationists.

The majority of the religion cases before the Court in the 1970s and 1980s involved the establishment clause, but the justices decided several free exercise cases as well. Perhaps the most notable involved a challenge by the Old Order Amish to a state's compulsory education law in *Wisconsin v. Yoder* (1972).[33] The Amish objected to provisions of the state law requiring attendance past the eighth grade. They believed, and the state did not challenge the sincerity of their belief, that sending adolescent children to high school would endanger their spiritual salvation. Although the Court recognized that the Amish marched totally out of step with contemporary society, Chief Justice Burger affirmed their constitutional right to do so. Enforcement of the law would raise "a very real threat of undermining the Amish community and religious practices as they exist today; they must either abandon belief and be assimilated into society at large, or be forced to migrate to some other and more tolerant region." Given the relatively small number of children involved, the state's interest in educating its citizens would not suffer if it granted the Amish an exception.

Yoder appeals to most people because it seems to carry out the intent of the free exercise clause. A small, powerless faction, wanting to be left free from state regulations that it believed impinged upon its religious beliefs, appealed to the highest court in the land, seeking protection of the First Amendment, and proved victorious. But it also raises the question, as did *Sherbert v. Verner* (1963) in the Warren era, of whether such findings impinge upon establishment clause values. By relieving the Amish of the secular obligation imposed by the school laws, did the Court impinge upon the command of the establishment clause, which bars any classification that would either impose a burden *or a benefit* on religion? Do *Sherbert* and *Yoder* represent the free exercise clause version of accommodation, another breach in the wall of separation?

The problem derives from the Court's criteria for establishment clause cases, namely, that a religious purpose alone—the first prong of the *Lemon* test—constitutes a First Amendment violation. The fact is that many practices in this country have a religious cast, and the Court has had to bend its criteria in order to sustain these practices. Yet in the free exercise decisions, the Court on several occasions permitted states to provide exemptions or, as in *Yoder*, required them to do so. As Jesse Choper succinctly put it:

On the one hand, the Court has read the establishment clause as saying that if a law's purpose is to aid religion, it is unconstitutional. On the other hand, the Court has read the free exercise clause as saying that, under certain circumstances, the state must aid religion. Logically, the two theses are irreconcilable.[34]

It is far from clear whether the Court could have adopted a single standard to govern both clauses in a logically consistent manner, but the tension between the two clauses is apparent, and it erupted in the so-called peyote case.[35]

Oregon dismissed two employees in a drug rehabilitation program because they ingested peyote at a religious ceremony of the Native American Church. Although a number of states have exemptions for peyote when used in religious ceremonies, Oregon does not. The state then denied the two men unemployment compensation because they had been dismissed for misconduct, the use of a criminally proscribed substance. The Oregon Supreme Court overturned that decision, holding that the First Amendment bars criminal punishment of good-faith religious use of peyote.

The state appealed, and in the Supreme Court Justice Antonin Scalia, writing for a bare 5–4 majority, balanced the individual's free exercise claims against the state's need to control harmful substances, the same type of balancing that the Court had used since *Sherbert v. Verner* in 1963. To allow peyote use on the basis of a free exercise claim would in effect grant a preference to a particular religious group, allowing it to break general laws that applied to everyone else. Scalia went all the way back to *Reynolds v. United States* (1879) to support his claim that the Court had "never held that an individual's religious beliefs excused him from compliance with an otherwise valid law prohibiting conduct that the State is free to regulate."

The case elicited a great deal of comment, in part because in previous instances where the Court had balanced individual free exercise against state interest, it had struck the balance in favor of the individual. Scalia in essence abandoned the balancing test when it involved criminal as opposed to civil sanctions, a position vociferously opposed by the minority.

Although some evidence would indicate that the strength of fundamentalist religious groups has waned in the past few years, especially following lurid revelations of sexual and financial wrongdoing by television evangelists, the effort to inject more religion into civic life continues to bring First Amendment problems before the courts. In the past several terms it would appear that personnel changes on the Court have swung the pendulum more to the side of accommodation than strict separation, yet the separationists have also won some battles.

The Court, for example, upheld the 1981 Adolescent Family Life Act, which provided grants to religiously affiliated organizations to operate programs designed to reduce the incidence of and problems associated with teenage pregnancy and sexual activity. Chief Justice William Rehnquist, in *Bowen v. Kendrick* (1988), found the "religious" parts of the program incidental to its secular purpose, much to the amazement of those who recognized that the program deliberately fostered particular religious values.

The justices also wrestled with public displays of crèches and menorahs on public grounds. In Pittsburgh the Allegheny courthouse had for years been the site of a Nativity scene, erected by the city's Holy Name Society, which adorned the massive grand staircase in the building's rotunda. The crèche featured an angel holding a banner proclaiming "Gloria in Excelsius Deo." A few blocks away, in front of another public building, Chabad, the national organization of Hasidic Jews, had put up an eighteen-foot menorah, the candelabra associated with Chanukah. Nearby were a Christmas tree and a sign saluting liberty, "a nice gesture," opined the city attorney, "consistent with the holiday spirit."

By a 5–4 vote, the majority ruled that the crèche carried a Christian message that violated the First Amendment. However, in *Allegheny County v. A.C.L.U. Greater Pittsburgh Chapter*, the Court allowed the menorah to stand by a 6–3 vote. The key element in Justice Harry A. Blackmun's analysis proved to be the venerable *Lemon* test, in particular whether a governmental practice advanced or inhibited, or appeared to endorse, particular religious beliefs. The crèche, standing as it did by itself, seemed to the majority to cross the line. The menorah, on the other hand, displayed along with the Christmas tree and the liberty sign, appeared not as an endorsement of any religion, but as recognition of the nation's cultural diversity.

The issue of religious displays on public property has been a sore point for both civil liberties groups as well as religious organizations, and there are almost as many views as there are groups. The more conservative sects tend to favor accommodation, while the more liberal religious groups call for a strict separation of church and state.

The decision in the crèche and menorah cases, along with a ruling that a Texas law exempting religious publications from sales and use taxes violated the First Amendment, poised the Court on what some commentators believed to be the beginning of a major turnabout in establishment clause jurisprudence. Justices White, Rehnquist, and Scalia had already made clear their support of greater accommodation between religion and the state; Justice O'Connor had strongly criticized the Lemon test, and Justices Kennedy and Souter also appeared willing to follow a more accommodationist policy.

When the Court decided to hear a challenge to nondenominational prayers at a public high school graduation, many people assumed it would be a major turning point. But by a 5-4 vote in *Lee v. Weisman* (1992), the Court reaffirmed that prayer as part of an official public school function remains forbidden by the establishment clause. Justice Kennedy delivered the opinion, which not only reaffirmed the original school prayer decision in *Engel* but also held the *Lemon* test still applicable.

There now appears to be a new centrist bloc on the Court, consisting of Justices O'Connor, Kennedy, and Souter, which, while it may prove to be somewhat more amenable to minor accommodation, seems determined to uphold the precedents built up over the last four decades since *Everson*. There will still be line drawing, and there will no doubt still be a debate between those who desire a "high and impregnable wall" between church and state, and those who advocate nonpreferential but closer ties.

Public Safety and
the Right to Bear Arms

Robert J. Cottrol and Raymond T. Diamond

A well regulated Militia, being necessary to the
security of a free State, the right of the people to
keep and bear Arms, shall not be infringed.
Second Amendment, U.S. Constitution

The often strident debate over the Second Amendment is like few other constitutional controversies. It is a constitutional debate that has taken place largely in the absence of Supreme Court opinion. It is a scholarly debate that members of the academy have until rather recently been reluctant to join. It is a historical controversy dominated more by partisans on different sides of the gun control debate than by professional historians. It is an arena of jurisprudence that awaits both its jurist and its philosopher.

Briefly stated, the debate over the Second Amendment is part of the larger debate over gun control, and as such it focuses on whether or not the framers intended to limit the ability of government to prohibit or severely restrict private ownership of firearms. It is a debate fueled, in part, by the fear generated by this nation's high crime rate, including an average of 20,000 homicides committed annually with firearms. The presence of firearms in roughly half the households in the country, many of them owned for protection, heightens the potential impact of the debate.

From this debate two interpretations of the Second Amendment have emerged. Advocates of stricter gun controls tend to stress the amendment's militia clause, arguing that the purpose of the amendment was to insure that state militias would be maintained against federal encroachment. Advocates of this view, the collective rights theory, argue that the framers' sole concern was with the concentration of military power in the hands of the federal government. Opponents of stricter gun controls stress the amendment's second clause, claiming that the framers intended a militia of the whole, or at least a militia consisting of the entire able-bodied white-male population. For them this militia of the whole was expected to perform its duties with privately owned weapons. Advocates of this view also urge that the militia clause should be read as an amplifying rather than a qualifying clause; that is, while maintaining a "well-regulated militia" was a major reason for including the Second Amendment in the Bill of Rights, it should not be viewed as a sole or limiting reason. The framers also had other reasons for proposing the amendment, including a right to individual self-defense.

The right to keep and bear arms has become controversial in the late twentieth century, yet for much of our history the right was extolled as a fundamental cornerstone of American liberty and one that could not be denied free people. This widespread agreement occurred in part because of the frontier conditions that existed from the colonial period through much of the nineteenth century. The role of privately owned arms in achieving American independence, particularly in the early years of the Revolution, strengthened this consensus. The often violent and lawless nature of American society also contributed to the widespread view that the right to possess arms for self-defense was fundamental.

But the Second Amendment and the right to keep and bear arms cannot be understood solely through an examination of American history. Like other sections of the Bill of Rights, the Second Amendment was an attempt to secure an existing right. The framers of the Bill of Rights did not believe they were creating new rights. Instead, they were attempting to prevent the newly formed federal government from encroaching on rights already considered part of the English constitutional heritage.[1]

To understand what the framers' intended the Second Amendment to accomplish, it is necessary to examine their world and their view of the right to bear arms as one of the traditional "rights of Englishmen." The English settlers who populated North America in the seventeenth century were heirs to a tradition over five centuries old governing both the right and the duty to be armed. At English law the idea of an armed citizenry responsible for the security of the community had long coexisted, perhaps somewhat uneasily, with regulation of the ownership of arms, particularly along class lines. The Assize of Arms of 1181 required the arming of all free men. Lacking both professional police forces and a standing army, English law and custom dictated that the citizenry as a whole, privately equipped, assist in both law enforcement and military defense. By law all men ages 16 through 60 were liable to be summoned into the sheriff's posse comitatus. All persons were expected to participate in the hot pursuit of criminal suspects, the "hue and cry," supplying their own arms for the occasion. There were legal penalties for failure to participate. The maintenance of law and order was a community affair, a duty of all citizens.[2]

And all able-bodied men were considered part of the militia and were required, at least theoretically, to be prepared to assist in military defense. The law required citizens to possess arms. Towns and villages were required to provide target ranges in order to maintain the martial proficiency of the yeomanry. Despite this, the English discovered that the militia of the whole maintained a rather indifferent proficiency and motivation. By the

sixteenth century the practice was to rely on select bodies of men inten-
sively trained for militia duty rather than on the armed population at large.

Although English law recognized a duty and a right to be armed, both
were highly circumscribed by English class structure. The law regarded the
common people as participants in community defense, but it also regarded
them as a dangerous class, useful perhaps in defending shire and realm but
also capable of mischief with their weapons, mischief toward each other,
their betters, and their betters' game. Restrictions on the type of arms
deemed suitable for common people had also long been part of English law
and custom. Game laws had long been one tool used to limit the arms of
the common people. The fourteenth-century Statute of Northampton restricted the ability of people to carry arms in public places. A sixteenth-cen-
tury statute designed as a crime control measure prohibited the carrying of
handguns and crossbows by those with incomes of less than 100 pounds a
year. After the English Reformation, Catholics were also often subject to
being disarmed as potential subversives.

The need for community security had produced a traditional duty to be
armed at English law, but it took the religious and political turmoil of seventeenth-century England to transform that duty into a political right. The
attempts by Stuart Kings Charles II and James II to disarm large portions of
the population, particularly Protestants and suspected political opponents,
met with popular resistance and helped implant into English and later
American constitutional sensibilities the belief that the right to possess
arms was of fundamental political importance. These efforts led to the
adoption of the seventh provision of the English Bill of Rights in 1689:
"That the subjects which are Protestants may have arms for their defence
suitable to their conditions and as allowed by law."[3]

By the eighteenth century, the right to possess arms, both for personal
protection and as a counterbalance against state power, had come to be
viewed as one of the fundamental rights of Englishmen on both sides of the
Atlantic. Sir William Blackstone, whose *Commentaries on the Laws of England*
greatly influenced American legal thought both before the Revolution and
well into the nineteenth century, listed the right to possess arms as one of
the five auxiliary rights of English subjects without which their primary
rights could not be maintained:

> The fifth and last auxiliary right of the subject, that I shall at present mention,
> is that of having arms for their defence, suitable to their condition and degree
> and such as are allowed by law. Which is also declared by the same statute
> . . . and is indeed a public allowance, under due restrictions, of the natural
> right of resistance and self-preservation, when the sanctions of society and
> laws are found insufficient to restrain the violence of oppression.[4]

If some five centuries of English experience had transformed the duty to be
armed for the common defense into a right to be armed, in part, to resist po-

tential political oppression, a similar evolution in thought had occurred in the American colonies between the earliest seventeenth-century settlements and the American Revolution. Early English settlement in North America had a quasi-military character, an obvious response to harsh frontier conditions. Governors of settlements often held the title of militia captain, reflecting both the civil and military nature of their office. In order to provide for the defense of often isolated colonies, special effort was made to insure that white men, capable of bearing arms, were brought into the colonies.

Far from the security of Britain and often facing hostile European powers at their borders, colonial governments viewed the arming of able-bodied white men and the requirement for militia service as essential to a colony's survival. The right and duty to be armed broadened in colonial America. If English law qualified the right to own arms by religion and class, those considerations were significantly less important in the often insecure colonies. If by the seventeenth century the concept of the militia of the whole was largely theoretical in England, in America it was the chief instrument of colonial defense. While the English upper classes sought to restrict the ownership of arms on the part of the lower classes as a means of helping to enforce game laws, any significant effort to restrict hunting in North America with its small population and abundant game would have been considered absurd. From the beginning, conditions in colonial America created a very different attitude toward arms and the people.

Race provided another reason for the renewed emphasis on the right and duty to be armed in America. Britain's American colonies were home to three often antagonistic races—red, white, and black. For the settlers of British North America, an armed and universally deputized white population was necessary not only to ward off dangers from the armies of other European powers but also to ward off attacks from the indigenous Indian population that feared the encroachment of English settlers on their lands. And an armed white population was essential to maintain social control over blacks and Native Americans who toiled unwillingly as slaves and servants in English settlements. This helped broaden the right to bear arms for whites. The need for white men to act not only in the traditional militia and posse capacities but also to keep order over the slave population helped lessen class, religious, and ethnic distinctions among whites in colonial America. That need also helped extend the right to bear arms to classes traditionally viewed with suspicion in England, including indentured servants.

The colonial experience helped strengthen the appreciation of early Americans for the merits of an armed citizenry. That appreciation was of course further strengthened by the experience of the American Revolution. The Revolution began with acts of rebellion by armed citizens. And if sober historical analysis reveals that it was actually American and French regulars who ultimately defeated the British and established American independence, the image of the privately equipped rag-tag militia successfully challenging the British empire earned a firm place in American thought

and helped influence American political philosophy. For the generation
that authored the Constitution, it reinforced the lessons their English an-
cestors had learned in the seventeenth century. It revitalized Whiggish notions that standing armies were dangerous to liberty. It helped transform
the idea that the people should be armed and security provided by a militia
of the people from a matter of military necessity into a political notion, one
that would find its way into the new Constitution.

This view that an armed population contributed to political liberty as
well as community security found its way into the debates over the Constitution and is key to understanding the Second Amendment. Like other
provisions of the Constitution, the clause that gave Congress the power to
provide for organizing, arming, and disciplining the militia excited fears
among those who believed that the proposed Constitution could be used to
destroy both state power and individual rights. It is interesting, in light of
the current debate over the meaning of the Second Amendment, that both
Federalists and Anti-Federalists assumed that the militia would be one that
enrolled almost the entire white-male population between the ages of 16
and 60 and that militia members would supply their own arms.

But many feared that the militia clause could be used both to do away with
the state's control over the militia and to disarm the population. Some expressed fear that Congress would use its power to establish a select militia.
Many viewed a select militia with as much apprehension as they did a standing army. The English experience of the seventeenth century had shown that
a select militia could be used to disarm the population-at-large. Richard Henry
Lee of Virginia expressed the fear that a select militia might serve this end.[5]

In their efforts to answer critics of the Constitution, Alexander Hamilton
and James Madison addressed the charges of those critics who argued that the
new Constitution could destroy both the independence of the militia and
deny arms to the population. Hamilton's responses are particularly interesting because he wrote as someone who was openly skeptical concerning the
military value of the militia of the whole. The former Revolutionary War artil-
lery officer conceded that the militia had fought bravely during the Revolution, but he argued it proved no match when pitted against regular troops.
Hamilton urged the creation of a select militia that would be more amenable to
military training and discipline than the population as a whole. Despite this
he conceded that the population as a whole should be armed.

But if Hamilton gave only grudging support to the concept of the militia
of the whole, Madison, author of the Second Amendment, was a much
more vigorous defender of the concept. In *The Federalist*, Number 46, he left
little doubt that he saw the armed population as a potential counterweight
to tyranny:

> [L]et a regular army, fully equal to the resources of the country, be formed; and
> let it be entirely at the devotion of the federal government: still it would not be

going too far to say that the State governments with the people on their side would be able to repel the danger. The highest number to which according to the best computation, a standing army can be carried in any country does not exceed one hundredth part of the whole number of souls; or one twenty-fifth part of the number able to bear arms. This proportion would not yield, in the United States an army of more than twenty-five or thirty thousand men. To these would be opposed a militia amounting to near half a million citizens with arms in their hands, officered by men chosen among themselves, fighting for their common liberties and united and conducted by governments possessing their affections and confidence. It may well be doubted whether a militia thus circumstanced could ever be conquered by such a proportion of regular troops. Those who are best acquainted with the late successful resistance of this country against the British arms will be most inclined to deny the possibility of it. Besides the advantage of being armed, which the Americans possess over the people of almost every other nation, the existence of subordinate governments, to which the people are attached and by which the militia officers are appointed, forms a barrier against the enterprises of ambition, more insurmountable than any which a simple government of any form can admit of notwithstanding the military establishments in the several kingdoms of Europe, which are carried as far as the public resources will bear, the governments are afraid to trust the people with arms.[6]

This desire to maintain a universal militia and an armed population played a critical part in the adoption of the Second Amendment. The amendment, like other provisions of the Bill of Rights, was designed to prevent the newly created federal government from encroaching on rights already enjoyed by the people. It is important to remember that firearms ownership, for self-defense and hunting, was widespread with few restrictions, at least for the white population. It is also significant that the universally accepted view of the militia, at the time, was that militiamen would supply their own arms. One year after the ratification of the Bill of Rights Congress passed legislation reaffirming the notion of a privately equipped militia of the whole. The act, titled "An Act more effectually to provide for the National Defence by establishing an Uniform Militia throughout the United States," called for the enrollment of every free, able-bodied white-male citizen between the ages of 18 and 45 into the militia. The act required every militia member to provide himself with a musket or firelock, a bayonet, and ammunition.[7]

The decades between the adoption of the Second Amendment and the Civil War brought little opportunity for judicial interpretation of the constitutional provision. There were few restrictions concerning either the keeping or the bearing of arms in antebellum America. Most laws restricting the possession of firearms were to be found in the slave states of the antebellum South. These laws generally prohibited the possession of firearms on the part of slaves and free blacks. Outside of the slave states the right to keep and bear arms was generally not impaired, not even for free Negroes.

There was no federal legislation restricting firearms ownership, and since *Barron v. Baltimore* (1833) held that the Bill of Rights only limited the power of the federal government, there was no occasion before the Civil War for the federal courts to pronounce upon the matter.

If in the antebellum era there was an absence of federal court decisions on the Second Amendment, there was nonetheless widespread agreement concerning the scope and meaning of the provision among antebellum commentators and in the limited number of state court decisions that examined the issue. Noted jurist and legal commentator St. George Tucker contrasted the Second Amendment's robust guarantee of a right to keep and bear arms with the more restrictive English guarantee, noting that class restrictions and game laws had not limited the American right in the way that the English right had been limited. Supreme Court Justice Joseph Story also regarded the right as fundamental:

> The right of the citizens to keep, and bear arms has been justly considered, as the palladium of the liberties of a republic; since it offers a strong moral check against the usurpation and arbitrary power of rulers; and will generally, even if they are successful in the first instance, enable the people to resist, and triumph over them.[8]

If leading antebellum commentators saw the right as central to a free people, federal courts were largely silent on the subject. The only pronouncement from the Supreme Court on the subject before the Civil War came in Chief Justice Taney's opinion in *Dred Scott v. Sandford* (1857). Taney indicated that African Americans, slave or free, could be denied the right to possess arms just as they could be denied freedom of speech, assembly, and travel. Despite the silence of the federal courts on the subject, state courts developed a jurisprudence of the right to keep and bear arms, interpreting relevant provisions of state constitutions. These cases attempted to balance the right to bear arms against competing interests in public safety. Generally state courts upheld prohibitions against carrying concealed weapons. Some state courts limited the right to carry arms to those weapons that were suitable for use in "civilized warfare," an attempt to prohibit the carrying of weapons that were thought to be used exclusively for criminal purposes. Most of these cases involved restrictions on carrying concealed firearms. In one antebellum case the Georgia Supreme Court decided that the Second Amendment applied to that state.[9]

It took the turmoil of the Civil War and Reconstruction to bring the Second Amendment before the Supreme Court. The end of the Civil War brought about a new conflict over the status of former slaves and the power of the states. The defeated white South sought to preserve as much of the antebellum Southern social order as could survive Northern victory and national law. Southern states were not prepared to accord to the newly emancipated black population the general liberties enjoyed by white citizens. Indeed, former slaves did not even have the rights that Northern states had long given free black citizens.

In 1865 and 1866 Southern states passed a series of statutes known as the black codes. These statutes were designed, in part, to insure that traditional Southern labor arrangements would be preserved. They often required blacks to sign labor contracts that bound black agricultural workers to their employers for a year. Blacks were forbidden from serving on juries and could not testify or act as parties against whites. Vagrancy laws were used to force blacks into labor contracts and to limit freedom of movement. And as further indication that the former slaves had not yet joined the ranks of free citizens, Southern states passed legislation prohibiting blacks from carrying firearms without licenses, a requirement to which whites were not subjected. The Mississippi statute provides a typical example of restrictions of this kind:

> *Be it enacted,* . . . that no freedman, free Negro or mulatto, not in the military service of the United States government, and not licensed so to do by the board of police of his or her county, shall keep or carry firearms of any kind, or any ammunition, dirk or bowie knife, and on conviction thereof in the county court shall be punished by fine, not exceeding ten dollars, and pay the cost of such proceedings and all such arms or ammunition shall be forfeited to the informer; and it shall be the duty of every civil or military officer to arrest any such freedman, free Negro or mulatto found with any such arms or ammunition, and shall cause him or her to be committed to trial in default of bail.[10]

Such measures caused strong concerns among Northern Republicans. Many charged that the South was trying to reinstate slavery and deny former slaves those rights long considered essential to a free people. The news that the freedmen were being deprived of the right to keep and bear arms was of particular concern to champions of Negro citizenship. For them the right of the black population to possess weapons went beyond symbolic importance. It was important both as a means of maintaining the recently reunited union and as a means of insuring against the virtual re-enslavement of those formerly in bondage. Faced with a hostile South determined to preserve the antebellum social order, Northern Republicans were particularly alarmed at provisions that preserved the right to keep and bear arms for former Confederates while disarming blacks, the one group in the South with clear unionist sympathies. This helped convince many Northern Republicans to seek national enforcement for the Bill of Rights.

The debates over the Fourteenth Amendment and the civil rights legislation of the Reconstruction era suggest the determination of Congress to protect the right to keep and bear arms and other provisions of the Bill of Rights against state infringement. Representative Jonathan Bingham of

Ohio, who authored the Fourteenth Amendment's privileges or immunities clause, and other Republican supporters of the Fourteenth Amendment expressed the view that the clause applied the Bill of Rights to the states. The Southern efforts to disarm the freedmen and to deny other basic rights to former slaves played an important role in convincing the 39th Congress that traditional notions concerning federalism and individual rights needed to change.[11]

If the events of Reconstruction persuaded the 39th Congress of the need for applying the Bill of Rights to the states, the Supreme Court in its earliest decisions on the Fourteenth Amendment moved to maintain the antebellum federal structure. The Supreme Court's first pronouncements on the Second Amendment came about after the enactment of the Fourteenth Amendment and concerned the extent to which the latter amendment extended the protection of the right to keep and bear arms. The first case, *United States v. Cruikshank* (1874), stemmed from charges brought by federal officials against William Cruikshank and others for violating the rights of two black men, Levi Nelson and Alexander Tillman, to assemble peaceably and with interfering with their right to bear arms. The Court in a majority opinion authored by Chief Justice Morrison R. Waite held that the federal government had no power to protect citizens against private action that deprived them of their constitutional rights. The opinion held that the First and Second Amendments were limitations on Congress, not private individuals. For protection against private criminal action the individual was required to look to state governments.[12]

The next case in which the Court examined the Second Amendment, *Presser v. Illinois*, more directly involved the question of whether or not the Fourteenth Amendment limited state action. That case involved a challenge to an Illinois statute that prohibited individuals who were not members of the organized militia from parading with arms. Although Justice William Woods, author of the majority opinion, noted that the statute did not infringe on the right to keep and bear arms, he nonetheless used the case to pronounce the view that the Second Amendment was a limitation on the federal and not the state governments. Although much of the Woods opinion can be viewed as dicta extraneous to the central issue, *Presser* has remained one of the major devices by which Second Amendment claims have been denied in recent times.[13]

So the nineteenth century ended with large-scale agreement concerning the fundamental nature of the right to keep and bear arms and with no definitive Supreme Court pronouncements setting the limits of the right or defining what might be reasonable regulation within the context of the right. That was to be expected for several reasons. Most legislation that affected people in the nineteenth century was state and local legislation and, despite the intentions of the framers of the Fourteenth Amendment, the Court would by and large not begin the process of applying the Bill of Rights to the states until well into the twentieth century. Also, in the nineteenth century firearms regulation would remain rare, partly a reflection of the need for firearms for self-defense in a largely rural, indeed frontier society, where professional police forces were relatively scarce. It was also partly a reflection of the fact that nineteenth-century Americans largely saw the private ownership of arms as an essential liberty. It would take the social changes accompanying urbanization in twentieth-century America to bring increased regulation and new attitudes concerning arms and the Second Amendment.

Although there was widespread agreement in early twentieth-century America concerning the importance of the right to bear arms, this agreement was tempered by the belief that whole classes of people were unfit to exercise the prerogative. In the South, state governments, long freed from the federal scrutiny that existed in the Reconstruction era, used laws regulating concealed weapons to accomplish what had been attempted through the black codes in the aftermath of the Civil War. Discriminatory enforcement of these laws often left blacks disarmed in public places while whites remained free to carry firearms. This state of affairs helped make possible the early twentieth-century reign of terror known as Jim Crow.

But the South was not the only region where social prejudice restricted the right of disfavored minorities to possess firearms. If the white South saw armed blacks as a threat, politicians in other regions saw a similar threat arising from large-scale Southern and Eastern European immigration. The new immigrants, like others before them, often met hostile receptions. They were associated with crime and anarchy and stereotyped as lazy and mentally unfit. Many native-born Americans feared the immigrants would bring anarchist-inspired crime from Europe, including political assassinations and politically motivated armed robberies. These fears led in 1911 to passage of New York's Sullivan Law. This state statute was aimed at New York City, a place where the large, foreign-born population was believed to be peculiarly susceptible to crime and vice. The Sullivan Law went far beyond typical gun control measures of the day. It prohibited the unlicensed carrying of concealed weapons and required a permit for the ownership or purchase of pistols. Violation of the statute was a felony. The first person convicted under the statute was a member of one of the suspect classes, an Italian immigrant.[14]

But these restrictions were anomalies in early twentieth-century America. For most citizens access to firearms was largely unimpaired and there was little occasion for either the courts or constitutional commentators to say much concerning the Second Amendment.

This situation would change after the First World War. Prohibition brought about the rise of organized gangs engaged in the sale of bootlegged alcohol. Territorial rivalries among the gangs led to open warfare on the streets of the nation's major cities. That warfare was made even more terrifying by the introduction of a fearsome new weapon, the Thompson submachine gun. A fully automatic weapon, developed too late for use in

World War I, the "Tommy Gun" was one of the first submachine guns in widespread use. Used by violent criminals in their wars on each other, the Thompson also claimed the lives of a fair number of members of the general public as well.

The end of the twenties and the end of prohibition did not bring a halt to notorious misuse of automatic weapons. The rise in the 1930s of such desperadoes as John Dillinger, "Pretty Boy" Floyd, "Ma" Barker, George "Machine Gun" Kelly, and Clyde Barrow and Bonnie Parker became a part of American folklore. The exploits of such criminals were made more vivid and terrifying by the new medium of talking motion pictures. Thus, the horrors of criminal misuse of automatic weapons were forcibly brought home to the public.

These events caused the Roosevelt administration to propose the first federal gun control legislation. The National Firearms Act of 1934 required registration, police permission, and a prohibitive tax for firearms that were deemed gangster weapons, including automatic weapons, sawed-off shotguns, and silencers. It is interesting in light of the current debate that the Roosevelt administration deemed the act a revenue measure, conceding that an outright ban on such weapons would probably be a violation of the Second Amendment.

The 1934 act gave rise to the Supreme Court's last decision to date on the Second Amendment, *United States v. Miller*. It was a curious case. Both sides of the Second Amendment debate have claimed that the decision authored by Justice James C. McReynolds supports their views. Interestingly, the Court only heard arguments by the government. The federal government appealed a decision by a federal district court invalidating the National Firearms Act of 1934 in a case involving the unlicensed transportation of an unregistered sawed-off shotgun. The Court focused on the weapon in question:

> In the absence of any evidence tending to show that the possession of a [sawed-off shotgun] at this time has some reasonable relationship to the preservation or efficiency of a well regulated militia, we cannot say that the Second Amendment guarantees the right to keep and bear such an instrument. Certainly it is not within judicial notice that this weapon is any part of the ordinary military equipment or that its use could contribute to the common defense.[15]

Advocates of the collective rights view have emphasized the *Miller* Court's focus on the militia, claiming that it was an indication that the Court saw the Second Amendment as only being concerned with the preservation of state militias. But the *Miller* Court's discussion of the militia indicates that the Court saw a clear relationship between the individual right and the maintenance of the militia:

The signification attributed to the term Militia appears from the debates in the Convention, the history and legislation of Colonies and States, and the writings of approved commentators. These show plainly enough that the Militia comprises all males physically capable of acting in concert for the common defense. "A body of citizens enrolled for military discipline." And further, that ordinarily when called for service these men were expected to appear bearing arms supplied by themselves and of the kind in common use at the time.[16]

Probably the most accurate way to view what the Court did in *Miller* is to see it as an updating of the nineteenth-century civilized warfare doctrine. McReynolds's decision relied on the antebellum Tennessee case *Avmette v. State*, which allowed the state to restrict the carrying of weapons not suited for the common defense. The Supreme Court in *Miller* remanded the case to the lower courts to determine whether or not a sawed-off shotgun was a weapon appropriate for militia use. That determination was never made.

Although *Miller* was the Court's most comprehensive exploration of the Second Amendment, it had little effect on either firearms regulation or the general public's view concerning the right to keep and bear arms. For nearly two decades after *Miller* little existed in the way of federal firearms regulation. State and local legislation existed, but with few exceptions such as the New York Sullivan Law, these were usually traditional regulations governing the manner of carrying weapons, not outright prohibitions. There was little serious attempt to mount constitutional challenges to these restrictions. The Second Amendment was thus bypassed in the postwar Supreme Court's process of applying most of the provisions of the Bill of Rights to the states. Justice Hugo Black, who was an advocate of the view that the Fourteenth Amendment made all of the Bill of Rights applicable to the states, argued that the Second Amendment should also apply to the states, but the Court has not heard a case on that issue since *Presser*. It is probably accurate to say that at least until the 1960s most people, including attorneys and judges, accepted the view that the Second Amendment protected an individual right but otherwise thought very little about the matter because firearms restrictions, even on the state and local levels, were slight.

It would take the turmoil of the 1960s and the tragedy of three assassinations to bring about the birth of the modern gun control movement and create the current debate over the meaning of the Second Amendment. The assassination of President John F. Kennedy in 1963 brought calls for stricter national controls over the sale of firearms. Urban riots and the assassinations of civil rights leader Martin Luther King and Senator Robert F. Kennedy helped lead to the passage of the Gun Control Act of 1968, the first federal legislation that seriously affected the purchasing of firearms for large numbers of Americans. This legislation limited the purchase of firearms through the mails and also restricted the importation of surplus military rifles. The act also prohibited the purchase of firearms by those with felony convictions, even though the legislation provided no means of checking a purchaser's record. Some of the provisions of the 1968 act would later be modified by legislation passed in 1986.

The 1968 act proved to be something of a watershed. Since then a national debate over gun control and a subsidiary debate over the meaning of the Second Amendment have become perennial features in American politics. The rise of a highly visible gun control movement during the last two decades has been something new in American political life. Some adherents of this new political movement have asked for relatively moderate measures, such as national screening to limit the ability of persons from suspect backgrounds, including persons with criminal records or histories of mental instability, from purchasing firearms. Such measures are essentially extensions of firearms regulations that have long existed in many states, attempts to limit firearms use by undesirable persons. These kinds of regulations have long existed even in states with state constitutional protection for the right to bear arms and courts willing to enforce such guarantees. The more modest measures pose little threat to the general public's right to possess firearms.

But in the last two decades others have argued for more radical measures. Their view has been that state and local government and most especially the federal government can and should outlaw the general public's right to possess whole categories of firearms that had previously been owned by large numbers of law-abiding citizens. In the 1970s and 1980s the argument was made that handguns, particularly cheap ones known popularly as "Saturday Night Specials," should be banned. More recently many gun control advocates have argued for bans on "assault rifles," a term employed without great precision to include semiautomatic rifles with military features or virtually all semiautomatic rifles, depending on the user's definition.

This advocacy of wholesale restrictions on firearms ownership has raised significant constitutional and social issues. Much of the effort to reinterpret the Second Amendment as a collective right has been an attempt to justify firearms restrictions that at earlier periods in American history would have been regarded as unconstitutional. But the modern gun control debate has been more than an argument over constitutional history and theory. It has also involved a clash over social policy and cultural values as well. The argument for radical gun control measures has in part been fueled by criminological concerns. The United States has the highest homicide rate of all Western industrialized nations. That rate is tragically high in our increasingly dangerous inner cities. Part of the case for sweeping gun control measures is an argument that such measures might help reduce that crime rate.

But if the debate has taken place on the constitutional and criminological levels, it has also taken place on cultural and symbolic levels. For some people, wholesale prohibitions on firearms ownership not only will have certain criminological benefits but will also contribute to the betterment of American civilization. The modern gun control movement has, in part, been a moral crusade, a rejection of the traditional view that widespread ownership of firearms is a reflection of American liberty. Instead many advocates of radical gun control have argued that such measures are necessary as one way of breaking with the nation's atavistic past, a past that has included high levels of violence and vigilantism.

The rise of the modern gun control movement has also had an ironic and clearly unintended consequence. It has transformed the National Rifle Association, before the 1960s a relatively small group of shooting enthusiasts, into a large, politically powerful organization that has, despite recent setbacks, enjoyed considerable success in blocking gun control legislation. The transformation of the NRA into a major political organization and the rise of even more radical organizations opposing gun control has contributed to the vigorous and often rancorous nature of the debate.

Despite the vigor of the debate in the last two decades, the Supreme Court has remained largely silent on the issue. A number of lower federal courts have upheld firearms restrictions against Second Amendment claims, often giving the collective rights view in their decisions. Most of these cases have involved claims made by persons with criminal backgrounds or who were convicted of firearms offenses while committing other crimes and are not particularly good indications of the extent to which the Second Amendment protects the public at large. In 1982 the Seventh Circuit Court of Appeals sustained a general prohibition against handgun ownership in Morton Grove, Illinois, against a Second Amendment challenge.[17] The Supreme Court refused to hear an appeal on the matter and make a modern pronouncement on the Second Amendment. With recent statewide bans on "assault rifles" in California and New Jersey it is possible that the Court may hear a case on the issue within the next decade, although the Court since *Miller* has generally been reluctant to look at the issue.

In a very real sense we are having the wrong Second Amendment debate. There should be discussion over whether or not the Second Amendment is an anachronism that should simply be repealed. A case could be made along those lines and indeed was recently made by columnist George Will, a supporter of stricter gun controls.[18]

But there is little support for any effort to repeal the Second Amendment. Public opinion polls consistently show high support not only for the individual rights interpretation but for maintaining the right to keep and bear arms as one of the rights of American citizens. Overwhelming majorities of the American population support the right of individuals to own firearms as well as support measures that would keep guns out of the hands of criminals, the mentally unbalanced, and others likely to abuse the right. And it is this public consensus that should be the starting point of a new, more productive debate over the Second Amendment. Such a debate would be more fruitful than the current debate over the collective rights theory, which in order to be accepted requires a highly strained reading of history and relevant Supreme Court cases.

That more fruitful debate would move us toward what should be our central concern with respect to public safety and the right to keep and bear arms, principally, in a nation where the Constitution protects the private ownership of firearms and in a society where private ownership of firearms is very much a part of culture and tradition, what is reasonable regulation of firearms? We will not attempt to answer that question, although we suspect that an honest answer would not totally please either advocates of stricter gun controls or their opponents. Evidence from social science studies indicates that few firearms crimes are committed by people who do not have prior histories of involvement in criminal activity, mental instability, or violent behavior. Little evidence has been produced indicating criminological or constitutional justification for measures designed to disarm people who do not have suspect backgrounds. The debate should thus focus on ways of developing fair and effective procedures for screening out those who should be prevented from purchasing firearms and how to do so in ways that would not seriously impair the rights the Second Amendment was designed to protect. Whether such procedures should involve waiting periods, registration, background checks, licensing procedures, or combinations of these possibilities should be part of the debate. Whether such procedures, or indeed harsher ones, would be effective in light of this nation's historical experience with ineffective prohibitions is of course problematic, and this too should be part of the debate.

Ironically, an acceptance of the individual rights component of the Second Amendment may be necessary for effective gun control measures. The political difficulty in securing effective national screening measures is directly related to the fear on the part of many who value the right to keep and bear arms that such measures are merely way stations on the road to firearms prohibition. That fear has been fed by those who have sought to read the Second Amendment's guarantee out of the Bill of Rights. The recognition that the Constitution does indeed protect the right to keep and bear arms may be the first step in the needed process of fashioning laws that both contribute to public safety and preserve a right long valued in this society.

The Enigmatic Place of Property Rights in Modern Constitutional Thought

James W. Ely, Jr.

The notion that property ownership is essential for the enjoyment of liberty has long been a fundamental tenet of Anglo-American constitutional thought. Property is more than the physical possession of an object. The concept of ownership encompasses a range of interests, including the right to use, develop, and dispose of one's property. Envisioning property ownership as establishing the basis for individual autonomy from government coercion, the framers of the Constitution placed a high value on the security of property rights. Echoing the philosopher John Locke, John Rutledge of South Carolina advised the Philadelphia convention that "Property was certainly the principal object of Society."[1] Further, the framers believed that respect for property rights was crucial to encourage the growth of national wealth. In the main the framers relied upon a variety of institutional arrangements, such as the separation of powers, to guard the rights of property owners. Still, the Constitution and Bill of Rights contain important provisions designed to restrain legislative attacks on property rights.

Not surprisingly, therefore, throughout most of American history the Supreme Court functioned as a guardian of property and economic rights against legislative encroachments. The Court's defense of traditional property rights in the 1930s, however, threatened the New Deal program to combat the Great Depression, eventually causing President Franklin D. Roosevelt to propose his plan to "pack" the Court. This constitutional crisis was avoided when in 1937 the justices abruptly abandoned scrutiny of economic regulations. Known as the constitutional revolution of 1937, this shift had a profound impact on property rights. Deference to the economic and social judgments of lawmakers became the new orthodoxy. Thus, judicial review of economic legislation since 1937 has been largely perfunctory.[2] Liberal constitutionalism moved in other directions, with scant attention to property rights. Indeed, after the New Deal it became rather fashionable for scholars to ignore or belittle the significance of constitutionally protected property. Desirous of achieving a more egalitarian distribution of wealth and pursuing environmental objectives, liberal scholars have formulated doctrines to eviscerate private property. In recent years, however, there have been signs that the Supreme Court was in the process of reinvigorating the property clauses of the Constitution.

In a 1981 lecture, Judge James Oakes predicted a revival of judicial interest in the constitutional protection of property rights.[3] In many respects the decade of the 1980s was propitious for such a development. National political currents broadly moved in a conservative direction. The contemporary political climate, as evidenced by the trend to curtail taxation, favored the security of property rights. The changing composition of the Supreme Court boded well for property rights as justices appointed by Republican presidents proved more concerned with property issues than their liberal predecessors.

There were also important intellectual currents sympathetic to the defense of property rights. Classical economic thinking, which stressed the efficiency of free markets, was increasingly employed in the analysis of legal issues. The law and economics movement stressed the deficiencies of governmental regulation of economic activity. Warning that regulations often imposed heavy compliance costs, hampered competition, and restricted economic opportunity, this school of thought argued that the operations of the free market should ordinarily determine the price of goods and services. Another group of legal scholars, spearheaded by Richard A. Epstein and Bernard Siegan, has mounted a sustained challenge to the liberal jurisprudence that has dominated thinking about property rights since the New Deal. Urging the federal courts to defend the free market and prevent government transfers of private wealth, they have been instrumental in reopening public debate regarding the constitutionality of economic regulations. Among other arguments, these scholars have reasserted the vision of the framers that economic and individual rights were fundamentally inseparable.

The resulting intellectual ferment has stirred a lively dialogue in the legal literature. Scholars, however, have drawn a bewildering variety of conclusions as to the direction in which property rights are headed. Some see little sign of renewed judicial interest and are confident that no property rights rebellion is in sight. Other observers proclaim the "death of property," meaning that the notion of absolute ownership has disintegrated in the twentieth century. One scholar has even plaintively asked: "Property rights: Are there any left?"[4] In sharp contrast, other scholars foresee a veritable renaissance of property rights. The "back to the future" theme has been sounded, sometimes with dread, in much current scholarship. Concerned about the scholarly and judicial revival of interest in property rights, Bernard Schwartz frets that the courts are "more receptive to attacks on economic regulation than they have been in half a century."[5] Similarly, another commentator detects "an ongoing effort by a part of the Court to make some new version of economic laissez-faire the law of the Constitution once again." Thus, he concludes that "the ghosts and goblins of laissez-faire seem to be at the ready, waiting for some unforeseen combination of time, chance, and circumstance to call them up for full service once more."[6]

How can we explain these discordant voices in the literature? What is the status of private property rights in an age of pervasive economic regulations? Will the scholarly rehabilitation of laissez-faire constitutionalism have an impact on judicial decisions? Is the stage being set for the reemergence of constitutionally protected property and economic rights?

This intense scholarly debate obscures the fact that the Supreme Court rendered relatively few decisions dealing squarely with the issue in the 1980s and early 1990s. Much of the existing commentary, therefore, has centered on a handful of cases dealing primarily with the contract clause and the takings clause of the Fifth Amendment. A focus on the Supreme Court, however, may not give us the full picture with respect to property rights. As is well known, many property issues are presented in state and lower federal courts. There is some evidence that these courts have become more assertive in defending property against legislative infringement. In this essay, I propose to briefly review current law dealing with the property clauses of the Constitution and to assess the probable course of future developments with respect to property rights.

Due Process Clause

The Fifth and Fourteenth Amendments provide that no person shall be "deprived of life, liberty, or property, without due process of law." For many years after the Civil War the Supreme Court gave a substantive interpretation to the due process clauses, reasoning that these guarantees went beyond procedural protection and encompassed certain fundamental but unenumerated rights. Foremost among these were the right to acquire and use property and the right to make contracts and to pursue common occupations. This doctrine, known as economic due process, reflected a close identification between constitutional values and the free market economy. Congress and the states could control property usage and business activity under the police power to protect health, safety, and morals, but the Supreme Court required lawmakers to justify such regulations. The justices did not accept legislative assertions of regulatory purpose at face value and invalidated laws deemed unreasonable or arbitrary as a violation of due process. In effect the doctrine of economic due process allowed the courts to exercise a broad supervisory review over economic and social legislation.[7] Most regulatory statutes passed constitutional muster, but the Court struck down laws that interfered with the workings of the market. Thus, in the early decades of the twentieth century the justices invalidated statutes establishing hours of work, imposing a minimum wage for women, and curtailing the entry of new businesses into the marketplace.

Economic liberty was the standard against which legislation was measured, and restraint was approved only if found necessary to promote public health, safety, or morals.

As a consequence of the constitutional revolution of 1937, the Supreme
Court repudiated economic due process and retreated from judicial review
of economic and social legislation. In *United States v. Carolene Products Co.*
(1938) the Court placed the rights of property owners in a subordinate category entitled to a lesser degree of protection.[8] The justices declared that
economic regulations would receive only minimum judicial scrutiny under
a permissive "rational basis" test. In a striking reversal of previous decisions, economic legislation was accorded a presumption of validity. It is
difficult to reconcile *Carolene Products* with either the text of the Constitution or the Supreme Court's long defense of property rights. The language
of the due process clauses draws no dichotomy between the protection
given property and other liberties. Indeed, the framers of the Constitution
and Bill of Rights believed that property rights and personal liberty were
indissolubly linked.[9] There are still other problems with *Carolene Products*.
Although couched in terms of deference to lawmakers, the decision in fact
exemplified judicial activism by ranking rights into categories not expressed in the Constitution. This judicial distinction has produced the curious result that under the due process clauses there is in fact no meaningful judicial review of legislation affecting the rights of property owners.

Moreover, the asserted justification offered for the Court's double standard for reviewing property rights differently than claims of individual liberty was questionable. The Court's belief that heightened scrutiny for
claims of individual rights was necessitated by the failure of the political
process, while economic regulations reflected majoritarian preferences in a
properly functioning legislative process, has proved to be particularly du-
bious. Much of the economic legislation upheld under the teachings of *Carolene Products* was classic protectionist legislation enacted not for the public's benefit but at the behest of special interest groups. One particularly
egregious example was a state statute requiring a prescription from an op-
tometrist before an optician could fit eyeglass lenses into new frames, thus
burdening consumers to benefit a select group. Insofar as *Carolene Products*
based its jurisprudence on a theory of the political process, it is a theory
that scholars have increasingly revealed as in clear conflict with reality.

From a historical and jurisprudential perspective the ruling in *Carolene
Products* is highly problematic, but the outcome harmonized with the emergence of liberal constitutionalism after 1937. By weakening the constitutional barriers that secured property ownership, the Court enlarged legislative control over economic matters and facilitated programs designed to
redistribute wealth.

Despite the call by several prominent scholars for a revitalization of economic due process, the Supreme Court has shown no sign of reestablishing
due process as a safeguard for property owners or of resuming its tradi-

tional role as an arbiter of economic legislation. Some state courts, on the other hand, continue to review economic regulations by applying a substantive interpretation of due process to strike down excessive or arbitrary statutes.

Contract Clause

The Constitution declares that "No state shall . . . pass any . . . Law impairing the Obligation of Contracts." Chief Justice John Marshall fashioned this provision into an important shield for existing economic arrangements against state legislative interference. Although not part of the Bill of Rights, the contract clause was at the heart of a great deal of constitutional litigation during the nineteenth century. One prominent legal historian even hailed the contract clause as "the bulwark of American individualism against democratic impatience and socialist fantasy."[10] In the twentieth century, however, the contract clause gradually declined in importance. To some extent its functions were superseded by the doctrine of economic due process. The contract clause was largely left for dead after a sharply divided Supreme Court, in *Home Building and Loan Association v. Blaisdell* (1934), sustained the validity of a state mortgage moratorium statute during the Great Depression. Asserting that the clause's "prohibition is not an absolute one and is not to be read with literal exactness," the Court ruled that an important public purpose could justify state interference with contracts.[11] In effect the Supreme Court subordinated the contract clause to the authority of the states to adopt regulatory measures.

Accordingly, it aroused a flurry of interest when the Supreme Court in the late 1970s applied the contract clause for the first time in nearly forty years. In two decisions the Court struck down both a state impairment of its own financial obligations as well as legislative interference with private contractual arrangements. The justices further ruled that state action that impaired its own obligations should be held to a high level of judicial scrutiny. Some observers predicted a major revival of the contract clause. By the mid 1980s, however, the Court appeared to retreat from rigorous application of the contract clause. Several decisions seemingly returned to a more deferential attitude toward state infringement of existing contractual arrangements in order to serve perceived public needs.

Nonetheless, it may be premature to dismiss the contract clause as a constitutional restraint on legislative power. The decisions of the Supreme Court applying this provision have, if nothing else, made it clear that the contract clause cannot be regarded as a dead letter. In turn, this has emboldened some state and lower federal courts to use the contract clause as a basis to curb legislative power. Consequently, in the 1980s and early 1990s there have been several state and lower federal court decisions invalidating legislation that attempted to alter mortgage foreclosure proceedings, change the terms of existing leasehold arrangements, or modify state employee pension plans.[12] Likewise, courts have ruled that statutes that altered the terms of existing employment or distributorship agreements violated the contract clause. Recently the Second Circuit Court of Appeals struck down a New York statute that imposed a "lag payroll" on state judicial employees to finance the creation of new judgeships. The Court reasoned that this scheme impaired the collective bargaining agreements governing the payment of salaries and that it attempted to compel a handful of employees rather than taxpayers to pay for the additional judges.[13]

Although it seems unlikely that the contract clause will regain its former eminence in constitutional jurisprudence, the clause will continue to serve a secondary role in protecting property rights and contractual expectations. The Supreme Court, however, is likely to be cautious in finding state laws to violate the contract clause. In 1992, for instance, the justices held that a Michigan statute that retroactively raised the amount of workers' compensation benefits payable to injured workers did not impair collective bargaining agreements because these contracts did not expressly cover such benefits.[14]

Takings Clause

The takings clause of the Fifth Amendment provides: "nor shall private property be taken for public use, without just compensation." Contemporary champions of property rights have centered their greatest hopes on a more vigorous application of the takings clause. Reflecting both common-law principles and colonial practice, the clause limited the government's power of eminent domain by mandating that individual owners were entitled to compensation when property was appropriated for public purpose.[15] The rationale behind the takings clause is that the financial burden of public policy should not be unfairly concentrated on individual property owners but shared by the public as a whole through taxation. Thus, the desire to achieve a public objective does not justify confiscation of private property without compensation. Consistent with the traditional high standing of property rights, the takings clause was the first provision of the Bill of Rights to be applied to the states under the due process clause of the Fourteenth Amendment.[16]

The most vexing problem in modern takings jurisprudence is whether governmental actions, short of formal condemnation, effectuate a taking for which compensation is required. Virtually all commentators agree that current takings analysis is a muddle. The Supreme Court has contributed to the confusion by applying the clause in an essentially ad hoc manner with seemingly inconsistent results. The justices have found it difficult to formulate meaningful standards to determine whether there has been a taking. Nonetheless, courts appear to be moving toward a broader view of the takings clause and scrutinizing governmental actions affecting property more carefully.

One line of Supreme Court cases addresses the issue of physical intrusion upon private property by the government or by persons with governmental authorization. In *Loretto v. Teleprompter Manhattan CATV Corp.* (1982) the Supreme Court held that a New York law requiring the installation of cable television facilities on a landlord's property effectuated a taking for which compensation was required. Explaining that a physical invasion of property was particularly serious, the Court established a rule that any permanent physical occupation of property, however slight, amounted to a per se taking.

Recently lower federal courts adopted an expanded notion of physical taking and ruled that local rent control ordinances can constitute a physical occupation of the landlord's property. These courts have invalidated rent control ordinances that in effect granted tenants leases of indefinite duration at controlled prices. Reasoning that such tenant succession rights drastically interfered with the landlord's right to use or control his property, the Ninth Circuit Court of Appeals observed that a municipality could not "eviscerate a property owner's rights and shield its action from constitutional scrutiny by calling it rent control."[17] In 1992, however, the Supreme Court cast doubt on this approach to a physical taking. The justices ruled in *Yee v. City of Escondido* (1992) that governmental action constitutes a physical taking only when it requires a landowner to submit to occupation of his land. The Court sustained a mobile home rent control ordinance because the landowner had voluntarily rented the property and retained the right to change land usage. But the justices cautioned that a "different case would be presented were the statute, on its face or as applied, to compel a landowner over objection to rent his property or to refrain in perpetuity from terminating a tenancy."[18]

A more difficult question is posed by land use regulations that limit the use of property or seek to redistribute wealth. Under the doctrine of regulatory taking, a regulation may so diminish the value or usefulness of private property as to constitute a taking. The Supreme Court recognized this concept in the landmark decision of *Pennsylvania Coal Co. v. Mahon* (1922). Justice Oliver Wendell Holmes declared: "The general rule at least is, that while property may be regulated to a certain extent, if regulation goes too far it will be recognized as a taking." He cautioned that "the natural tendency of human nature" was to extend regulations "until at last private property disappears."[19] Despite the *Mahon* ruling, the Supreme Court has found it difficult to distinguish between appropriate restrictions and unconstitutional takings. Accordingly, the justices have been reluctant to actually apply the doctrine of regulatory taking.

The issue of regulatory takings has been most frequently raised in the context of land use controls. Historically landowners could use their property for any lawful purpose, restrained only by the common-law prohibition against creating a nuisance. By the early twentieth century, however, urbanization and industrialization had created novel land use problems. With more congested living conditions, the manner in which one person used his or her land

directly affected his or her neighbors. When nuisance law proved inadequate
to cope with urban land use problems, states and localities began to control
more systematically land usage. Yet public restrictions on the use of privately
owned land raised difficult constitutional questions. Landowners often complained that the cost of achieving social objectives was unfairly placed on their
shoulders rather than imposed on the general public.

During the 1920s zoning emerged as a land control technique. Zoning
was justified as an exercise of the police power to safeguard public health
and safety. But such regulations restricted an owner's dominion over the
land and often impaired its value. In *Village of Euclid v. Ambler Realty Company* (1926) the Supreme Court upheld the constitutionality of a comprehensive zoning ordinance that divided a locality into districts, residential
and commercial, restricting the type of building construction in each district. Reasoning that such limitations served the health, safety, and morals
of the public, the Court ruled that state police power included the authority
to classify land and prevent the erection of commercial buildings in residential areas. To bolster its decision the Court drew an analogy between
zoning and the power to abate a common-law nuisance.

Almost from the outset regulatory bodies moved beyond the purported
health and safety rationale to control land usage. Many zoning restrictions,
such as the requirement of large lot sizes for homes and height restrictions
on buildings, serve to preserve residential amenity features and to inflate
the cost of housing. Such regulations often have an exclusionary impact on
lower-income persons and contribute to urban sprawl.[20] Nonetheless, the
Supreme Court upheld an ordinance that restricted construction of a five-
acre tract to five single family residences. The Court held that the application of zoning laws effected a taking only "if the ordinance does not substantially advance legitimate state interests . . . or denies an owner
economically viable use of his land."[21] Likewise, the Court has sustained
the designation of structures as historic landmarks despite the fact that
such action prevented the owner from modifying the building and caused
a large reduction in its value.

Increasingly controversial in recent years has been the practice of many
communities to levy fees or require donations of land in order to approve
new building projects. This practice is based on the notion that a land developer should reimburse a community for the impact of a project on local
services such as schools, parks, and water services. At first these exactions
were closely related to actual impact of a new development. Faced with
growing resistance to higher taxes, however, many local governments
have aggressively turned to exactions as an alternative source of general
revenue. The connection between building projects and exactions has become progressively more cloudy. For instance, localities have required land
developers to pay fees to support public transportation, to dedicate land
for public parks, and to subsidize the construction of low-income housing.
Such exactions constitute a kind of special tax levied upon developers but

ultimately paid by newcomers through higher land prices. Sensitive to the concerns of current residents, local zoning authorities find it politically convenient to place these costs on outsiders like nonresident land developers.

In addition to zoning, legislation to protect the environment can drastically curtail a landowner's ability to take advantage of property ownership. For instance, landowners must obtain a government permit before the filling of any wetland. The imposition of a permit requirement in order to develop land does not by itself constitute a taking. But the permit process is often expensive and lengthy, and denial of a permit may well prevent any development of the land. Similarly, some states restrict the construction of structures on beachfront property. Such environmental regulations, which sometimes leave the owner with no economically viable use of land, have been challenged as a taking of property. Still other laws seek to mandate public access to privately owned beach property, thus diminishing the owner's control of the land.

As this discussion indicates, zoning and environmental regulations have made substantial inroads upon the traditional rights of owners to make use of their land. It appeared that there was no meaningful constitutional limit on the power to regulate land. Perhaps concerned about the increasingly complex web of land use controls, the Supreme Court took a fresh look at the question of regulatory taking in 1987. As a result, the justices strengthened the position of property owners against governmental authority to reduce the value of their property by regulation. In the notable case of *Nollan v. California Coastal Commission* (1987) the Supreme Court, for the first time since the 1920s, struck down a land use regulation. The case arose when a state agency conditioned a permit to rebuild a beach house upon the owner's grant of a public easement across the beachfront. The Court held that the imposition of such a condition constituted a taking because the requirement was unrelated to any problem caused by the development. Further, the Court indicated a willingness to examine more carefully the connection between the purpose and the means of regulations. Writing for the Court, Justice Antonin Scalia added: "We view the Fifth Amendment's property clause to be more than a pleading requirement and compliance with it to be more than an exercise in cleverness and imagination."[22]

Moreover, in *First Evangelical Lutheran Church v. County of Los Angeles* (1987) the justices ruled that a property owner may be entitled to compensation for the temporary loss of land use when controls are later invalidated. This decision raised the prospect of damage awards against excessive regulations. In response to these "fundamental changes in takings law," President Ronald Reagan issued an Executive Order in 1988 directing that federal agencies evaluate the effect of their actions "on constitutionally protected property rights" in order to reduce the risk of unlawful regulations.[23] Legislation to strengthen the legal position of property owners has also gained ground in Congress. In 1991 the Senate passed the Private Property Rights Act, which provides that no federal regulations shall become effective until the attorney general has certified that regulatory activity complies with the Executive Order on taking private property.[24] The measure is pending in the House of Representatives.

It is too early to assess fully this new direction in takings law. Many have interpreted the *Nollan* decision as signaling a heightened degree of judicial supervision of land use regulations. Certainly some lower federal and state courts have begun to take a closer look at conditions imposed on landowners. For instance, courts since *Nollan* have invalidated as an unconstitutional taking of property the requirement that a subdivision developer dedicate land for a proposed parkway and the refusal of a city to permit construction of a convenience store unless the owner granted an expanded right-of-way for street purposes. In both cases the court could find no nexus or connection between the development and the imposed condition. Likewise, a zoning ordinance that required that a large amount of privately owned land be retained in natural state as a greenbelt was held to constitute a taking of property.

Numerous lawsuits have been instituted by property owners challenging environmental regulations that severely restrict the use of their land. During the early 1990s courts have found a regulatory taking when environmental regulations denied an owner any economically viable use of the land. For example, landowners have received sizable compensation when the denial of a wetlands fill permit virtually eradicated the value of their property. Even more telling, in 1991 the Court of Appeals for the Federal Circuit held that the Surface Mining Control Act effectuated a taking by prohibiting a mining company from exercising its right to mine coal deposits. The Court ordered the government to pay more than $60 million to the affected landowner. The Supreme Court declined to review this ruling, thus leaving in effect the lower-court order to pay compensation.[25]

The dramatic impact of this new takings jurisprudence is perhaps best illustrated by the decision of the New York Court of Appeals in *Seawall Associates v. City of New York* (1989). At issue was a municipal ordinance that prohibited conversion or demolition of single-room occupancy housing and that required the owners to lease such rooms for an indefinite period. The declared purpose behind this ordinance was to alleviate the plight of the homeless. The Court of Appeals struck down the ordinance as both a physical and regulatory taking of property without compensation. Finding that the ordinance abrogated the owners' fundamental right of possession and right to exclude others, the court concluded that the law effected a per se physical taking. Moreover, the court invalidated the ordinance as a regulatory taking. The court ruled that the rental provisions denied the owners economically viable use of their property and that the ordinance did not substantially help the homeless. In the court's view, the tenuous connection between the means adopted by the city and the ends of alleviating homelessness could not justify singling out a few property owners to bear this burden. Rather, this was the type of social obligation that should be placed on the taxpayers as a whole.

Challenges to the constitutionality of land use regulations and exactions will likely become more frequent. Although the courts continue to uphold most regulatory schemes, there is clearly judicial movement toward a less deferential attitude concerning controls on land usage.[26]

Indeed, the Supreme Court has recently put sharp new teeth into the regulatory taking doctrine. At issue in *Lucas v. South Carolina Coastal Commission* (1992) was a South Carolina ban on beachfront construction.[27] Designed to prevent beach erosion and preserve a valuable public resource, the law prevented the owner of two residential lots from erecting any permanent structure on his land. He contended that this prohibition destroyed the economic value of his property and effectuated a taking for which just compensation was required under the Fifth Amendment.

By a six-to-three vote, the Supreme Court, in an opinion by Justice Scalia, held that regulations that deny a property owner "all economically beneficial or productive use of land" constitute a taking notwithstanding the public interest advanced to justify the restraint. Justice Scalia cogently explained that the total deprivation of economic use is the practical equivalent of physical appropriation of land. Moreover, he expressed concern that regulations which prevent economic use "carry with them a heightened risk that private property is being pressed into some form of public service under the guise of mitigating serious public harm." The Court did recognize a narrow exception to the rule that eliminating all economic use of land effectuates a taking. No compensation would be required if the owner was barred from putting the land to use by already existing common-law principles of property law or nuisance. In separate dissenting opinions, Justices Harry A. Blackmun and John Paul Stevens advanced a limited conception of property rights. They argued that state legislatures have wide latitude to control land use and rejected any categorical rule that a regulation which renders land valueless is a taking.

In one sense, the *Lucas* decision did not break any new doctrinal ground. But the case nonetheless represents a watershed because the Supreme Court applied for the first time its previously announced rule that the deprivation of all economic use constituted a regulatory taking. The effect will likely be to make it more difficult for government to ban any development of parcels of land without paying compensation. Most land use regulations do not have the effect of denying all economic use. But environmental regulations, such as wetlands restrictions, which require land to be left in natural state would appear vulnerable. At the heart of the issue is whether the burden of achieving environmental objectives should be shared by the general public or placed upon individual property owners.

Although *Lucas* has strengthened the protection of private property under the Fifth Amendment, contemporary takings jurisprudence has not evolved consistently in a manner favorable to property owners. In *Hawaii Housing Authority v. Midkiff* (1984) the Supreme Court virtually eliminated the "public use" requirement as a restriction on the exercise of eminent domain power. At issue was a Hawaii land reform statute that authorized tenants under long-term leases to acquire by compulsory purchase the landlord's title to the land. The justices emphasized that courts must defer to legislative determinations of public use, even if eminent domain is employed to transfer private property from one person to another. In effect, legislators hold untrammeled authority to decide whether eminent domain is appropriate in a particular situation.[28] The Supreme Court has also been adept at raising procedural barriers in cases involving regulatory takings, thus avoiding a decision on the merits. Moreover, state courts in California, an important jurisdiction in fashioning land use regulations, have remained hostile to regulatory takings claims and have sustained highly intrusive land use controls.

The significance of a reinvigorated takings clause is by no means confined to land use. Takings jurisprudence has an important bearing on industries in which rates are set by government agencies rather than operation of the free market. The authority of the federal and state governments to regulate charges has long been recognized, but the Supreme Court has insisted that such imposed rates must be reasonable and provide for a fair return on investment. The justices have recently shown renewed interest in judicial review of utility rate making under the takings clause. In *Duquesne Light Co. v. Barasch* (1989) the justices emphasized that "the Constitution protects utilities from being so limited to a charge for their property serving the public which is so 'unjust' as to be confiscatory."[29]

Insurance regulations have also run afoul of the takings clause. During the 1980s automobile and medical malpractice insurance dramatically increased in cost. Anxious to stabilize rising insurance premiums, state laws have sought to freeze prices or even to mandate a reduction in existing rates. Such legislation in effect compelled insurers to sell certain policies at a loss. Both federal and state courts, however, have ruled that lawmakers cannot fix rates at an arbitrary level that is so unreasonable as to deprive insurers of a fair return.

Local rent control ordinances have long been a source of controversy because they clearly involve a compelled wealth transfer. In an attempt to hold down the cost of rental housing, such measures fix rent payments and thereby prevent landlords from leasing residential property at market prices. It follows that rent control laws effectively require landlords to subsidize tenants. Historically, however, courts have rarely taken a hard look at rent regulations. The Supreme Court has upheld the general validity of rent ceilings but insisted that the regulatory schemes must yield landlords a reasonable return on investment. Applying this test, in the early 1990s several state and lower federal courts struck down local rent controls as confiscatory in violation of the takings clause. Moreover, several members of the current Supreme Court seem disenchanted with rent control absent emergency housing conditions and have suggested that ordinarily the marketplace should determine rents. Some observers believe that the Supreme Court may be poised to reconsider the constitutionality of rent control. Certainly the imposition of ever more onerous rent regulations, such as tenant hardship provisions and restrictions on the demolition or conversion of rental property, is bound to collide with the renewed judicial sensitivity to the rights of property owners.

The takings clause, of course, does not prevent governmental interference with existing property relationships. Rather, the Fifth Amendment simply requires that owners receive just compensation, defined as an equivalent, for any property taken by government action. In an era of tight budgets and widespread resistance to higher taxes, however, lawmakers are often tempted to achieve public benefits by placing regulatory burdens on a relative handful of property owners instead of society as a whole through higher taxes. Takings jurisprudence, therefore, has a potentially significant impact on economic regulations and proposed social reforms. As a practical matter, reformist zeal tends to wither when taxpayers are called upon to pay for the results. Consequently, many regulations of property will be jeopardized if the Supreme Court mandates the payment of compensation.

Nonetheless, important libertarian considerations undergird the Supreme Court's fledgling moves to strengthen the rights of property owners under the takings clause. In the first place, reinvigorated enforcement of the just compensation requirement would enhance democratic accountability. Governmental officials would be compelled to address directly the financial implications of land use controls and social programs and not rely on regulations as a politically attractive substitute for general taxation. Officials could use public revenue, for instance, to provide low-income housing or to purchase beachfront property by eminent domain. This would afford citizens an opportunity to debate the desirability of such policies and to decide how much they are prepared to pay if property is taken to accomplish them. Secondly, the takings clause, like the other provisions of the Bill of Rights, was crafted to protect individual liberty by restricting the reach of government power. To the founding generation respect for the rights of property owners reinforced the basic constitutional design of limited government. Experience in the twentieth century amply demonstrates that individual liberties do not flourish in nations where private property is not recognized.

Equal Protection

The Fourteenth Amendment provides in part that no state shall "deny to any person within its jurisdiction the equal protection of the laws." Although the states have been accorded wide latitude to classify and regulate economic activity, courts have recently shown renewed willingness to employ the equal protection clause to protect economic interests from inequitable treatment. In *Allegheny Pittsburgh Coal Co. v. Webster County* (1989) the

Supreme Court, for the first time since the 1930s, invalidated a tax assessment on real property on grounds it had a discriminatory impact. The justices unanimously held that taxes must be evenly applied to comparable properties and that the systematic undervaluation of some property in the same tax class denied other taxpayers equal protection. Similarly, a lower federal court invalidated a municipal ordinance that prohibited a sidewalk shoeshine business while permitting other types of street vendors.

But the Supreme Court remains highly deferential to state tax laws in the face of equal protection challenges. In 1978 California voters adopted a constitutional initiative, known as Proposition 13, which placed strict limits on the rate at which real property taxes could be annually increased. Since the tax burden is calculated in terms of acquisition value, the result has been dramatic disparities in the taxes paid by long-term and recent owners of property of similar market value. Nonetheless, in *Nordlinger v. Hahn* (1992) the Supreme Court found that there were reasonable policy considerations to support this disparate tax treatment and that therefore Proposition 13 did not violate the equal protection clause.[30] The justices distinguished *Allegheny Pittsburgh* on grounds that in that case the tax authorities purported to tax all property at a uniform current value, but in fact did not enforce the tax scheme evenly.

Conclusion

Despite the renewed judicial interest in economic liberty, the place of property rights in modern constitutional thought remains uncertain. The modern welfare state rests on the assumption that redistribution of resources is an appropriate governmental function. The current Supreme Court, perhaps fearful of igniting a political firestorm, has shown no inclination to challenge any major national economic regulations. Yet it is impossible to reconcile unfettered legislative control of private property with either the language of the Constitution or the course of constitutional history.

Indeed, the Constitution and the Bill of Rights affirmed the central place of property ownership in American history. In defending the rights of property owners, courts have reflected not only the views of the framers but also values deeply embedded in the political culture. Questioning the fashionable dichotomy between personal and economic liberty, Justice Scalia observed: "Few of us, I suspect, would have much difficulty choosing between the right to own property and the right to receive a Miranda warning."[31]

Recent events in Eastern Europe have vividly underscored the historic tie between property ownership and personal liberty. Realizing that private property tends to diffuse political power, the newly independent nations of Eastern Europe have taken steps to restore private ownership and to privatize segments of industry. Fortunately for Americans, the framers of our Constitution and Bill of Rights understood the vital role of property rights 200 years ago.

Reversing the Revolution
Rights of the Accused in
a Conservative Age

David J. Bodenhamer

In 1987 and 1988 the little-known Office of Legal Policy in the Department of Justice released eight reports on criminal procedure. Under the series title "Truth in Criminal Justice," the papers addressed an assortment of constitutional issues, from pretrial interrogation to habeas corpus to inferences from silence. The reports, wrote the assistant attorney general for legal policy, challenged "a judicially created system of restrictions of law enforcement that has emerged since the 1960s" and sought a return to "the ideal of criminal investigation and adjudication as a serious search for truth."[1]

The series clearly reflected the Reagan administration's position that liberal judges had unduly bridled police and prosecutors in combating crime, at grave cost to public safety. According to this view, the Warren Court in the 1960s had abandoned the discovery of truth, the traditional goal of American criminal procedure, in a misguided and unjustified expansion of defendants' rights. These rights enabled criminals to escape punishment — and worse, to continue a life of crime — not through a trial determination of guilt or innocence but rather on some technicality that bore little relationship to what actually happened. As Attorney General Edwin Meese argued in his preface to each report, "Over the past thirty years . . . a variety of new rules have emerged that impede the discovery of reliable evidence at the investigative stages . . . and that require the concealment of relevant facts at trial." The law needed reform, he proclaimed; above all else, "criminal justice . . . must be devoted to discovering the truth."[2]

To achieve this end, the reports called for the reversal of landmark decisions from the 1960s. Few important cases escaped condemnation: *Mapp v. Ohio* (1961), *Massiah v. United States* (1964), and *Miranda v. Arizona* (1966), among others, introduced extra-constitutional, judicially created rules that impeded effective law enforcement. These decisions and others from the Warren Court, the reports claimed, unfairly burdened criminal investigation, allowed an explosive rise in the crime rate, and diminished the importance of the criminal trial, traditionally the testing ground for competing claims of truth. Order would be restored and the trial regain its central

role in American jurisprudence when police and prosecutors had the freedom to present evidence of guilt or innocence. Convicting the guilty, after
all, was the primary mission of the criminal justice system. Only the punishment and prevention of crime vindicated the innocent individual's right
to security. But "[i]f truth cannot be discovered and acted upon, the system
can only fail in its basic mission."[3]

This criticism of the 1960s due process revolution was not new to the politics of the 1980s. Richard Nixon made "law and order" a major theme of
his 1968 presidential campaign, proclaiming that the Warren Court let
"guilty men walk free from hundreds of courtrooms." His first appointment to the Supreme Court, the new Chief Justice, Warren Burger, shared
Nixon's view: while still on the appellant bench, he wrote that the Court's
actions made guilt or innocence "irrelevant in the criminal trial as we floun-
der in a morass of artificial rules poorly conceived and often impossible of
application."[4] Election after election saw politicians trot out variations of
this theme, often with great success. The criticism remained politically potent during the Reagan-Bush years—witness the infamous Willie Horton
commercial in 1988—because it appeared to explain the dramatic increase
in violent crimes, especially by black males.

Yet throughout much of the 1970s and 1980s the Warren Court reforms
remained essentially intact. The Burger Court, with a more conservative
cast, refused to extend the due process revolution and even trimmed some
newfound rights, but it did not repudiate the earlier Court's legacy. Even
the Rehnquist Court followed suit initially, despite the new Chief Justice's
view that the Warren Court had erred often by deciding cases without constitutional justification.

In the 1990s the Court switched direction. Bolstered by the retirement of
William Brennan, a liberal holdover from the Warren era and a strong intellectual force on the bench, the Court signaled a reversal on issues of defendants' rights. The new conservative majority abandoned several precedents, some established only a few years earlier. More significant was a
different tone to the Court's opinions, a determination to ensure that rights
of the accused did not prevent successful prosecution of guilty suspects.
Perhaps more by circumstance than design, the Court's shift paralleled the
recommendations of the Department of Justice. After two decades of conservative electoral success, constitutional law finally merged with political
opinion.

But what of this change in course? The politics are clear, but what about
the interpretation of the past upon which it rests? The Warren Court's decisions on criminal procedure were not as revolutionary, as far reaching, or
even as consequential as critics have maintained. This conclusion may not
be true for the Rehnquist Court. An emphasis on convicting the guilty, for
example, departs significantly from legal traditions that far predate the
Warren Court, and a belief that protection of formal trial procedures best
ensures justice is at odds with American experience. To understand why

the counterrevolution may be more radical than the revolution itself, it is first necessary to recall the past.

Prelude to a Revolution

From the beginning of the nation, the states, not the central government, were primarily responsible for the integrity of criminal due process. State constitutions and state courts defined and protected the rights of the accused. The Bill of Rights applied only to federal trials. Even the passage of the Fourteenth Amendment with its language suggesting national oversight of due process did not change this division of responsibility. Well into the twentieth century the Supreme Court adhered to the position first announced in *Hurtado v. California* (1884) that the Fourteenth Amendment did not bind the states to the procedural guarantees of the federal Constitution. Most rights belonging to Americans were attributes of state citizenship and thus were not subject to national regulation or control. Criminal due process referred only to the procedures employed by the state. If criminal prosecutions followed the process required by state law, then the result by definition was justice.

Few people found the lack of national supervision troublesome, at least not if they were part of the white majority, because Americans shared a common set of legal values, institutions, and procedures. Chief among them was a commitment to due process of law, which in ideal form pledged procedural fairness in all actions from indictment to trial and punishment. Underlying this notion of fairness was a belief expressed through centuries of Anglo-American experience that the primary purpose of criminal justice was to protect the innocent, not to convict the guilty. The fifteenth-century English maxim remained a guide for nineteenth-century Americans: it was better for twenty guilty persons to escape punishment than one person to suffer wrongly.[5]

Even as Americans celebrated their commitment to due process, criminal justice was taking new and different shape. The grand jury came under sharp attack in the mid-nineteenth century, and by the 1880s almost twenty states, mostly western, allowed the prosecutor to charge a person directly through an information rather than the traditional indictment. Newly created police departments shifted the focus of law enforcement from reacting to citizen complaints to detecting crime by patrols and investigations. But it was the trial, long the centerpiece of the criminal process, that experienced the most dramatic challenge. Not only did bench trial, or trial by the judge alone, begin to rival jury trial in several jurisdictions as an acceptable means of trying a case, most defendants avoided trial altogether by pleading guilty in exchange for less severe punishment. State surveys in the 1920s revealed a heavy dependence on plea bargaining, especially in big city courts: in Chicago, for example, 85 percent of all felony convictions resulted from a guilty plea. The percentages in other cities were almost as high or higher.

Plea bargaining changed the face of American justice. It made efficient prosecution and conviction of the guilty, not protection of the innocent, the primary goal of the legal system. There were informal, subterranean, and highly particularistic standards for fixing guilt and innocence: confessions became the desired end and police interrogations the preferred means for obtaining them. State supreme courts often protested: plea bargaining was a perversion of due process; it represented the sale of justice; and its secrecy mocked the pledge of neutral justice in a public trial. Other critics characterized plea bargaining as an auction, and legal scholars denounced it as a license to violate the law. But the practice continued. Public concerns about order, especially in the face of rapid urbanization and a flood of immigration from Eastern Europe and Asia, made the control of crime paramount.

These changes led to dissatisfaction during the first decades of the twentieth century with the traditional policy of no federal oversight in matters of criminal justice. Increasingly events pressured the Supreme Court to extend the protection of the Bill of Rights to criminal defendants under the Fourteenth Amendment, just as it had begun to do for the rights of free speech and free press. The Red Scare following World War I demonstrated the need as states failed to protect even the most basic rights of defendants, especially ethnic and racial minorities. During the 1920s, studies of criminal justice, including a major national investigation by the Wickersham Commission, revealed the open contempt many police departments held for the rights guaranteed by state and federal constitutions. And the wholesale lynching of blacks in the South finally became a national disgrace.

By the 1930s numerous organizations, notably the American Civil Liberties Union and the National Association for the Advancement of Colored People, pressed for nationalization of the Bill of Rights. In 1932, they scored an initial success. *Powell v. Alabama*, the famous Scottsboro case, established that the due process clause of the Fourteenth Amendment guaranteed the assistance of counsel to defendants charged with capital crimes in state courts. Even so, the Supreme Court continued to resist attempts to incorporate the protections of the Fourth, Fifth, Sixth, and Eighth Amendments into a national standard. The Fourteenth Amendment, the justices held in *Palko v. Connecticut* (1937), imposed on the states only rights essential to a "scheme of ordered liberty."[6] In criminal matters the assurance of fair trial alone was fundamental to liberty. States could employ widely different procedures without violating due process. Not even trial by jury was essential to fairness, even though the founding fathers had deemed it the bulwark of their liberties.

From the 1930s through the 1950s the Supreme Court grappled with the meaning of the phrase "due process of law." The fair-trial test meant that the Court would decide case by case which rights of the accused enjoyed constitutional protection. It also suggested that the values and attitudes of individual judges would determine which state procedures created such hardships or so shocked the conscience that they denied fair treatment. Still, the test provided a method for extending the Bill of Rights to the states, and the catalog of nationalized rights—provisions of the Bill of Rights binding on the states—grew extensively by the end of the three decades, especially given the previous absence of such guarantees, although the list pales when compared to current practice. Fundamental rights included limited protection against illegal searches and seizures (Fourth Amendment), coerced confessions (Fifth), public trial, impartial jury, and counsel (Sixth), and cruel and unusual punishments (Eighth). Even so, the interpretation of these rights was not as far reaching as later Courts would find, and some rights—double jeopardy, protections against self-incrimination, and jury trial, among others—remained totally under state control.

The Court's continued reliance on the fair-trial test, although maintaining a theoretical line between state and federal power, led to much confusion regarding which criminal procedures were acceptable. Some state practices it permitted, others it rejected, but no clear standard emerged to guide law enforcement. Adherence to the test increasingly exposed the Court to charges that defendants' rights depended on judicial caprice. Such an *"ad hoc* approach," Chief Justice Earl Warren cautioned in 1957, "is to build on shifting sands."[7] It was also at odds with the Court's decisions on First Amendment freedoms. These rights applied fully and identically to central and state governments alike under the due process clause of the Fourteenth Amendment. Why should not the same standard govern rights of the accused? *Palko v. Connecticut*, progenitor of the fair-trial doctrine, Justice Brennan reminded his colleagues, contained no "license to the judiciary to administer a watered-down, subjective version of the individual guarantees of the Bill of Rights."[8]

By the late 1950s four justices—Warren, Black, Douglas, and Brennan—were ready to abandon the fair-trial approach to the Fourteenth Amendment. The 1960s witnessed their triumph. Too much had changed nationally to continue an interpretation that defined rights in terms of state boundaries. State prosecutors and local police alike had grown weary of a tribunal in distant Washington deciding long after trial that state practices violated the Constitution. Law schools and bar associations desired more uniform rules. Commentators and legal scholars also questioned why the Fourth, Fifth, Sixth, and Eighth Amendments were not as fundamental as the freedom to speech and press.

In a nation where interstate highways collapsed distances and chain stores erased a sense of place it was only a matter of time before national standards replaced local practice. For criminal law the shift came in a rush of Supreme Court decisions in the 1960s. In what was termed the "due process revolution," the Bill of Rights became a national code of criminal procedure. Suddenly, rights of criminal defendants became more real, more immediate, and, for many people, more threatening.

Nationalizing the Rights of the Accused

Between 1961 and 1969 the Supreme Court accomplished what previous courts had stoutly resisted: it applied virtually all of the procedural guarantees of the Bill of Rights to the states' administration of criminal justice. Adopting the strategy of selective incorporation, the justices explicitly defined the Fourteenth Amendment phrase, due process of law, to include most of the rights outlined in the Fourth, Fifth, and Sixth Amendments. The result was a nationalized Bill of Rights that dimmed the local character of justice by applying the same restraints to all criminal proceedings, both state and federal. The majority justices did not seek to diminish states' rights; they desired instead to elevate subminimal state practices to a higher national standard. But in the process the Court reshaped the nature of federalism itself.

Leading the due process revolution was an unlikely figure, Chief Justice Earl Warren. He was a former California district prosecutor, attorney general, and governor whose pre-Court reputation was of a crusader against corruption and for vigorous law enforcement. The judiciary scarcely entered into his calculus of what constituted proper government, and as a politician he certainly did nothing to challenge traditional meanings of due process. In fact, Warren led the campaign to intern Japanese Americans during World War II, an action that denied, among other constitutional guarantees, the right to a fair hearing.

Warren's reputation took a sharp turn as Chief Justice, in large measure because he brought a different style and philosophy to the Court. His longstanding belief in active government challenged the majority justices' embrace of judicial restraint, which included deference for legislative actions, respect for federalism and the diversity of state practice, and reliance upon neutral decision making based on narrow case facts rather than broad constitutional interpretation. Warren specifically dismissed as "fantasy" the notion that judges can be impartial. "As defender of the Constitution," he wrote, "the Court cannot be neutral."[9] More important, Court decisions must reach the right result, a condition defined by ethics, not legal procedures. He firmly believed that the Constitution embodied moral truths that were essential to enlightened government. The Court had a duty to apply these principles, even if doing so contravened the expressed wishes of the legislature. And finally, its role was to champion the individual, especially those citizens without a meaningful political voice.

By the 1960s the Court was ready to follow the Chief Justice's lead. Act-

ing with unprecedented boldness, a majority on the Warren Court pro-
moted policies it deemed essential to a just society. Equality joined individualism in the pantheon of modern liberal values. Liberty, long defined as
the restraint of power, now required positive governmental action. Individual freedom rested upon the protection and extension to all citizens of
the fundamental guarantees found in the Bill of Rights and the Fourteenth
Amendment. In its emphasis on equality and national standards, the Court
was not alone. Liberalism experienced a resurgence under the presidencies
of Kennedy and Johnson, and the rhetoric of civil rights and social justice
framed the agenda of the ascendant Democratic Party. So for most of the
decade, the justices drew support from a liberal political coalition that
preached a similar message.

Popular myth has it that the Court's decisions on criminal justice were
highly controversial and came only through the determined efforts of a
bare majority of judges. This view distorts what actually happened. Take,
for example, *Gideon v. Wainwright* (1963), which declared that the Sixth
Amendment right to counsel applied to the states under the due process
clause of the Fourteenth Amendment and that states had to provide a lawyer for felony defendants too poor to hire one. The decision was unanimous, even though it reversed a 1942 precedent (*Betts v. Brady*) allowing a
state to refuse such assistance in non-capital cases unless its refusal denied
a fair trial. More striking was the fact that twenty-three states filed *amicus
curiae*, or friend-of-the-court, briefs asking the Court to mandate the assistance of counsel in serious criminal cases. Their assessment of the Court's
previous deference to the states was damning. It had resulted only in "confusion and contradictions" that failed totally "as a beacon to guide trial
judges."[10] The states themselves demanded the nationalization of this important guarantee of the Bill of Rights.

Other decisions affecting the conduct of state trials also met general acceptance, even when the justices divided narrowly. For example, the Court
decided in *Malloy v. Hogan* (1964) that the privilege against self-incrimination was part of the due process clause of the Fourteenth Amendment.
And the next year, 1965, in *Pointer v. Texas*, the Court ruled that the Sixth
Amendment right of an accused to confront a witness against him was a
fundamental right that the Fourteenth Amendment required of all states.
Neither case occasioned much public comment, certainly not the storm of
protests often depicted by opponents of the decisions.

In truth, there was never much objection to the Warren Court's restraints
on state trial practices. News coverage of the landmark decisions was limited; few columnists discussed the changes. Most people undoubtedly
viewed the trial as the centerpiece of American justice, especially when
placed in contrast to totalitarian practices during the height of the cold war.
(The absence of a trial in the vast majority of criminal cases scarcely dinted
public awareness.) At least for trial rights they concurred with Justice

Arthur Goldberg's opinion in *Pointer* that states had no "power to experiment with the fundamental liberties of the people." Diversity here denied equal justice.

The greatest protest against the Court's extension of federal trial rights came from state judges who considered the decisions an infringement of their prerogative. Conservative legal commentators also objected, claiming that the theory of selective incorporation[11] used to justify the decisions was constitutionally incorrect, primarily because it undermined the federal system's division of authority between state and central governments. But these criticisms were blunted by most states' acceptance of the Court's direction. Uniform rules for trials did not threaten the core of state power, and they removed much of the uncertainty that accompanied numerous appeals.

Pre-trial rights were a wholly different matter. The Court discovered early that any challenge of state police practices would be highly controversial. In *Mapp v. Ohio* (1961) the liberal justices narrowly (5–4) applied the federal exclusionary rule to the states. Even though the case facts revealed a blatant disregard of search and seizure guarantees, the Ohio Supreme Court had upheld the state law permitting the use of illegally seized evidence to convict Dollree Mapp of possession of obscene material. The Supreme Court disagreed. One of its earlier decisions, *Wolf v. Colorado* (1948), had extended the Fourth Amendment to the states but without the federal rule of procedure that required the exclusion of any evidence gained in violation of the amendment's guarantees. Now with the amendment's protection went the means to enforce it, the exclusionary rule. "To hold otherwise," Justice Tom Clark reasoned, "is to grant the right but in reality withhold its privilege and enjoyment."[12]

Clark, a former U.S. Attorney General, did not believe the decision would impede law enforcement—although, he argued, the Constitution demanded it regardless—but critics of *Mapp* concluded otherwise. They condemned the Court as unrealistic: police engaged in dangerous work that often required quick action; failure to follow the correct procedures should not doom the evidence of crime, especially when state law and state courts permitted it. Indeed, *Mapp* undermined state ability to maintain order, opponents argued, by breaching the federal principle that left criminal matters to state control. The majority justices had overreached their authority and fashioned their decision not on constitutional precedent but on their sense of a right result.

These criticisms surfaced with more force a few years later when the Court extended the right of counsel to the pretrial stages of criminal process, first in *Massiah v. United States* (1964) and then in *Escobedo v. Illinois* (1965) and *Miranda v. Arizona* (1966). The justices concluded that Fifth Amendment guarantees against self-incrimination and coerced confessions and the Sixth Amendment right to counsel were meaningless unless applied to a police investigation at the point where it focused directly on an individual suspected of crime. Any information gained illegally by denying these protections was not admissible at trial. Significantly, the decisions affirmed and extended the precedents of earlier Courts, stretching back at least to 1945, that automatically overturned convictions achieved through coerced or involuntary confessions, even if the confessions were true and the guilty defendant went free as a result.[13] But for opponents of the decisions the Court had departed dramatically from past practice, impeding the investigation of crime and jeopardizing public safety.

Miranda was by far the most controversial decision, the one still cited as the premier example of a Court gone wrong. Chief Justice Warren's opinion extending the Fifth Amendment protection against self-incrimination to suspects under police interrogation exemplified his ethically based, result-oriented jurisprudence. The opinion first detailed the unfair and forbidding nature of police interrogations. Police manuals and statements by law enforcement officers revealed that beatings, intimidation, psychological pressure, false statements, and denial of food and sleep were standard techniques used to secure the suspect's confession. For Warren, these tactics suggested that "the interrogation environment [existed] . . . for no other purpose than to subjugate the individual to the will of the examiner."[14] Ethics alone made reprehensible any practice that tricked or cajoled suspects from exercising their constitutional rights, leaving them isolated and vulnerable. But such police tactics also violated the Fifth Amendment protection against self-incrimination.

The longest part of the opinion was a detailed code of police conduct. The new rules quickly became familiar to anyone who watched television crime dramas: the suspect must be informed of the right to remain silent; that anything he says can be used against him; that he has the right to have counsel present during questioning; that if he cannot afford an attorney, the court will appoint a lawyer to represent him. These privileges took effect from the first instance of police interrogation while the suspect was "in custody at the station or deprived of his freedom in a significant way." And the rights could be waived only "knowingly and intelligently," a condition presumed not to exist if lengthy questioning preceded the required warnings.[15]

Warren's language vividly portrayed the unequal relationship between interrogator and suspect, an imbalance that the Chief Justice believed did not belong in a democratic society. "The prosecutor under our system," he commented later, "is not paid to convict people [but to] protect the rights of people . . . and to see that when there is a violation of the law, it is vindicated by trial and prosecution under fair judicial standards."[16] The presence of a lawyer and a protected right of silence created a more equal situation for the accused; thus, these conditions were essential to the constitutional conception of a fair trial.

Police officers, prosecutors, commentators, and politicians were quick to denounce the *Miranda* warnings. They charged that recent Court decisions had "handcuffed" police efforts to fight crime. This claim found a receptive audience among a majority of the general public worried about rising crime rates, urban riots, racial conflict, and the counterculture's challenge to middle-class values. The belief that the pretrial reforms threatened public safety even acquired a certain legitimacy from members of the Supreme Court itself. "[I]n some unknown number of cases," Justice Byron White warned in his dissent from the *Miranda* decision, "the Court's rule will return a killer, a rapist or other criminal to the streets . . . to repeat his crime whenever it pleases him."[17]

These alarms were exaggerated. Numerous studies have since demonstrated that the decision, like the ones in *Mapp* and *Massiah*, did not restrain the police unduly and, in fact, had little effect on the disposition of most cases. Access to an attorney, usually an overworked and underpaid public defender, may have smoothed negotiations between suspect and prosecutor, but it did not lessen the percentage of cases resolved by plea bargains, nor did it result in lengthy delays, greater bureaucracy, or more dismissals of guilty suspects.

Even as a matter of law, *Miranda* was not as revolutionary as critics claimed. The Supreme Court from the 1930s had held that voluntariness of a confession was essential for its acceptance as evidence, and since 1945 it automatically reversed convictions based on involuntary confessions, regardless of whether or not the confession was in fact true. There were various terms used to describe the voluntariness test: "free will" and "unconstrained choice" signified a voluntary confession; "breaking the will" and "overbearing the mind," an involuntary one. But, as Justice John Marshall Harlan noted in his dissent in *Miranda*, the Court's gauge for determining whether or not a confession was voluntary had been steadily changing, usually in the direction of restricting admissability.[18] *Miranda* scuttled this case-by-case determination. It established uniform rules of procedure, and equally important, accepted as constitutional any confessions gained under these rules.

Although controversial, the reforms in pretrial procedures gradually brought needed improvements in police practices. Police procedures came more fully into public view, resulting in heightened awareness of official misconduct and greater expectations of professionalism. In response, many police departments raised standards for employment, adopted performance guidelines, and improved training and supervision. The Court's actions had begun to bear fruit, much in the manner desired by the majority who believed that hard work and respect for the law, not deception or lawbreaking, were the requirements of effective law enforcement.

The Court, ever aware of public criticism, made concessions to secure more widespread acceptance of its rulings. Most important was the decision not to apply new rulings retroactively. The justices acknowledged that this course denied equal justice to prisoners convicted under abandoned procedures, but they admitted candidly that wholesale release of prisoners was politically unacceptable. Another concession was the adoption of a "harmless error" test to determine the impact of an unconstitutional act at trial: constitutional errors would not void convictions if "beyond a reasonable doubt that error did not contribute to the verdict obtained."[19] The Court also hesitated to restrict the police unduly. It held in 1966, the same year as *Miranda*, that the government's use of decoys, undercover agents, and paid informants was not necessarily unconstitutional. The justices further approved the admissability of evidence secured by wiretaps and sustained the right of police "in hot pursuit" to search a house and seize incriminating evidence without a warrant. Even *Miranda* itself represented a compromise response to concerns that the earlier *Escobedo* decision required the presence of counsel during the preliminary stages of a police inquiry, before the investigation centered on a suspect in custody.

These moderating decisions failed to quiet the Court's critics, but mounting pressure did not deter the justices from making further reforms in state criminal procedures. *In re Gault* extended certain due process requirements to juvenile courts. Several important cases incorporated the remaining Sixth Amendment guarantees—specifically, the rights to compulsory process, speedy trial, and trial by jury—into the due process clause of the Fourteenth Amendment as new restraints on state criminal process. The Court continued to insist that poverty should be no impediment to justice by requiring that the state furnish transcripts to indigent defendants. And it strengthened its long-established position that confessions be truly voluntary. Much more controversial were the continuing reforms of pretrial procedures. In 1967 several search and seizure decisions especially brought further protest from "law and order" advocates who accused the Court of coddling criminals, a charge that gained momentum during the 1968 election when two presidential candidates—Richard Nixon and George Wallace—made it a major theme in their campaigns.

Such cases, whether controversial or not, departed sharply from the decades-old tradition that defined criminal justice as a local responsibility. Each decision underscored the dramatically changed relationship between the federal Bill of Rights and the state's authority to establish criminal procedures. Earlier Courts had accepted state experimentation with any part of due process unless the justices considered it essential to a scheme of ordered liberty. This standard permitted states to define fairness in a variety of ways, and these definitions may or may not include the guarantees of the federal amendments. But the Warren Court concluded that rights of the accused were rights of American citizenship. The justices rejected theory and diversity in favor of history and uniformity, as Justice White made clear in his majority opinion in *Duncan v. White* (1968), denying the right of a state to withhold jury trial in cases of serious crime: "state criminal processes are not imaginary and theoretical schemes but actual systems bearing virtually every characteristic of the common-law system that has been developed in England and this country." The issue, he continued, was not whether a procedure "is fundamental to fairness in every criminal system that might be imagined but is fundamental in the context of the criminal processes maintained by the American states."[20]

The next year, 1969, the Court reversed, fittingly, *Palko v. Connecticut*, the landmark case that had justified state experimentation with criminal procedures. The issue, as it had been in 1937, was double jeopardy. The question: did the Fifth Amendment restrain the states? This time the answer was yes. Writing for the majority in *Benton v. Maryland*, Justice Thurgood Marshall noted that recent cases had thoroughly rejected the premise in *Palko* that a denial of fundamental fairness rested on the total circumstances of a criminal proceeding, not simply one element of it. Once the Court decides a particular guarantee is fundamental to American justice, he continued, then failure to honor that safeguard is a denial of due process. Equally important, these essential protections applied uniformly to all jurisdictions. Here, then, was the core of the due process revolution: rights of the accused did not vary from state to state; they were truly national rights.

Slowing the Revolution

By 1969 the Court's transformation of criminal procedure was at its end. Neither popular nor political opinion supported further reform. The previous year, stung by rioting in American cities and pressured to curb the recent sharp upturn in crime and violence, Congress had responded by passing the Omnibus Crime Control and Safe Streets Act, the most extensive anticrime legislation in American history. The measure contained a number of provisions designed to reverse recent Court decisions, especially the *Miranda* rule. And now there was a new Chief Justice, Warren Burger, appointed by Richard Nixon to redeem his campaign pledge to restore a conservative cast to the Supreme Court.

Contrary to expectations, there was no counterrevolution in the law governing defendant's rights, even after three conservative appointees replaced Warren Court justices. Upon Burger's retirement in 1986, the major criminal procedure decisions of the Warren Court remained intact. The lasting influence of the due process reforms owed little to the Chief Justice, who did not share his predecessor's concern with rights of the accused. Indeed, he had often attacked the Court's decisions while on the appellate bench. His announced goal was to shift the burden of reform to the state legislatures. "To try to create or substantially change civil or criminal procedure by judicial decision," he argued, "is the worst possible way to do it."[21]

The Burger Court did not renounce the due process revolution, but the justices were more tolerant of police behavior and less receptive to further expansion of rights of criminal defendants. Symbolic of the change was the

Court's interpretation of the Fourth Amendment's requirement that search warrants be based upon probable cause. Previous decisions had challenged the validity of a warrant issued on the basis of rumors or even an anonymous informant's tip, yet in *United States v. Harris* (1971) a divided Court held that a suspect's reputation alone was sufficient to support a warrant application. Writing for the majority, Chief Justice Burger denounced "mere hypertechnicality" in warrant affidavits and urged a return to more practical considerations in actions against criminals.[22]

Subsequent cases confirmed the new direction. Not only did the Court lower the threshold requirements for a valid search, thus permitting police greater latitude, it redefined the exclusionary rule. Framers of the exclusionary rule, first announced in 1914, may have expected it to influence police behavior, but the principle itself, they believed, was part of the Fourth Amendment. Not so, concluded the Court in 1974. In ruling that grand jury witnesses may not use unlawful searches to keep them from testifying, the Court characterized the exclusionary rule as a "judicially created remedy designed to safeguard Fourth Amendment rights generally through its deterrent effect." It was not a "personal constitutional right," and its use presented "a question, not of rights but of remedies" — one that should be answered by weighing the costs of the rule against its benefits.[23]

This new cost-benefit analysis led ultimately to a good-faith exception to the exclusionary rule, announced in *United States v. Leon* (1984): evidence produced by an officer's reasonable or good-faith reliance on the validity of a warrant was admissible in court, even if the warrant later proved defective. The good-faith exception rested explicitly on a balancing of the costs and benefits involved: using evidence captured innocently under a defective warrant exacted a small price from Fourth Amendment protection when compared to the substantial cost society would bear if an otherwise guilty defendant went free. Left unanswered was the question of whether the exception was necessary. Opponents of the decision argued not; since *Mapp*, evidence was excluded or prosecutions dropped in fewer than 2 percent of all cases. Strict adherence to the exclusionary rule had resulted in better police work. If the good-faith exception invited a more casual approach to law enforcement, they feared, the Fourth Amendment would once again become a meaningless guarantee.

In most other areas of criminal procedure, the Court maintained but did little to advance the rights of the accused extended during the Warren era. Arguing that the law requires only a fair trial, not a perfect one, the Court upheld a conviction even though the police, when giving the required *Miranda* warnings, neglected to tell the defendant of his right to appointed counsel if he could not afford one. It also allowed admissions secured without the required warnings to be used to impeach the defendant's credibility, though not to obtain his conviction, if he took the stand in his own behalf. In Sixth Amendment cases the Court guaranteed the right to counsel in all trials that could result in imprisonment; but following the lead of

Congress in the Crime Control Act of 1968, it refused to grant the protection to unindicted suspects in a police lineup. Similarly, the justices extended the guarantee of a jury trial to include all petty misdemeanors pun-
ishable by six months or longer imprisonment, yet allowed states to
experiment with the size of juries and accepted 10–2 and 9–3 verdicts in
non-capital cases.[24]

Reversing the Revolution

Initially, the Rehnquist Court followed its predecessor in cases involving
rights of the accused. It declined to extend defendants' rights and insisted
on balancing individual protections with the need for effective law enforcement, but it did not reverse Warren Court decisions. Law officers gained
greater latitude in applying the *Miranda* rules when, in *Colorado v. Connelly*
(1986), the Court adopted a less strict standard to determine the voluntariness of a confession. Police must give the required warnings and stop all
questioning if a suspect demanded a lawyer, but they could use nonthreat-
ening tactics, such as pretending sympathy with the suspect, to secure a
valid confession.[25] Strengthening the ability of the police to fight crime was
also the result in *United States v. Salerno* (1987), upholding the Bail Reform
Act of 1984 that allowed the government to deny bail if release of a defendant would endanger lives or property. Even though an apparent departure from the presumption of innocence, the law itself provided numerous
procedural safeguards, including representation of counsel. These protections, the justices concluded, provided a reasonable balance between the
rights of the accused and the need for public safety.

This incremental rebalancing of societal and individual interests gave
way to a more comprehensive reassessment of rights of the accused during
the 1990 term. For over two decades politicians' demands for a law-and-
order judiciary had reaped electoral windfalls, but not until the appointment of three conservative justices—Kennedy, Scalia, and Souter—did
politics and constitutional law join so conclusively. Suddenly the calculus
of decision making had changed, and it emboldened the new conservative
majority to challenge Warren Court precedents.

Several cases signaled the new direction. The most dramatic departure
came in confession law, long a bellwether of constitutional attitudes toward the defendant. Since the 1940s the Court had reversed convictions
based in whole or in part upon an involuntary confession, even when there
was ample evidence apart from the confession to support the conviction. In
Arizona v. Fulminante, the 5–4 majority abandoned this precedent. They applied instead the harmless-error test to such evidence. This new approach
classified evidence of a coerced confession not as an automatic violation of
due process but simply as a trial error. Like other mistakes at trial, involuntary confessions must now be examined in the context of all the facts

presented at trial to determine if its use was harmless, or inconsequential to the verdict.

The dissenting justices claimed that the majority had misapplied the harmless-error rule—first announced, ironically, by the Warren Court—which specifically noted three errors that could not be categorized as harmless error: depriving a defendant of counsel, trying a defendant before a trial judge, and using a coerced confession against a defendant. In his controlling opinion, Chief Justice Rehnquist dismissed this argument. The first two errors, he concluded, were "structural defects affecting the framework within which the trial proceeds, rather than simply an error in the trial process itself."[26] An involuntary confession did not taint the entire trial; it was like other evidence and was subject to the same rules of admissability. This argument was strained: it ignored the far-reaching effects of a coerced confession, which, unlike other types of evidence, cast a shadow over the entire case, both for prosecution and defense. But the Chief Justice ignored these distinctions. There was a more important reason to adopt the harmless-error rule: it was essential to preserve the central truth-seeking purpose of the criminal trial.[27] The goal was to convict the guilty, not restrain the government. Settled constitutional interpretations of due process stymied that function; the harmless-error rule would promote it.

Not only had the Court shifted its doctrinal stance but its very tone was markedly different, as another decision announced the same day made clear. *Powers v. Ohio* held, 7 to 2, that peremptory challenges used to excuse blacks from the jury violated the equal protection clause of the Fourteenth Amendment, no matter whether the defendant was white or black. Although the defendant in this instance was not a member of the affected class, fairness demanded a race-neutral selection of jurors.

Justice Scalia rejected the majority opinion in a scathing dissent. He argued that judges could not look into the reasons for a peremptory challenge, and he reserved his sharpest criticism for what he viewed as unwarranted judicial rule making. "The Court's decision today," he argued, "is unprecedented in law, but not in approach. It is a reprise . . . of *Miranda v. Arizona*, in that the Court uses its key to the jail-house door not to free the arguably innocent, but to threaten release upon society of the unquestionably guilty unless law enforcement officers take certain steps that the Court newly announces to be law." At least, he continued, *Miranda* related to the defendant's rights, not his guilt. "Even if I agreed that the exercise of peremptory strikes constitutes unlawful discrimination (which I do not), I would not understand why the release of a convicted murderer who has not been harmed by those strikes is an appropriate remedy."[28] Scalia exaggerated the effect of the decision: the majority simply reversed the conviction and sent the case back to lower court for retrial. But the tone of his dissent—and its underlying premise—expressed a dominant philosophy of the Rehnquist Court: criminal justice existed to convict the guilty, and judicial decisions that frustrated this end were impermissible.

Judicial restraint and a respect for federalism are other key themes of the new conservative majority. The first principle requires deference to legislative authority; the second, to state practice. Judges can only interpret whether or not the law is constitutional in its form and application. Few jurists dispute this standard. Not even the Warren Court at the height of its rule making in *Miranda* believed that it had violated these bounds. But the Rehnquist Court has made these concepts a touchstone of its philosophy. In practice, the justices will retreat from broad constitutional decisions and determine case by case whether a practice is acceptable. This approach marks a return to the fair-trial standard that guided the pre-Warren Court. Fairness is the essential constitutional requirement of due process, and states may achieve this result in a variety of ways. Indeed, the justices have concluded, the federal principle demands that the Court respect the states' authority to control criminal process.

By what measures will the justices determine fairness? Tradition and reason were the two criteria used in *Schad v. Arizona* (1991), a case involving the constitutionality of certain instructions to the jury. In determining what is due process, Justice David Souter wrote for the majority, "history and current practice are significant indicators of what we as a people regard as fundamentally fair and rational . . . , which are nevertheless always open to critical examination."[29] There is nothing unique in these standards—the Warren Court used similar language—and it still leaves much to judicial interpretation. Too much, according to Justice Scalia, along with the Chief Justice the dominant intellectual force on the high bench. In his concurring opinion he wanted to restrict the criterion of judgment to history alone: "It is precisely the historical practices that *define* [emphasis in original] what is 'due.' 'Fundamental fairness' analysis may appropriately be applied to *departures* from traditional American conceptions of due process; but when judges test their individual notions of 'fairness' against an American tradition that is broad and deep and continuing, it is not the tradition that is on trial, but the judges."[30]

The contrast with the Warren Court could hardly be more dramatic. Earl Warren had called for the "constant and creative application" of the Bill of Rights to new situations. This process implied continual revision of the catalog of rights, leaving "a document that will not have exactly the same meaning it had when we received it from our fathers" but one that would be better because it was "burnished by growing use."[31] The Rehnquist Court rejects this emphasis. Historical continuity, not change, is the new guiding principle.

Federalism too is a lodestar for the Court. *Coleman v. Thompson* (1991), which with other recent decisions sharply restricts a state prisoner's access to federal courts, is illustrative. The first sentence in Justice Sandra Day O'Connor's opinion for the 6–3 majority—"This is a case about federalism"—establishes the grounds for the denial of federal habeas review when the prisoner missed the filing deadline for a state court appeal because of his attorney's error. But the text scants a discussion about the proper division of power and ignores any question of rights in favor of a cost-benefit analysis: "most of the price paid for federal review of state prisoner claims is paid by the State . . . in terms of the uncertainty and delay added to the enforcement of its criminal laws." Habeas corpus, while a bulwark against unfair convictions, entails significant costs, "the most significant of which is the cost in finality in criminal litigation." And in overruling *Fay v. Noia* (1963), the Warren Court decision that expanded federal review of habeas petitions, "we now recognize the important interest in finality served by state procedural rules, and the significant harm to the States that results from the failure of the federal courts to respect them."[32]

Justice Harry Blackmun, joined by Justices Marshall and Stevens, rebuked his colleagues in a stinging dissent: "[D]isplaying obvious exasperation with the breadth of substantive federal habeas doctrine and the expansive protection afforded by the Fourteenth Amendment's guarantee of fundamental fairness in state criminal proceedings, the Court today continues its crusade to erect petty procedural barriers in the path of any state prisoner seeking review of his federal constitutional claims." Where was the concern for the petitioner Coleman's rights, especially since he was under sentence of death? These rights are not an issue of federalism; they are constitutional guarantees and as such are superior to state interests. Federal review exists not to diminish state authority but "to ensure that federal rights were not improperly denied a federal forum." Most unsettling was the majority's "blind abdication of responsibility" and its willingness to replace "the discourse of rights . . . with the functional dialect of interests." The Court "now routinely, and without evident reflection, subordinates fundamental constitutional rights to mere utilitarian interests." [33] The goal of finality alone was not sufficient to compromise the protection of rights.

Federalism implies a diversity of practice, and the Court has repeatedly demonstrated its willingness to accept different criminal procedures for different states, even if it means reversing precedents it has only recently affirmed. Such was the case in *Payne v. Tennessee* (1991). Various states in the 1980s had enacted laws that permitted sentencing juries in capital cases to consider evidence about the victim when deciding whether or not to impose the death penalty. These statutes clearly represented a political response to public beliefs that the law favored the criminal and cared little for the victim of crime. In 1987 and 1989 the Court rejected victim-impact evidence as a violation of the Eighth Amendment's ban on cruel and unusual punishment. *Payne* abruptly jettisoned these precedents.

Judicial opinions usually begin with a brief, dispassionate statement of the facts, but not so in this case. Rarely has a Court opinion made the description of a crime more vivid. Chief Justice Rehnquist, for the 6–3 majority, quoted extensively from the evidence at trial, emphasizing the bloody crime and the dissolute nature of the defendant: Payne appeared to be "sweating blood," he had "a wild look about him. His pupils were contracted. He was foaming at the mouth." Rehnquist had set the stage for overturning *Booth v. Maryland* and *South Carolina v. Gathers*, the controlling precedents. These cases "unfairly weighted the scales in a criminal trial." Citing as authority the opinion of his fellow dissenting justices in the earlier cases, he rejected the notion that evidence about the victim leads to arbitrary decisions in capital cases, a result forbidden by the Eighth Amendment. In any event, the states must remain free "in capital cases, as well as others, to devise new procedures and new remedies to meet felt needs." Blind adherence to past mistakes would not accomplish these ends, especially when the precedents "were decided by the narrowest of margins, over spirited dissents."[34] Nowhere in evidence was the Warren Court's concern that due process protected the citizen from the overbearing power of the state. The new jurisprudence increasingly echoed the conservative politics of the past two decades. Now it was the society that had to be protected from the effect of a citizen's constitutional rights.

The change in the Court's attitude and approach was painfully obvious to Justice Marshall, the sole holdover from the Warren era. "Power, not reason, is the new currency of this Court's decisionmaking," he protested in dissent. "Neither the law nor the facts supporting *Booth* and *Gathers* underwent any change in the last four years. Only the personnel of this Court did." The admission of victim-impact evidence, although unconstitutional in Marshall's view, was less consequential than the majority's disregard of stare decisis, or the doctrine that the Court will look to its precedent when deciding cases. Joined by Justice Blackmun, he charged that the Court had declared itself free to "discard any principle of constitutional liberty which was recognized or reaffirmed over the dissenting votes of four Justices and with which five or more Justices *now* disagree." The implications of this departure were radical and staggering: "the majority today sends a clear signal that scores of established liberties are now ripe for reconsideration."[35]

Marshall's view was more than the lament of an isolated liberal justice. The Court's recent decisions foreshadowed an end, if not a reversal, of the due process revolution, especially given the appointment of Clarence Thomas, another conservative jurist, beginning with the 1992 term. Justice Scalia's concurring opinion in *Payne*—and the majority's actions throughout the 1991 term—suggested that the Court in future cases would be less inclined to continue or extend constitutional protection to what it now viewed as mere procedural rules. "Considerations of stare decisis are at their acme in cases involving property and contract rights, where reliance interests are involved; the opposite is true in cases such as the present one involving procedural and evidentiary rules."[36] If so, then the Court will reject a legacy that far predates the Warren Court. It was, after all, Justice Felix Frankfurter, one of this century's staunchest advocates of judicial restraint, who fifty years ago cautioned that "the history of American freedom is, in no small measure, the history of procedure."[37]

Much more certain is the Court's new direction, at least for rights of the accused. Federalism and the diversity of state practice it implies has once again become a touchstone for the conservative majority, even though the due process revolution occurred in part because of the failure of states to protect the minimal liberties guaranteed by their own constitutions. It also came at the request of states, who believed that uniform rules would end the uncertainty and ambiguity that attended law enforcement. One consequence of this deference to the states will be a diminishment of the notion of equal justice. But it is questionable, as the Warren Court realized, whether local standards of due process are appropriate or meaningful in a highly mobile national society, especially when states have repeatedly created artificial distinctions between their citizens. Judicial restraint will be another banner under which the Court will march, albeit selectively. When the Congress refused Chief Justice Rehnquist's request to trim the federal habeas power, he simply accomplished the same result by judicial decision.

What may be most troubling, however, is the suggestion that the goal of criminal justice, indeed its sole standard, is convicting the guilty. This attitude makes rights of the accused subject to experimentation, dependent upon the will of a popular majority. But rights are fundamental. They are essential to our conception of personal liberty. They exist, as Madison recognized two centuries ago, to protect individuals against arbitrary government and oppressive majorities. The Bill of Rights will never prevent all injustices, nor does the original expression of them contain all the rights found necessary to due process. But neither are they subject to diminishment without the loss of liberty. This should be the lesson from our past: we are most faithful to the framers—and to our own freedom—when we strive to advance their legacy of protecting each citizen from the power of overzealous government.

Police Practices and the Bill of Rights

Laurence A. Benner and Michal R. Belknap

There is nothing that late twentieth century Americans fear more than crime. Fueled by drug addiction and the turf battles of urban street gangs, criminal activity—especially violent criminal activity—has increased alarmingly in recent years. Politicians and pundits echo the demands of ordinary people that government get tough on criminals. In the midst of what is often characterized as a "war" on crime, those provisions of the Bill of Rights that protect persons accused of criminal conduct sometimes seem like impediments to the reestablishment of law and order. Yet, the Fourth and Fifth Amendments are as vital as they are controversial.

While limiting what the police can do in combating crime, these amendments also protect individual liberty. As the renowned political scientist Edward S. Corwin once pointed out, liberty is "the absence of restraints imposed by other persons upon our own freedom of choice and action."[1] Such restrictions can come from two sources. One is other people, such as the mugger who takes away a woman's physical and financial options by hitting her over the head and stealing her money. When they arrest and confine those who might mug us, the police and the courts safeguard us against the deprivation of our liberty by such individuals. What we too often forget, however, is that in order to ensure this freedom from crime, the police may decide to restrain us, invade our privacy, or subject us to interrogation. When that happens, it is not another private citizen but the government itself that limits our liberty. History has shown that the more unchecked power government has, the greater the likelihood that it will abuse such power. The Fourth and Fifth Amendments exist to ensure that in trying to protect us from each other, government does not abuse its powers and become a bigger threat to our freedom than the crime it is combating.

To understand the important role these provisions play in protecting our freedom, we might consider what society would be like without them. Suppose, for example, that the local Narcotics Task Force receives an anonymous tip that a meeting between drug traffickers regarding a substantial shipment of cocaine will take place in a home located somewhere in the 200 block of Second Street. Can the police enter and search all of the homes in that block in order to locate the drug dealers? Can they use electronic surveillance to eavesdrop upon the conversations occurring in all of those homes for the same purpose? Without the Fourth Amendment, which requires individualized justification for such intrusions, there would be no constitutional constraints protecting innocent citizens from such dragnet police practices.

Suppose further that a public demonstration is held to protest the local mayor's failure to investigate allegations that several of his aides have taken bribes. Police arrest several of the demonstrators on charges of disturbing the peace and place them in small, windowless interrogation rooms. One demonstrator is repeatedly shocked with an electric stun gun in an effort to make him reveal the names of the leaders of the demonstration. Another demonstrator is threatened that unless she cooperates the authorities will seek to have her declared an unfit mother and take away her children. In a third room a suspected demonstration leader is continually questioned around the clock without food, water, or sleep by relay teams of interrogators. His requests to see his lawyer are denied and his pleas to be left alone ignored. Such practices occur regularly in other countries. Isolated instances of such tactics occur only as aberrations in our system of criminal justice because the Fifth Amendment gives each citizen the right to refuse to be subjected to custodial interrogation.

The framers of the Bill of Rights believed that "in a free society, based on respect for the individual, the determination of guilt or innocence by just procedures, in which the accused made no unwilling contribution to his conviction, was more important than punishing the guilty."[2] They chose to enshrine in the Constitution provisions that would preserve their liberty, their privacy, and the accusatorial system of criminal procedure that the United States had inherited from England.

Even if the first Congress had not written down in the Fourth and Fifth Amendments guarantees against unreasonable searches and seizures and compulsory self-incrimination, eighteenth-century Americans would have had no doubt that they enjoyed these protections. The generation that wrote the Bill of Rights believed in the existence of natural rights, which no government might invade because they were part of the fundamental law of the land that courts would enforce for the protection of individual liberty. Although the principles that the Fourth and Fifth Amendments represented were widely accepted, the specific limitations embodied in those additions to the Constitution lay dormant for many years after the Bill of Rights became part of the Constitution in 1791. During the nineteenth century there was little federal criminal law. Most crimes were defined and punished by the states, and in *Barron v. Baltimore* (1833) the Supreme Court held that the provisions of the Bill of Rights applied only to the national government. Since under that decision the states did not have to comply with the strictures of the Fourth and Fifth Amendments, the impact of those provisions on American criminal justice was minimal.

This situation changed dramatically in the 1960s, due to judicial reinterpretation of the Fourteenth Amendment. That amendment, ratified in 1868, provides that no state shall "deprive any person of life, liberty, or property, without due process of law." For a number of years controversy raged within the Supreme Court over whether this language had the effect of prohibiting the states from abridging those rights already protected against federal interference by the Bill of Rights. The issue was whether the guarantees in the first eight amendments were part of the "liberty" that states could not take away without "due process of law." Most of the Court's rulings "incorporating" provisions of the Bill of Rights into the due process clause of the Fourteenth Amendment came while Earl Warren was Chief Justice (1953–1969). In *Mapp v. Ohio* (1961) the Warren Court incorporated the Fourth Amendment exclusionary rule, banning evidence obtained as a result of unreasonable searches and seizures, and in *Malloy v. Hogan* (1964) it did the same with the Fifth Amendment's prohibition of compulsory self-incrimination. Indeed, between 1961 and 1969 it made applicable to the states virtually all of the criminal procedure guarantees of the Bill of Rights.

The Fourth Amendment

The text of the Fourth Amendment provides:

> The right of the people to be secure in their persons, houses, papers and effects against unreasonable searches and seizures, shall not be violated, and no Warrants shall issue, but upon probable cause, supported by Oath or affirmation, and particularly describing the place to be searched, and the persons or things to be seized.

The historical background giving rise to the Fourth Amendment reveals that this constitutional guarantee originated as a direct result of abusive law enforcement practices suffered by the colonists at the hands of the British. Envisioned by the founders of this nation as an essential bulwark against similar abuses of governmental power in the future, the amendment protects two distinct rights—the right to personal liberty and the right to privacy. In the language of the amendment, a governmental restraint upon personal liberty by physical force or show of authority is called a "seizure." A governmental invasion of a protected privacy interest is called a "search." Combined together, the right to be free from such governmental intrusions has been referred to as the "right to be let alone."[3]

The right to be let alone, however, is not absolute. The constitutional guarantee only protects against "unreasonable" governmental searches and seizures. The fundamental question addressed by the Fourth Amendment then is this: Under what circumstances must the individual's right to be let alone yield to the common good? The founders resolved this ques-

tion by employing a standard known as probable cause, which required individualized justification. Today the perceived crisis in crime control has
created enormous pressure to abandon this strict protective mechanism in
order to give greater powers to law enforcement. In response to this pressure, the courts have created an increasing number of exceptions to the
probable cause requirement and limited the operative terms of the amendment by redefining what constitutes a search or a seizure. The result of this
judicial reinterpretation has been to diminish greatly the scope of protection that once sprang from this constitutional guarantee.

As previously noted, late-eighteenth-century Americans were not legal
positivists who believed that they were creating new rights against government when they adopted the Bill of Rights. Rather, they believed the
source of such rights lay in a higher, fundamental law, based upon custom,
principles of natural law, and reason. Their intent in drafting the Fourth
Amendment was therefore to create a mechanism that would prevent the
violation of what they viewed as a self-evident and fundamental right to be
secure from unjustified governmental invasions of personal liberty and privacy. The procedural mechanism they employed for safeguarding this basic freedom had three essential elements: (1) prior judicial authorization; (2)
a requirement that there be individualized justification (probable cause) for
the intrusion; and (3) a requirement that the facts constituting the justification be sworn to under oath.

Probable cause has historically required more than mere suspicion. Using the time-worn, traditional definition, we may say that probable cause
exists for a seizure when trustworthy information is sufficient to give rise to
a reasonable belief that a crime has been committed and that the person to
be seized has committed the offense. Probable cause for a search exists
when reliable information gives rise to a reasonable belief that evidence of
wrongdoing will be found at the premises to be searched. The key aspect of
the probable cause standard is that a general justification (such as a lauda-
tory public purpose) will not do. The justification must relate specifically to
the individual who is called upon to surrender the liberty or privacy interest in question. This individualized justification standard was not an invention of the founders. Rather it had roots going back to English common law
and even ancient Roman law.

Historical Roots of the Fourth Amendment

Under Roman criminal procedure at the time of Cicero, criminal prosecutions were normally private law suits instituted by the aggrieved party. The
accuser had to state his complaint to the court and support it by taking an
oath. If the court found that there was probable cause, the accuser could
obtain an official writ (the precursor of our warrant) authorizing him to
search places for evidence of the crime.[4]

By the seventeenth century, English common law had refined these early protections and developed all of the requirements we find in the literal text of the Fourth Amendment today. These included (1) prior judicial approval (2) to search a particularly described place (3) for particularly described items, (4) based upon probable cause (5) established by information obtained under oath.[5] The "common law" was, of course, the accumulation of judicial decisions made in cases involving disputes between private citizens. One of the recurring themes throughout the Anglo-Saxon struggle for human rights, however, was the continual (and often unsuccessful) attempt to force the sovereign to recognize these same legal rules of procedure. For example, numerous monarchs from Henry VIII to Charles I used the power of arbitrary search and seizure to stifle dissent. Henry VIII devised a particularly effective method of controlling freedom of expression by licensing his supporters as royal printers. He then issued warrants that officially authorized them to search for and destroy all unlicensed books and papers. During the religious persecutions of the sixteenth century the notorious Court of Star Chamber also employed the practice of issuing such "general warrants" in its war against nonconformists. Such warrants were not supported by oath, nor were they based upon probable cause or any form of individualized justification. Indeed they specified no person or place. Rather they simply authorized the holder of the warrant to search any place for the purpose of discovering heretical books or pamphlets.[6] The use of such general warrants by government officials was finally declared illegal in England shortly before the American Revolution.[7]

Despite the abolition of general warrants in England, a particularly egregious form of general warrant, known as the writ of assistance, was used by British authorities in the American colonies to enforce tariffs designed to implement a mercantilist imperial commercial policy. Armed with a writ of assistance, a customs officer could, at his whim, exercise blanket authority to search any house, business, or warehouse for imports on which the required duties had not been paid. Because the British trade regulations unfairly burdened colonial commerce, for many years they went largely unenforced. However, in 1760, while Britain was at war with France, the government ordered strict enforcement of all trade sanctions in the colonies. What had been a semi-legitimate business practice now was prosecuted as smuggling. In the years just prior to the Revolution well-known patriots either smuggled or defended smugglers in court. For example, Boston merchant John Hancock, later a signer of the Declaration of Independence, was defended in 1769 by a future president, John Adams, on charges stemming from the importation of French wine in violation of the Townshend Acts. Hancock's ship the "Liberty" had been boarded pursuant to a writ of assistance and, under the "zero tolerance" policy of the day, subjected to forfeiture, an event that provoked a riot by the citizens of Boston.[8]

Because of the frequent abuse of the arbitrary search powers granted to

Crown officers by the writs of assistance, when the writs expired following the death of George III, a group of Boston merchants went to court to attempt to block the issuing of new ones. James Otis, who resigned his position as Advocate General of the Admiralty to represent the merchants without fee, gave an impassioned argument. Calling them "remnants of Starchamber tyranny," Otis argued that by stripping away the common-law protections provided by the probable cause standard and the oath requirement, the writs annihilated the sanctity of the home and placed "the liberty of every man in the hands of every petty officer."[9] Although Otis failed to prevent the reissuance of the writs of assistance, John Adams, who attended the argument, later observed that it had been a spark helping to ignite the revolutionary spirit of the colonists. "Every man . . . appeared to me to go away, as I did, ready to take up Arms against Writs of Assistance," he wrote. "Then and there the child Independence was born."[10]

After the Revolution, the founders did not forget the lessons of the past. Indeed, being extremely mistrustful of governmental power, they sought explicit recognition of the fundamental principle that a governmental intrusion upon an individual's right to be let alone was "reasonable" only if there was individualized justification founded upon probable cause. This is seen most clearly in the original version of the Fourth Amendment submitted by James Madison: "The rights of the people to be secured . . . from all unreasonable searches and seizures, shall not be violated by warrants issued without probable cause supported by oath or affirmation. . . ."[11]

It is readily apparent that this formulation reflects the fear of general warrants and highlights the importance of probable cause as the operative mechanism for curbing unreasonable governmental intrusions. Due to a quirk of history, however, the text of the Fourth Amendment has not come down to us in this form. During debate on the amendment in the first Congress, Representative Egbert Benson of New York objected that Madison's formulation was not strong enough. He moved that the language "by warrants issued without probable cause" be changed to assert affirmatively, "and no warrants shall issue, but upon probable cause." The House rejected this proposed change by a considerable majority. However, Benson, who was the chairman of a Committee of Three appointed to arrange the amendments in final form, had the last word, because the version the House sent to the Senate included his rejected change. No one apparently caught the error and the amendment was subsequently passed by the Senate and ratified by the states in that form.[12]

This seemingly minor change, which was intended to strengthen the Fourth Amendment, instead weakened it by recasting the amendment in the form of two distinct clauses. What was once a unitary thought—that a search or seizure is reasonable only if it is based upon individualized justification in the form of probable cause—became fragmented. The declaration that the right to be free from unreasonable searches and seizures should not be violated was now an independent clause (known today as the "reasonableness clause"), totally separated from the probable cause requirement.

By destroying the direct linkage between the probable cause standard and protection from unreasonable searches and seizures, Benson's change created an ambiguity. At the time the Fourth Amendment was adopted, probable cause was universally required for any search or seizure, regardless of the circumstances. The tampered text of the Fourth Amendment, however, seemed expressly to require probable cause only in cases involving warrants. A warrant was at that time, of course, an indispensable prerequisite to the search of a home or business. There being no organized police force in eighteenth-century America, the warrant symbolized the authority of the holder to conduct the search. A warrant was not always required, however, for a seizure. For example, a fleeing felon, caught in the act of committing his crime, could be arrested upon hue and cry without stopping to get an arrest warrant. This dichotomy laid the basis for an interpretation that would subsequently permit the erosion of the probable cause standard—the very mechanism the framers had employed to protect the liberty and privacy of future generations.

Judicial Interpretation of the Fourth Amendment

Early interpretation of the Fourth Amendment held true to the original intent of the founders. Courts held that for a search or seizure to be "reasonable" under the Fourth Amendment the police must, at a minimum, have individualized justification for the intrusion, amounting to probable cause. In recent decades, however, the Supreme Court, viewing the amendment as an impediment to effective law enforcement, has divorced the warrant clause, which contains the probable cause requirement, from the reasonableness clause, which does not. This has enabled the Court to isolate and make exceptions to the founders' requirement that all searches and seizures be based upon particularized probable cause. It has achieved this result through development of the "Special Needs Doctrine." Under this doctrine, if special circumstances make compliance with the warrant or probable cause requirement difficult, the Court employs a balancing test to determine whether the search or seizure is "reasonable" without them. If the needs of law enforcement "outweigh" the liberty or privacy interest invaded, then the Fourth Amendment is not violated.

The first case to apply the balancing test to a confrontation between police and a citizen was *Terry v. Ohio*.[13] There the Court held that police could seize a person and subject him or her to a "patdown" search for weapons, in the absence of probable cause, if there was "reasonable suspicion" the person was about to engage in violent criminal activity. The Court reasoned that the need to prevent violent crime and the need for investigating officers to protect themselves from the threat of a hidden weapon out-weighed the liberty and privacy interests infringed by the minimally intru-sive search and seizure. Certainly no one can argue with the result of this decision. Once the shield formed by the probable cause standard was pierced, however, it was difficult to prevent further mutilation. Later cases, for example, expanded this exception to permit stops of motorists on the basis of reasonable suspicion of nonviolent criminal behavior. Still, up to this point the Court had simply lowered the degree of individualized jus-tification from probable cause to mere suspicion. Its next step, however, created an exception that jettisoned the concept of individualized justifica-tion altogether.

The seminal case that made such a radical departure from the founders' original understanding was *United States v. Martinez-Fuerte*.[14] This case con-cerned the operation of a permanent immigration checkpoint set up near San Clemente, California. Employing the balancing test, the Court said that the seizure of a motorist and his passengers (simply because they looked Hispanic), and their brief detention for questioning, was only min-imally intrusive. The need to contain the tide of illegal immigration, on the other hand, was great. Hence, such seizures were "reasonable" under the Fourth Amendment, even though based solely upon racial appearance and not justified by any degree of particularized suspicion of wrongdoing. To-day, as a result of the extension of this "checkpoint" line of cases, the sus-picionless seizure of all motorists is permissible. For example, in 1990, the Court upheld the validity of sobriety checkpoints at which motorists are stopped and questioned, even though there is no indication that the driv-ers are intoxicated. Such "stops" must be brief, and probable cause is still required for an actual arrest. Nevertheless, for the innocent citizen who casts not even a shadow of suspicion, the right to travel freely throughout this country without fear of unjustified intrusion has diminished signifi-cantly.

In light of the greater value placed upon privacy, and the direct historical connection to abuses suffered under the writs of assistance, the Court ini-tially was reluctant to balance away the probable cause requirement when it came to searches. True, the Terry decision had authorized a patdown for weapons based only upon reasonable suspicion, and such *Terry* searches had been extended to the passenger compartment of a car, but attempts to expand this exception beyond its officer-safety rationale were unsuccess-ful. With the ascension of William Rehnquist to the position of Chief Jus-tice, and the appointment of three new associate justices by President Ron-ald Reagan, a crime control advocate, this reluctance soon dissipated.

The Rehnquist Court began by abolishing the warrant and probable cause requirements for "administrative" searches of both business pre-mises and personal offices of public employees. In upholding the warrant-less search of commercial premises, the Supreme Court ruled that busi-nesses have diminished privacy interests in their premises. Therefore, the

Court said, the warrant and probable cause requirements were not applicable, even though the police had used their authority to conduct an "administrative" records search as a pretext to conduct a general search for evidence of criminal activity. In another case, the office of a government physician was searched without a warrant or probable cause by a supervisor investigating allegations of malfeasance. The Court found that the "realities of the workplace" made the warrant requirement impractical and that a probable cause requirement would impose "intolerable burdens" upon government agencies. Holding the privacy interests of hundreds of thousands of federal, state, and local governmental employees in the balance, the Court found that their right to privacy in their offices was insignificant because they could leave their personal belongings at home.[15]

The most far-reaching search decisions affecting the American worker, however, have been the drug-testing cases. At issue in *Skinner v. Railway Labor*[16] was the validity of federal regulations requiring a private employer (a railroad company) to compel its employees, upon pain of suspension for nine months, to submit to blood tests without any individualized suspicion of drug or alcohol abuse. The government maintained that the testing of railroad workers was necessary to determine the cause of train accidents and deter train crews from being intoxicated on the job. Similarly, in *National Treasury Employees Union v. Von Raab*[17] the U.S. Customs Service, in response to an executive order by President Reagan, had established a urinalysis testing program for a broad category of personnel, including not only customs agents but also clerical personnel and even co-op students. Acknowledging that the piercing of the skin and extraction of blood infringed upon a worker's right to be let alone and that urinalysis could reveal such private medical facts as whether one was pregnant or had epilepsy, the Court nevertheless found these privacy interests insignificant when balanced against the government's "special interest" in railway safety or a drug-free workforce.

In these cases, the testing requirement was either triggered by an event such as an accident or was limited to employees who applied for a particular job. However, subsequent lower court decisions have permitted random testing of employees at any time. There has, furthermore, been a spinoff effect from these decisions. They have encouraged private employers to undertake expansive testing to ferret out not only those who abuse drugs or alcohol but also those who smoke or have a high cholesterol level. For example, a payroll clerk in Indiana was reportedly fired because a company drug test found nicotine in her urine.[18]

The trend toward diminishing the right to privacy has, of course, not been limited to the workplace. For example, under the so-called automobile exception the protection of a neutral magistrate's judgment as to the existence of probable cause has all but disappeared. Warrantless auto searches have become the norm, even where the vehicle is a mobile home. The Court's most direct assault upon privacy, however, has been its redefinition of the Fourth Amendment's operative term "search." Under traditional analysis a physical trespass always constituted a search. Today, however, a "reasonable expectation of privacy" has become the divining rod for revealing what constitutes a "search." If the Court is of the opinion that a citizen's expectation of privacy is not "reasonable," then police conduct invading that privacy does not constitute a "search." If no "search" occurs, then the Fourth Amendment does not apply and the protections against arbitrary invasions of privacy afforded by the warrant and probable cause requirements are not available. Thus, the Court has held that even where police illegally trespass upon a farmer's land in order to see what was otherwise secluded from public view, there is no Fourth Amendment violation because the farmer, in the Court's view, has no reasonable expectation of privacy in the fields surrounding his home. Using this type of analysis, the Supreme Court has ruled that the police may rummage through our garbage, view our fenced-in back yards from the air in order to see what could not be observed from the street, place radio transmitters in our cars to follow our movements, keep track of whom we correspond with, monitor whom we talk to on the telephone, and even look at our checks, deposit slips, and bank statements, all without a warrant, probable cause, or even reasonable suspicion. Such police practices are now unchecked by any constitutional restraint because the Court has determined that any expectation of privacy we may have in such matters is not "reasonable." Therefore the police intrusion is not a "search" to which Fourth Amendment protection applies. Ironically, the Warren Court originally created the "reasonable expectation of privacy" test in order to expand the scope of the Fourth Amendment to make it applicable to electronic surveillance. In the hands of the Rehnquist Court, however, this "test" for defining a search has become a vehicle for doing precisely the opposite.

That police can abuse their powers in this era of lax constraints is highlighted by an incident in which officers reportedly took aerial reconnaissance photographs of a television commentator's country estate and placed him under continual surveillance for several weeks following his criticism of the local police chief on the air.[19] The danger of abuse will be magnified, moreover, if the trend toward relaxing controls extends to the government's use of high-tech surveillance equipment to spy on citizens at home. These innovations run the gamut from miniaturized radio transmitters to parabolic microphones and infrared radiation sensors. Perhaps most invasive of all, however, is the new laser-beam technology. By bouncing a laser beam off a closed window, police can eavesdrop on a conversation inside a home by digital transformation of the window pane vibrations. The Supreme Court has never definitively addressed the use of devices such as the laser beam, but it has hinted that a citizen has no right to complain if police observe or listen from a lawful public vantage point using technology generally available to the public. If laser technology becomes generally available at your local Radio Shack, should a policeman standing on a public sidewalk across the street from your home be able to use it to eavesdrop on your private conversations with your spouse?

The final outcome of the Supreme Court's sweeping decisions in the area of privacy remains uncertain. Nevertheless, several trends are clear. Except in cases involving searches or arrests made inside the home, the warrant requirement has become almost an anachronism. Through judicial interpretation, the Court has also gradually eroded probable cause as the cornerstone of Fourth Amendment protection by substituting for this objective, neutral principle a subjective balancing test. In "weighing" the needs of the state against the rights of the individual with the mythical scales of the balancing test, however, the justices have necessarily based their determination of "reasonableness" upon personal value judgments, because there are no longer any neutral guidelines. This trend is antithetical to the fundamental postulate, long thought essential to the survival of freedom, that ours is a government of laws administered according to neutral principles rather than a government of men operating according to their personal predilections. By substituting the subjective balancing test for the probable cause standard, the Court has moved toward transforming the Fourth Amendment from a rule of law into a rule of personal opinion. Amidst demands for a more vigorous war on crime, it, therefore, is not surprising that this balancing process has resulted in increasing governmental control and diminishing individual privacy.

Justice William J. Brennan repeatedly warned of the dangers of the trend toward diminishing our right to privacy. Recognizing that privacy is always an endangered freedom that must be vigilantly protected from the passions of the moment, he explained: "The needs of law enforcement stand in constant tension with the Constitution's protections of the individual. . . . It is precisely the predictability of these pressures that counsels a resolute loyalty to constitutional safeguards."[20]

The Exclusionary Rule: The Price of Liberty and Privacy

Supreme Court decisions have eroded not only the scope of Fourth Amendment protection but also the mechanism for enforcing the amendment: the exclusionary rule. When the police discover physical evidence of guilt as a result of a search or seizure that violates the defendant's Fourth Amendment rights, the exclusionary rule prohibits the government from using that evidence in court to convict her.

The Supreme Court first refused to admit evidence obtained in violation of the Fourth Amendment in 1886. In that case, the Court suggested that the admission of illegally obtained records into evidence by the trial court had rendered the trial an "unconstitutional proceeding" that was therefore void.[21] As refined by the Supreme Court in subsequent federal criminal cases, the exclusionary rule initially rested upon the duty of the federal courts to give force and effect to the human-rights provisions of the Constitution. Reaffirming the Fourth Amendment exclusionary rule in 1913, the justices declared:

> If letters and private documents can be seized [illegally] and used in evidence against a citizen accused of an offense, the protection of the Fourth Amendment . . . is of no value, and . . . might as well be stricken from the Constitution. The efforts of the courts and their officials to bring the guilty to punishment, praiseworthy as they are, are not to be aided by the sacrifice of those great principles established by years of endeavor and suffering which have resulted in their embodiment in the fundamental law of the land.[22]

The application of the exclusionary rule to state criminal proceedings was complicated by the fact that the Bill of Rights initially applied only to the federal government. Even after the Supreme Court held that the due process clause prohibited the states from engaging in unreasonable searches and seizures, it at first declined to require the adoption of the exclusionary rule, leaving the states to experiment with other enforcement mechanisms. Such alternatives never materialized, however. As the chief justice of the California Supreme Court commented in explaining why that court reluctantly changed its position and adopted the exclusionary rule as a matter of state law: "My misgivings . . . grew as I observed . . . a steady course of illegal police procedures that deliberately and flagrantly violated the Constitution. . . . [I]t had become all too obvious that unconstitutional police methods of obtaining evidence were not being deterred. . . ."[23] In 1961, after half of the states had adopted the exclusionary rule on their own, the U.S. Supreme Court made it a uniform requirement, as a matter of federal constitutional law, declaring: "[The rule] gives to the individual no more than that which the Constitution guarantees him, to the police officer no less than that to which honest law enforcement is entitled, and, to the court, that judicial integrity so necessary in the true administration of justice."[24]

The rule has become the subject of heated controversy. This is largely because of the popular perception that it unleashes guilty criminals back into society. Exaggerated claims that the exclusionary rule increases the crime rate, however, have not been born out by statistical studies. Indeed, a comprehensive investigation of the costs of the rule has shown that only 1.77 percent of all cases are "lost" due to its operation. This is because it is infrequently invoked, and even when evidence is excluded, conviction can still be obtained using other evidence that is untainted by constitutional violation. Moreover, an examination of the cases "lost" due to the rule reveals that over 85 percent were not crimes of violence but rather common drug offenses, such as possession of marijuana, for which incarceration was not a likely punishment. Thus, the vast majority of the defendants who "go free" as a result of the exclusionary rule would not have been imprisoned in any event, had they been convicted.[25] Nevertheless, the exclusionary rule has remained a favorite target of politicians. It is especially vulnerable to such attacks because it is a creature of judicial rule making, which lacks roots in the express language of the Fourth Amendment.

Today, as a result of judicial modifications, the exclusionary rule has become riddled with exceptions. For example, it does not apply to exclude evidence in grand jury proceedings, nor does it apply in deportation cases or other "civil" proceedings. By far the biggest limitation on the exclusionary rule, however, has been the "good faith" exception established in 1984. This retrenchment holds that so long as a police officer reasonably relied upon the validity of a search warrant, evidence obtained pursuant to that warrant will not be suppressed, even if the warrant was not based upon probable cause.

As is readily apparent from these exceptions, the exclusionary rule is no longer based upon conceptions of judicial duty and integrity. Indeed, in "good faith" exception cases, the judiciary itself has violated a citizen's rights by issuing a warrant without probable cause. Instead of resting upon a principled basis, the rule now has a strictly utilitarian rationale: the deterrence of illegal conduct by law enforcement. Under this approach, the Supreme Court engages in a cost-benefit analysis to determine when the exclusionary rule should apply. Thus, in the case creating the "good faith" exception, the Court reasoned that the cost of losing relevant evidence outweighed any benefit, because no deterrent purpose would be served by punishing the police for a judge's mistake in issuing a defective warrant. The airtight logic of this position is unassailable if deterrence of police misconduct is the sole objective of the exclusionary rule. However, this rationale does not satisfactorily explain how a judgment of conviction, imposed by the judicial branch, can be constitutionally valid if it rests upon evidence obtained as a result of a violation of the Constitution by one of its own members.

A further anomaly posed by the "good faith" exception arises from the fact that the right to be secure in one's home unless a search warrant is issued upon probable cause—the core value protected by the Fourth Amendment—would now seem to be a right without a remedy. Do effective alternatives to the exclusionary rule exist? Three have been suggested: civil suits for monetary compensation; disciplinary action against offending officers; and, in egregious cases, criminal prosecution.

A report by the Department of Justice, however, confirms what other studies have repeatedly shown: the failure of these alternatives either to compensate victims adequately or to serve as an effective deterrent. According to the report, while 12,000 civil actions were filed against federal law enforcement officers from 1971 to 1986, only five plaintiffs actually received an award of damages. Turning to internal discipline for Fourth Amendment violations, the report noted that the Department of Justice itself had conducted only seven investigations regarding its own agents since 1981 and had imposed no sanctions. Finding a similar dearth of criminal prosecutions, it characterized this alternative as "ill advised."[26] Another possibility is independent police review boards, which can be (and have been) established to investigate violations. In practice, however, the police have vigorously opposed any meaningful review by such "outsiders," and the political will has been lacking to give such boards adequate investigative powers or to permit them to impose sanctions directly upon offending officers.

Despite the demonstrated shortcomings of the various alternatives to the exclusionary rule, the Department of Justice report recommended that the rule be abolished and an improved civil remedy established as a deterrent. The major premise underlying its recommendations was that the exclusionary rule, by depriving a court of evidence relevant to a defendant's guilt, interferes with the "truth-seeking" function of the criminal justice process. Advocates of the exclusionary rule have pointed out, however, that if a fully effective alternative existed, it would cause the same interference that the rule itself does. This is because a fully effective deterrent, by "mak[ing] the police obey the commands of the Fourth Amendment *in advance*," would prevent them from ever obtaining the evidence in the first place.[27]

If the police always obeyed the Fourth Amendment, of course, the cost of the exclusionary rule would not be apparent. The problem with the exclusionary rule is that by removing the visible benefits of a violation of the Constitution, it forces us to come face to face with the price society must pay in order to preserve individual liberty and privacy. There are many who think that price is too high. As Daniel Webster admonished, however, "The first object of a free people is the preservation of their liberty. The spirit of liberty . . . demands checks; it seeks guards . . . it insists on securities. . . . This is the nature of constitutional liberty, and this is our liberty, if we will rightly understand and preserve it."[28]

The Fifth Amendment

Hailed as one of the great landmarks in humanity's struggle to make itself civilized, the privilege against self-incrimination reflects, more than any other aspect of criminal procedure, the moral relationship between the state and the individual. Under Talmudic law, which reflected the ancient oral teaching handed down from the time of Moses, confessions were normally not admissible against an accused in a criminal proceeding, even though voluntarily given. The Bible also records that the Apostle Paul exercised a status-based privilege under Roman law that protected citizens against compulsory self-incrimination. After arresting him following a riot in Jerusalem, the authorities ordered the apostle whipped until he confessed. Paul, however, asserted his right as a Roman citizen not to be subjected to interrogation by torture and was later released unharmed.[29]

During the Middle Ages, European systems of criminal justice came to rely heavily upon confessions for evidence of guilt and regularly used torture to obtain them. While there are examples of torture in English history, this interrogation technique never became an established part of British criminal justice. This is because by the twelfth century, England had developed an accusatorial rather than inquisitorial system of justice. Apparently to protect citizens from unnecessarily having to endure trial by ordeal or trial by battle because of unjustified allegations, the English adopted the principle that proceedings against a person suspected of crime might be commenced only by a formal complaint, made under oath, or by an indictment issued by an accusing jury (the forerunner of our grand jury). After the abolition of trial by ordeal, the use of the oath played a more prominent role in the resolution of guilt or innocence. Once a proper charge had been laid, the defendant was required to answer the charge under oath. If he denied it, he could also be interrogated under oath. Being questioned under an oath to tell the truth before God created a soul-threatening dilemma for the devout Christian. Assuming that a truthful answer would be incriminating, a defendant had the unhappy choice of either telling the truth and suffering immediate temporal punishment or committing perjury, a sin, and suffering eternal damnation. If a defendant refused to plead to the charge under oath, he could be imprisoned indefinitely.

In its earliest stages the "privilege" against self-incrimination only shielded the suspect from having to answer an allegation until it was substantiated by a formal charge supported by oath or indictment. When the flames of religious persecution engulfed England in the late sixteenth and early seventeenth centuries, even this limited privilege fell into total eclipse. Both the Court of High Commission, created by Queen Elizabeth to enforce religious conformity, and the infamous Court of Star Chamber attempted to root out heretics and dissenters by inquisitorial practices. Suspected nonconformists were compelled to take the soul-threatening oath and interrogated at length without benefit of formal charges. In reaction to such abuses of royal power, the privilege against self-incrimination reasserted itself and entered a second stage of development, emerging as the right to be free from compelled self-incrimination. During this stage the practice of judicially interrogating the accused at trial was abolished and the right to remain silent established as a principle of justice. Englishmen, and, somewhat later, English colonists, became convinced that accusatorial procedure was essential to protect the individual's right of self-determination. After independence every one of the eight states that annexed a bill of rights to its new constitution included protection against self-incrimination.

Subsequently, Americans crystallized this principle of justice in the Fifth Amendment's brief and picturesque expression that no person "shall be compelled . . . to be a witness against himself." While these words seem at first glance to prohibit only the use of torture, it was the compulsion created by the use of the oath, not torture, that gave rise to the privilege against self-incrimination in its present form. Early interpretation of the Fifth Amendment by the U.S. Supreme Court followed the English common law in holding that the slightest degree of influence exerted upon an accused to speak gave rise to a presumption of compulsion, rendering the confession inadmissible. Under the pressures of the Prohibition era of the 1920s, however, the Court limited the scope of the amendment's protection by employing a "trustworthiness" rationale in deciding confession cases. During this period the privilege yielded to the perceived necessities of law enforcement to such an extent that incriminating statements became admissible unless the methods used to extract them were so harsh that they created a danger that the confession was false. Under this rationale, lengthy, around-the-clock interrogation sessions, featuring relay teams of officers, psychological coercion, and other third-degree tactics (including even minor physical abuse, such as a kick in the shins) became permissible.

Concerned with the abuses that had developed under such a lax standard, the Supreme Court began to tighten restrictions upon federal law enforcement in the 1940s by mandating that a confession was inadmissible if it had been obtained during a period of unnecessary delay in bringing the defendant before a magistrate following arrest. Confronted with a 1908 precedent, holding that the Fifth Amendment did not apply to the states, the Court initially turned to the due process clause of the Fourteenth Amendment to deal with state interrogation practices. In a series of twenty-nine confession cases decided between 1936 and 1964, the Court progressively refined the meaning of due process until not only physical force but also certain forms of psychological coercion were forbidden in the back rooms of police stations. The problem with this due process "voluntariness" approach, however, was that it involved an Alice-in-Wonderland journey into the metaphysical realm of the human "will." If a confession was the product of free choice, it was "voluntary" and therefore admissible. If, on the other hand, the suspect's "will" had been broken by psychological pressure, then due process was violated and the "involuntary" confession was inadmissible. Because "voluntariness" varied with the ability of the suspect to withstand pressure, this *ad hoc* approach to constitutional adjudication failed to provide clear guidance to the police as to what practices were acceptable and made judicial review a morass of subjectivity.

Therefore, in 1964, the Court applied the Fifth Amendment directly to the states and also held in *Escobedo v. Illinois*[30] that a suspect had the right to have the assistance of counsel during custodial interrogation. The Court acknowledged that extending the right to counsel from the courtroom to the police interrogation room would diminish significantly the number of confessions obtained, but concluded:

> If the exercise of constitutional rights will thwart the effectiveness of a system of law enforcement, then there is something very wrong with that system.
> . . . We have learned the lesson of history, ancient and modern, that a system

of criminal law enforcement which comes to depend on the "confession" will in the long run, be less reliable and more subject to abuses than a system which depends on extrinsic evidence independently secured through skillful investigation.[31]

The *Escobedo* decision provoked an immediate outcry in law enforcement circles. It was feared that if defense lawyers invaded the inner sanctum of the police precinct, the confession would soon become a thing of the past. Confronted by this storm of controversy, the Court retreated from the path it had taken and struck a compromise in the now famous case of *Miranda v. Arizona*.[32] This compromise permitted the police to obtain uncounseled waivers of both the right to have counsel's advice and the right to be free from the compulsion created by custodial interrogation. In order to provide a mechanism for obtaining valid waivers, the Court created the so-called *Miranda* warnings. This procedural protocol, now printed on cards carried by every police officer, requires the police to advise suspects, prior to custodial interrogation, that they have a right to remain silent, that any statement they make can be used in evidence against them, and that they have the right to an attorney's advice before and during questioning, without charge if they are indigent.

Miranda held that no statement given by an accused during custodial interrogation is admissible against him if the police failed to give these required warnings. Within six years after this landmark ruling, however, President Richard Nixon realigned the Court by appointing four new members. Joined by two justices who had dissented in *Miranda*, this group ultimately formed a new majority that began making exceptions to the *Miranda* exclusionary rule. As a result of this reorientation, the Court held that the *Miranda* warnings were not themselves constitutional rights but mere judge-made prophylactic rules designed to deter police abuse. Balancing the cost of exclusion against its deterrent value, the Court found that statements obtained in violation of *Miranda* could be used for the limited purpose of impeaching a defendant who took the stand and told an inconsistent story. Similarly, when the Court created a "public safety" exception to the *Miranda* rules, it reasoned that the need briefly to interrogate an arrested suspect in order to locate his weapon "outweighed" the value of giving warnings. The Court also redefined "custodial interrogation"—the event that triggers the *Miranda* requirements—holding that warnings are not required prior to the roadside questioning of a person stopped for drunk driving because the driver is not in "custody" for the purposes of the *Miranda* rule.

While limiting the scope of *Miranda*, the Court also relaxed the standard for a valid waiver of the right not to have to submit to custodial interrogation and the right to have counsel present for advice. *Miranda* had held that to establish a waiver of the rights it created, the state would have to meet a "heavy burden." The Burger and Rehnquist Courts, however, have made this "the lightest heavy burden . . . to be found,"[33] allowing waiver to be inferred in the absence of an express verbal statement, permitting the police to deceive the accused as to the charge about which he was to be interrogated and authorizing them to withhold from a suspect information concerning his attorney's immediate availability. The Supreme Court has even held that an insane person, suffering from hallucinations, can voluntarily waive these so-called *Miranda* "rights."

Like *Escobedo*, the *Miranda* decision was initially decried by doomsayers, fearful that advising a suspect of his right to an attorney would result in fewer confessions, since lawyers would invariably advise suspects not to talk. These fears, however, have proven to be unjustified. After twenty-five years' experience with the rule, numerous empirical studies, including an American Bar Association survey of judges, prosecutors, and police officers, have established that *Miranda* creates no significant problem for law enforcement.[34] Indeed, defense attorneys continue to be astonished that their clients confess despite being given *Miranda* warnings. This should not be at all surprising. Central to the *Miranda* decision was the Court's conclusion that the police-dominated atmosphere surrounding custodial interrogation constitutes compulsion, rendering any statement made in such a setting a compelled one violative of the Fifth Amendment. Yet, precisely these same pressures operate on a suspect who is asked to waive his rights. Indeed, it seems illogical that a sane person would voluntarily subject himself to the pressures of a custodial interrogation at the hands of a trained interrogator if he had a truly free and unconstrained choice in the matter. Despite these shortcomings, *Miranda* nevertheless remains a symbol of society's respect for individual self-determination and human dignity. While its ritualized warnings may fail to dissipate the compulsion inherent in the custodial setting, by requiring an officer of the state to acknowledge that the lowly criminal suspect before him has certain rights, they serve to restrain impulses that in other eras have led to unchecked abuses.

Conclusion

The history of the Fourth and Fifth Amendments can best be understood as a struggle between two opposing conceptions of an ideal criminal justice system. One view, called the "crime control" model, sees the primary function of the criminal justice system as the apprehension and punishment of the guilty. Proponents of this view tend to value the efficiency and effectiveness of law enforcement more highly than human rights and to favor the restriction of liberty and privacy when it impedes the war on crime. Proponents of the opposing view, called the "due process" model, believe that the rights to liberty, privacy, and self-determination are essential to the continued existence of a free and democratic society. Since the coercive power of government is exercised through the criminal law, they insist that the primary function of the criminal justice system must be to safeguard those freedoms from erosion.[35]

One is a short-term view. It seeks to respond to what is perceived as an immediate crisis. The other is a long-term view. It seeks to prevent the abuses of power that history has shown repeatedly occur when power is left unchecked. One view assumes that the social order can best be preserved by controlling crime, the other presupposes that the social order will disintegrate if abuse and discrimination are not kept in check by fair procedures. Neither view holds a monopoly on the truth. The challenge for a society that seeks to ensure both freedom from the common street mugger and freedom from oppressive government is how to strike a proper balance between these two models.

A majority of the Warren Court, molded by the experience of the Second World War and the horrors of Nazi Germany and Stalinist Russia, championed the "due process" model. The Warren Court's extension of the federal Constitution's human rights guarantees to the states in the 1960s was motivated by an increasing awareness that the states were failing to protect ethnic and racial minorities from abusive and discriminatory law enforcement practices at a time when those groups were attempting to exercise their political rights and participate in the democratic process of mainstream America. The television images of police beating peaceful civil rights demonstrators and the documentation of abuses such as dragnet searches and coerced confessions in back rooms of police stations created public support for extending federal protection for such basic human rights. In the 1970s and 1980s, however, the public came to feel increasingly vulnerable to street crime, and the pendulum swung the other way. Many Americans began to regard these basic human rights as mere "technicalities" that allowed guilty criminals to escape just punishment. The replacement of members of the Warren Court with new justices, appointed by presidents who made "crime control" a political slogan, led to judicial reinterpretation of the Fourth and Fifth Amendments. In the 1990s the judiciary has continued to diminish liberty and privacy in order to promote efficient law enforcement. Although this objective is laudable, as Justice Louis Brandeis warned long ago: "Experience should teach us to be most on our guard to protect liberty when the Government's purposes are beneficent. . . . [T]he greatest dangers to liberty lurk in insidious encroachment by men of zeal, well-meaning but without understanding."[36]

The "Cruel and Unusual Punishment" Clause
A Limit on the Power to Punish or Constitutional Rhetoric?

Joseph L. Hoffmann

The Anglo-American legal system could hardly be described, at least historically, as "soft on crime." To give one example from English history: At the time when the prohibition of "cruel and unusual punishments" first appeared as a part of the English Bill of Rights of 1689 (and for many years thereafter), the prescribed punishment for treason was to hang the offender by the neck, cut him down while still alive, remove and burn his bowels in front of him, and then behead and quarter him. Women convicted of treason received a somewhat "lesser" punishment—they were burned alive at the stake.

The American colonies, for the most part, rejected such extreme methods of capital punishment. But early Americans found other painful or demeaning forms of corporal punishment completely acceptable. For instance, in 1791, when the United States adopted the prohibition of "cruel and unusual punishment" in the Eighth Amendment,[1] federal law provided that larceny be punished by thirty-nine lashes. Branding, pillorying, and ear-cropping were also common punishments in America in the late eighteenth century and beyond.

Today, 200 years after the adoption of the Bill of Rights, these punishments have passed from American law and practice. But the Eighth Amendment played no direct role in their abolition. Indeed, the U.S. Supreme Court did not even have cause to mention the "cruel and unusual punishment" clause in an opinion for more than seventy-five years after its adoption, and the justices relied upon the clause only rarely during the next century.

Sentencing reform in this country has been driven by the moral judgment of the American people, as expressed in the statutory enactments of legislatures, the discretionary decisions of prosecutors, the verdicts of juries, and the sentencing pronouncements of trial judges. With few exceptions, whenever a majority of Americans have decided that a punishment is unacceptably "cruel and unusual," either in the abstract or as applied to a particular crime, no constitutional provision or reviewing court has been needed to fix the problem—the punishment has simply fallen into disuse, either because the authorization for it was revoked or because juries and trial judges no longer tolerated its imposition.

These historical observations highlight the paradoxical nature of the cruel and unusual punishment clause: The clause seems, on the one hand, to be among the least essential elements of the Bill of Rights, because among those provisions it alone seems to be expressed in terms of the moral judgment of a majority of American society. Unlike the anti-majoritarian thrust of the First, Second, Fourth, Fifth, and Sixth Amendments, the Eighth Amendment appears to guarantee only what the majority already believes to be morally required. And if the words "cruel and unusual" indeed are defined in terms of society's current mores and are subject to change only when society itself has evolved, then (except for relatively rare cases of unauthorized punitive conduct by renegade officials) the cruel and unusual punishment clause would appear to serve a merely rhetorical purpose. As Justice Joseph Story once wrote, the Eighth Amendment "would seem to be wholly unnecessary in a free government, since it is scarcely possible that any department of such a government should authorize or justify such atrocious conduct."[2]

On the other hand, if it is possible to find independent content in the words "cruel and unusual," that is, content or meaning independent of the current mores of American society, then the clause would be among the *most* essential in the Bill of Rights. This is because the clause would then confer rights upon perhaps the least valued, and hence most vulnerable, of all minority groups within society—the class of convicted criminals. Is there any class more in need of protection from the majority will than those who have been convicted of crimes? Even the defendants protected by the Fourth, Fifth, and Sixth Amendments do not rank so low in society's eyes—after all, anyone can be wrongly accused of a crime. If those amendments work well, however, then only the guilty should be convicted and fall within the ambit of the Eighth Amendment. Moreover, no class is less likely to have its interests represented in the political arena than the class of convicted criminals. Convicts are themselves generally disabled from political participation, and very few people are likely to adopt their cause. To the contrary, any shrewd politician, whether legislator, prosecutor, or judge, knows that one easy way to win votes is to "get tough" on crime by supporting, or imposing, tougher punishment for criminals.

The Eighth Amendment and Constitutional Interpretation

The search for the meaning of the cruel and unusual punishment clause is, ironically, complicated by the relatively simple and straightforward language of the clause, as well as by its apparently single-minded focus on the moral dimension of a particular punishment. These special aspects of the clause make it especially difficult for the Supreme Court to invalidate a punishment under the Eighth Amendment; such a ruling, after all, requires the Court to reject the view of a societal majority, as expressed in a legislatively enacted criminal statute, that a certain punishment is morally acceptable.

Constitutional interpretation is rarely, if ever, easy; the average law library is filled with books that seek either to justify or criticize the legitimacy of judicial review (and occasional invalidation) of statutory enactments by democratically elected legislatures. But most of the provisions in the Bill of Rights at least appear to authorize the Court, either expressly or by implication, to make multifaceted policy judgments, balancing competing interests against one another in deciding how to apply the provision in question.

For example, the Fourth Amendment bans "unreasonable" searches and seizures, without specifying what are legitimate reasons. Thus, in deciding whether a search or seizure is unreasonable under the Fourth Amendment, the Court legitimately may (and often does) consider all relevant moral, political, social, and economic advantages and disadvantages of the challenged police practice.

The First Amendment's language, by comparison, is more absolute, seemingly allowing *no* laws to abridge the freedoms of speech, press, religion, assembly, or petition. Unlike the Fourth Amendment, the First Amendment appears to place entire subject areas outside the range of proper governmental action. But once one accepts the inevitability that even First Amendment rights must have limits—if they did not, how could the government prohibit yelling "fire" in a crowded theater?—then the question of how and where to draw the line involves the same broad range of moral, political, social, and economic concerns. The language of the First Amendment itself does not purport to dictate the terms of the inquiry into potential limits, nor does it attempt to establish which of the competing concerns should take priority in determining the importance of a proposed exception to the First Amendment's protections.

As a consequence of this multifaceted balancing approach to constitutional interpretation, both the First and the Fourth Amendments provide the Court with ample opportunities to disagree, in ways that at least appear to be principled and legitimate, with the views of a majority of Americans. For example, if the Court decides to strike down a popular program of mandatory drug testing of public employees as a violation of the Fourth Amendment, it can find that the majority has overstated the likelihood or the risks of drug usage by the employees. Or the Court can dispute the projected costs of alternative measures, such as individual determinations of likely drug use. Or the Court can hold that, contrary to the beliefs of the majority, the program would produce an unequal, discriminatory effect on protected classes within society. Or the Court may agree with all of the separate empirical judgments and predictions underlying the majority's view, yet disagree with how the majority strikes the balance of competing interests. All of these bases for invalidating the program, and many others, can appear, at least in the abstract, to be potentially legitimate exercises of the Court's judicial power.

The language of the cruel and unusual punishment clause, on the other hand, seems to compel the Court to make what might be called a "pure and simple" moral judgment: Is the challenged punishment "cruel and unusual," or is it not? Unlike the First Amendment, the Eighth Amendment contains an express limitation on the scope of its protections—it does not prohibit *all* punishments, only "cruel and unusual" ones. Unlike the Fourth Amendment, moreover, the Eighth Amendment's express limitation is defined in terms of a normative judgment about the moral quality of a challenged punishment: the clause does not broadly prohibit unreasonable punishments, nor does it specifically prohibit costly, discriminatory, or useless punishments. Concerns based on nonmoral judgments, such as the cost of possible alternative punishments or the importance of using a particular punishment to achieve a political or social goal, thus would seem to be excluded from the Court's consideration, at least based on the Eighth Amendment's language.

The purity and simplicity of the normative moral judgment seemingly required by the Eighth Amendment's language creates a difficult problem for the Court. According to most philosophers, the morality of a punishment necessarily rests, at least in large measure, on the consensus of a particular society at a particular place and time in history. This is true regardless of whether the philosopher purports to believe in a utilitarian justification for punishment—that punishment is justified because it reduces crime or serves some other societal end—or a retributive one—that punishment is justified simply because it is what the criminal deserves. In either case, most philosophers agree, it is simply impossible to conclude that a particular punishment is always cruel or always not cruel, either in the abstract or for a particular crime or criminal. The ultimate conclusion about the morality of a particular punishment is, like beauty, in the eye of the beholding society; what is viewed as cruel punishment by one society may not be cruel to another.

The history of American society over the past 200 years supports the philosophers' view that the morality of a punishment is based on the perceptions of a particular society. Indeed, if there is one commonly accepted principle of the Eighth Amendment, it is that the meaning of the cruel and unusual punishment clause cannot be fixed as of 1791, or at any other moment in time, but instead must be allowed to change in relation to changes in American values. Thus Chief Justice Warren Burger, who argued for a narrow view of the clause, explained:

> A punishment is inordinately cruel, in the sense we must deal with it in these cases, chiefly as perceived by the society so characterizing it. The standard of extreme cruelty is not merely descriptive, but necessarily embodies a moral

judgment. The standard itself remains the same, but its applicability must change as the basic mores of society change.[3]

And Chief Justice Earl Warren, who advocated a much broader reading of the clause in perhaps the most well-known and oft-cited of all Eighth Amendment commentaries, wrote: "The Amendment must draw its meaning from the evolving standards of decency that mark the progress of a maturing society."[4]

In construing the cruel and unusual punishment clause, any attempt by the Court to deviate from a fundamentally majoritarian or consensus-based view of morality is destined to appear unprincipled and illegitimate, at least in the eyes of the societal majority. And therein lies the Court's special Eighth Amendment dilemma: If the interpretation of the cruel and unusual punishment clause is tied too closely to the moral judgment of American society, the clause becomes unnecessary, as a mere restatement of the primacy of the majority's will in a democratic society. Yet any other method of construing the clause, and especially one that reaches a different result than most Americans would reach, places the Court on extremely thin ice, subject to the criticism that it is "legislating" moral standards rather than "adjudicating" them. Chief Justice Burger stated the problem well:

> There is no novelty in being called upon to interpret a constitutional provision that is less than self-defining, but, of all our fundamental guarantees, the ban on "cruel and unusual punishments" is one of the most difficult to translate into judicially manageable terms. . . . [I]t is essential to our role as a court that we not seize upon the enigmatic character of the guarantee as an invitation to enact our personal predilections into law.[5]

To be sure, the Court has, from time to time, proven willing to use the Eighth Amendment to strike down particular punishments; but all of the justices, on both sides of these "cruel and unusual punishment" cases, have agreed that the Court should proceed in such cases with an exceptional amount of caution and self-restraint.

The Eighth Amendment as a Prohibition of Certain Punishments

The fundamental issue before the Court in any case involving the meaning of the Eighth Amendment's cruel and unusual punishment clause is whether there exists a principled and legitimate method of interpreting the clause other than relying solely on the moral judgment of a majority of American society. To put it differently, if a societal majority finds a punishment morally acceptable, does that foreclose the Court from invalidating the punishment? Or is there a legitimate basis for the Court to deviate, at least on occasion, from society's moral judgment? The Court today addresses these fundamental issues in three principal contexts.[6]

First, the Eighth Amendment is sometimes invoked in cases involving challenges to the constitutionality of particular forms or methods of punishment—what might be called challenges to punishments "in the abstract." The claim in these cases is that the punishment itself is "cruel and unusual," regardless of the crime for which it is imposed and the moral culpability of the criminal who receives it.

What limited historical evidence exists concerning the original intent behind the cruel and unusual punishment clause suggests that this kind of case is at the core of the Eighth Amendment. The drafters of the Eighth Amendment were primarily concerned with barring the imposition of "cruel methods of punishment that [we]re not regularly or customarily employed,"[7] such as those invented by Lord Chief Justice Jeffreys to punish the perjurer Titus Oates during the reign of James II in England. Oates had been responsible for the deaths of many innocent Catholics, as a result of his false testimony that they were involved in a "Popish Plot" to overthrow the King. Among the punishments imposed by Lord Jeffreys (which were described in a 1689 dissent in the House of Lords as "cruel, barbarous, and illegal" and as violative of the cruel and unusual punishments clause of the English Bill of Rights)[8] were that Oates be stripped of his canonical and priestly habits, that he stand in the pillory annually, that he be whipped "from Aldgate to Newgate" and, two days later, "from Newgate to Tyburn," and finally that he be imprisoned for life.[9] These punishments were objectionable, not because they were necessarily disproportionate to the seriousness of Oates's crime, but because they had "no Precedent" and were "contrary to Law and ancient Practice."[10]

In American legal experience, constitutional challenges to particular forms or methods of punishment have not often succeeded. For over 175 years, American courts used a majoritarian interpretation of the cruel and unusual punishment clause and thus invalidated only a handful of relatively bizarre punishments. The leading Supreme Court cases, *Weems v. United States*[11] and *Trop v. Dulles*,[12] involved, respectively, a punishment known as *cadena temporal* and the punishment of forfeiture of citizenship imposed for wartime desertion of duty. (*Cadena temporal*, used only in the Philippines during American control, consisted of incarceration and "hard and painful labor" with chains fastened to the wrists and ankles at all times, along with severe civil disabilities and constant surveillance following the incarceration.) The decisions in these two cases involved relatively straightforward applications of the cruel and unusual punishment clause. Both punishments were quite severe, both were used only on very rare occasions, and neither enjoyed wide public support.

During the past twenty years, however, the cruel and unusual punishment clause has undergone a jurisprudential rebirth of sorts and has been the subject of numerous Court opinions. Perhaps the most controversial, and certainly the most well-known, recent claim of invalidity under the Eighth Amendment is the contention that the death penalty is, on its face, a "cruel and unusual" punishment. The Court has addressed this claim twice since 1970,[13] and several of the opinions written by the individual justices on the subject provide excellent examples of the various approaches to constitutional interpretation of the clause.

The most consequential direct challenge to the constitutionality of the death penalty was the 1972 case of *Furman v. Georgia*.[14] At the time, public support for the death penalty was at a historic low, and no executions had occurred for five years; nevertheless, polls suggested that a slight majority of Americans continued to support capital punishment. In *Furman*, five of the justices concluded that the death penalty, at least as it existed at the time, violated the Eighth Amendment. The challenge posed by such a ruling was daunting: how to explain to the American people that the death penalty was "cruel and unusual," when most people, or at least a substantial percentage of them, accepted the morality of the death penalty.

Only two justices confronted the issue head on and found the death penalty itself to be "cruel and unusual," regardless of the crime for which it was imposed. The opinions of Justices William Brennan and Thurgood Marshall, although well written and persuasive, reveal the inherent difficulty of declaring unconstitutional a punishment that a clear majority of Americans had not yet rejected on moral grounds.

Justice Brennan identified four principles that, in his view, marked a punishment as "cruel and unusual": (1) unusual severity, to the point of degrading the dignity of human beings; (2) arbitrary imposition; (3) rejection by contemporary American society; and (4) excessiveness, in the sense of inflicting unnecessary suffering. Recognizing the difficulty of finding the death penalty to violate any one of these four principles given its public support, Justice Brennan concluded that the four principles must be considered together. Any punishment that "seriously implicated" each of the principles would, under this "cumulative" test, be unconstitutional, even if it did not violate any of the principles standing alone. According to Justice Brennan, the validity of the death penalty was sufficiently in doubt, under each of the four principles, to justify adding them together and reaching a conclusion of unconstitutionality.

Justice Marshall also found the death penalty to be "cruel and unusual" on its face, but he used a more direct approach. Justice Marshall focused his opinion on two points: first, the death penalty was an excessive punishment, since it did not serve any legitimate penological purpose. Retribution, in Justice Marshall's view, might explain why society chose to punish, but it could not suffice as the moral justification for a punishment. Thus, the death penalty could not be based on retribution. Numerous studies, on the other hand, had failed to prove any deterrent value from the use of the death penalty, at least as compared to life imprisonment. Thus, the death penalty could not be based on deterrence. Finally, other possible purposes for the death penalty, such as incapacitation, encouraging guilty pleas, eugenics, and cost-saving, were, according to Justice Marshall, either unsupported by fact or unacceptable in principle.

Justice Marshall's second point responded honestly and forthrightly, if perhaps unconvincingly, to the majoritarian dilemma posed by the Eighth Amendment: he simply contended that public support for the death penalty was based on public ignorance of the various arguments against capital punishment expressed in the first half of his opinion. Moreover, he argued, the public was also unaware of the discriminatory application of capital punishment, the likelihood that innocent people are sometimes executed, and the deleterious effects of capital cases on the criminal justice system in general. Marshall concluded:

> It has often been noted that American citizens know almost nothing about capital punishment. . . . I believe that the great mass of citizens would conclude on the basis of the material already considered that the death penalty is immoral and therefore unconstitutional. . . . Assuming knowledge of all the facts presently available regarding capital punishment, the average citizen would, in my opinion, find it shocking to his conscience and sense of justice. For this reason alone capital punishment cannot stand.[15]

The arguments on the other side of the constitutional issue were made by the four dissenters in *Furman*, Chief Justice Burger and Justices Harry Blackmun, Lewis Powell, and William Rehnquist. Among their arguments, typical of previous responses to challenged punishments, were (1) federal courts should be loathe to strike down legislatively authorized punishments as "cruel and unusual," since elected state legislatures, and not life-tenured federal courts, are the barometers of public opinion; (2) the punishment of death was common in 1791 (and was referred to explicitly in the language of the Fifth Amendment and the due process clauses of the Fifth and Fourteenth Amendments), thus the framers must have believed that the death penalty was not "cruel and unusual"; (3) the fact that a majority of state legislatures, along with the federal government, authorize capital punishment is a reliable indicator of society's moral judgment; (4) public opinion polls show broad support for the death penalty; (5) the fact that juries rarely impose the death penalty is evidence not of societal rejection of the punishment but of the care and caution that juries properly bring to capital cases; (6) the efficacy of the death penalty is irrelevant under the Eighth Amendment; (7) even if it were relevant, the death penalty serves an appropriate retributive purpose; and (8) the evidence about deterrence is equivocal, suggesting that the Court should defer to the legislative resolution of the deterrence issue.

The three justices who joined with Brennan and Marshall in voting against the death penalty in *Furman* did so without even addressing the argument that the death penalty itself, in the abstract, was "cruel and unusual." Instead, each of the three concluded that there was something wrong with the way the death penalty was being administered by the states. This allowed the three to avoid a direct confrontation with society's underlying moral judgment about the death penalty. For example, Justice Douglas contended that racial and class discrimination plagued the administration of the death penalty. Justice Potter Stewart, on the other hand, wrote that arbitrariness, not discrimination, was the main problem: "These death sentences are cruel and unusual in the same way that being struck by lightning is cruel and unusual."[16] Finally, Justice Byron White concluded that the death penalty was being imposed so rarely by the states that it could not possibly serve a useful purpose: the problem, in other words, was its infrequent use.

Although no single opinion in *Furman* received majority support, the votes of Justices Brennan, Marshall, Douglas, Stewart, and White, when added together, produced a ruling that all existing death-penalty statutes were unconstitutional. Contrary to the views of Justices Brennan and Marshall, however, the *Furman* Court was not riding the crest of an anti-death-penalty wave. Nor did the *Furman* decision mark the end of the death penalty in America. Instead, in the years immediately after *Furman*, thirty-five states revised and reenacted their death-penalty statutes, hoping the changes would satisfy a majority of the Court that the death penalty could be administered within constitutional standards. And in 1976, in *Gregg v. Georgia*[17] and its companion cases, the Court upheld three of the new statutes (Georgia, Florida, and Texas) by a 7–2 vote, with Justices Brennan and Marshall dissenting.

After *Gregg*, most states adopted some variation of one of the three death-penalty statutes approved by the Court. Today, thirty-six states and the federal government have statutes that authorize the death penalty for at least some crimes.[18] Executions, which ceased in the late 1960s under the cloud of possible unconstitutionality, resumed in 1977 when Gary Gilmore faced a firing squad in Utah. Between the time when the post-*Furman* statutes went into effect and the end of 1990, over 3,700 convicted criminals were sentenced to death, and 143 persons were actually executed. At the end of 1990, 2,412 persons remained on Death Row awaiting execution.[19]

Since *Furman* and *Gregg*, the Court has not seriously reconsidered the claim that the death penalty itself violates the Eighth Amendment. And in light of the apparent nationwide increase in popular support for the death penalty during the 1980s, it is unlikely that a challenge to the constitutionality of the death penalty alone will attract the Court's attention in the near future. For this reason, those who advocate abolition of the death penalty have turned to state legislatures and state courts, in the hopes of achieving through the political process or the interpretation of state constitutional law what they concede they cannot presently achieve under the Eighth Amendment. One interesting approach that may someday bear political, if not judicial, fruit is the effort to test the strength of the asserted public support for capital punishment; a growing body of evidence suggests that such support drops dramatically when people are allowed to consider an alternative of life imprisonment without parole, coupled with a requirement to pay restitution to a murder victim's survivors.[20]

Even if judicial invalidation of capital punishment itself is unlikely at the present time, it is possible that the Court will decide to take up the question of whether particular methods of execution violate the cruel and unusual punishment clause. The Court upheld the constitutionality of death by shooting in 1879[21] and by electrocution in 1890.[22] And in 1985, over a vigorous dissent by Justice Brennan, the Court declined to review a direct challenge to the constitutionality of electrocution.[23] Basic social values may well be changing in this area, however. In recent years, several states have replaced electrocution with lethal injection as their primary method of execution. This shift has generally been based on the legislative (and public) belief that lethal injection is a more "humane" method of execution, causing less pain and suffering for the condemned person. If these statutory changes indeed reflect a growing societal consensus against electrocution, then the Court may soon have a good, and legitimate, reason to hasten the demise of electrocution by considering whether it is "cruel and unusual" punishment under the Eighth Amendment.

The Eighth Amendment as a Guarantee of Proportional Punishments

The second principal context in which the Court addresses Eighth Amendment "cruel and unusual punishment" issues is in cases involving a constitutional challenge to the imposition of a punishment for a particular crime or against a particular class of criminals. This is sometimes called an "as applied" challenge, and the nature of the claim is sometimes described as a "proportionality" claim; that is, a particular punishment is "disproportionate," either to the crime in question or to the moral culpability of the criminal.

At the outset, a very good historical argument can be made that proportionality claims do not fit within the scope of the cruel and unusual punishment clause. Indeed, such an argument was made recently by Justice Antonin Scalia, joined by Chief Justice Rehnquist, in the 1991 case of *Harmelin v. Michigan*.[24] Justice Scalia reviewed the origins of the Eighth Amendment, noting the link between the "cruel and unusual punishment" clause and the Titus Oates case. He also pointed out that state constitutions adopted just before or after the Bill of Rights, such as those of Pennsylvania (1776), South Carolina (1778), New Hampshire (1784), and Ohio (1802), specifically required that punishments be "proportioned"; in fact, the New Hampshire and Ohio constitutions each contained a cruel and unusual punishment clause *and* a proportioned punishment clause, suggesting that the clauses referred to different subjects. Finally, Scalia cited contemporary legislative and judicial discussions of the Eighth Amendment, which tend to show that the original intent was to prohibit punishments "without reference to the particular offense."[25] Thus, if a punishment is not "cruel and unusual" in the abstract, according to Scalia, it can be used for any crime without violating the Eighth Amendment; the legislature simply must be trusted not to authorize the use of, say, the death penalty for an overtime parking violation.

Justice Scalia's mastery of the historical evidence is impressive. Whatever the history books and he may say about the matter, however, the Court has long recognized proportionality claims as legitimate under the Eighth Amendment; a majority of the Court continued to recognize them in *Harmelin*; and the Court seems unlikely to reverse its course now. The *Weems v. United States* and *Trop v. Dulles* cases, previously cited as direct challenges to particular punishments, can also be read as early proportionality cases, although this construction may be a bit forced. In subsequent cases upholding challenged punishments, individual members of the Court wrote, albeit in dictum, that the Eighth Amendment embodies a proportionality principle. In 1962, in *Robinson v. California*,[26] the first case to apply the Eighth Amendment to the states, the Court rejected a ninety-day prison sentence for the crime of being addicted to narcotics. Since the sentence could not possibly have been "cruel and unusual" in the abstract, the Court must have found the punishment to be disproportionate to the crime. Finally, and most importantly, in *Solem v. Helm*,[27] in 1983, the Court struck down a life sentence without possibility of parole, under a recidivist statute, for a person convicted of seven nonviolent felonies. The *Helm* Court expressly based its holding on the proposition that the cruel and unusual punishment clause "prohibits not only barbaric punishments, but also sentences that are disproportionate to the crime committed."[28]

Given that the Court apparently continues to recognize a proportionality component within the Eighth Amendment, the issue remains: How is the Court to determine whether a punishment is "disproportionate," either for a particular crime or for a particular class of criminals?

The key to resolving a proportionality claim, according to *Helm* and several other Court decisions, is to identify those "objective factors" that determine whether or not a particular punishment is appropriate for a particular crime or criminal. The "objective factors" that have been identified by members of the Court to date are (1) the gravity of the offense as compared to the severity of the penalty, (2) the penalties imposed in the same jurisdiction for similar crimes, and (3) the penalties imposed in other jurisdictions for the same crime.

This effort to base proportionality decisions on "objective factors," rather than on the moral judgments of the justices themselves, is laudable. But the Court does not seem very close to achieving consensus about what should be considered an "objective factor," nor about how such factors should be balanced against each other. For example, three of the current justices, in a 1991 case upholding a mandatory life sentence without parole for a first offender convicted of simple possession of 650 grams of cocaine, suggested that the first of the three aforementioned factors is the most important one and that the second and third factors should be considered only if the Court believes the challenged punishment too severe.[29] In a 1989 case, on the other hand, four justices argued that proportionality analysis must end whenever the Court determines that a particular application of a punishment is not "unusual," in the sense that a substantial number of states authorize the same use of the challenged punishment.[30] And in the same case, four justices wrote that international standards of human decency are relevant to proportionality analysis under the Eighth Amendment; the remaining five justices disagreed.[31]

In addition, applying "objective factors" to a particular proportionality claim turns out, not surprisingly, to be a very complicated matter. Take, for example, the current controversy over the proposed use of the death penalty for major drug kingpins. Public opinion polls show strong public support for the proposal. Would such a use of the death penalty be constitutionally disproportionate to the crime?

The first "objective factor," a comparison of the seriousness of the offense and the penalty, does not even come close to answering the question. The gravity of the offense (namely, dealing in huge quantities of dangerous drugs) certainly ranks quite high, perhaps even higher than that of an average murder. After all, a drug kingpin may be indirectly responsible for the destruction of many lives. But the death penalty is also by far the most severe punishment known to American society, different in kind from other punishments. Should it be reserved solely for intentional killings? The Court came very close to this conclusion when, in 1977, it struck down, on proportionality grounds, the imposition of the death penalty for the rape of an adult woman who does not die.[32]

The second and third "objective factors" are even less helpful. It is unclear what crimes are similar for purposes of applying the second factor, nor is it clear whether any other punishments can ever be characterized as similar to the death penalty. With respect to the third factor, at least for the first court to authorize the death penalty for drug kingpins, there will be, by definition, no other jurisdictions that authorize the same penalty for the same crime. Does this mean that no jurisdiction can be the first to do so? This would turn the Eighth Amendment into a one-way ratchet: The penalty for a crime could go down, but it could never go back up.

The real problem is that the "objective factors" approach, despite its attractiveness, is so vague and indeterminate that it leaves the Court in the same bind of having to decide whether or not it can legitimately disagree with the majority's view of the morality of the challenged punishment. This problem has plagued the Court in recent decisions about the proportionality of the death penalty for juvenile murderers, murderers who are mentally retarded, and felony-murders in which the defendant neither intends to kill nor actually kills. In the case of juvenile murderers, for example, the Court has reviewed the issue numerous times over the past ten years, only to reach the unsatisfying conclusion that fifteen-and-a-half is too young to receive the death penalty but sixteen is not too young. The justices' opinions about the juvenile death penalty primarily deal with such seemingly trivial matters as how to count up the states that authorize or do not authorize such a penalty. Should states that do not authorize the death penalty at all count as opposing the death penalty for juveniles, or should they be excluded from the tally altogether? If this is the best the Court can do to resolve proportionality issues, it is perhaps worth asking whether the end result is worth the effort.

The Eighth Amendment as a Source of Procedural Rights

The third context in which the modern Court often applies the cruel and unusual punishment clause is probably the least obvious of the three principal applications considered here, and it is certainly the most difficult to justify, at least in terms of the language of the Eighth Amendment. As a result of the Court's decisions in *Furman* and *Gregg*, invalidating and revalidating the death penalty, not in the abstract but on the application of the punishment, the Eighth Amendment has become a potent constitutional limitation on the procedures by which the state and federal governments administer their respective death-penalty systems. The cruel and unusual punishment clause has, in effect, become a "super due process clause" for death-penalty cases only, imposing greatly heightened procedural standards to ensure the fairness and accuracy of both the guilt and sentencing stages of capital trials.

The basis for this procedural use of the "cruel and unusual punishment" clause is found in the *Furman* opinions of Justices Douglas, Stewart, and White. There, each of the three concluded that the death penalty, as it was administered, violated the Eighth Amendment, even though none of them found it to be invalid on its face. The clear implication was that the death penalty could be constitutionally imposed, but only if the procedures for imposing it were substantially improved over those that existed before *Furman*. Specifically, the main problem with the *Furman* death-penalty statutes, according to the opinions, was that they gave too much discretion to the sentencer without providing any guidance in the exercise of that discretion. The sentencer thus did not know what factors should or should not be considered in deciding between a death sentence and a life sentence. Without such guidance, the three believed, arbitrary and/or discriminatory sentencing results were inevitable.

This procedural interpretation of the Eighth Amendment has been sharply criticized. For example, the *Furman* dissenters wrote: "The approach of these concurring opinions has no antecedent in the Eighth

Amendment cases. It is essentially and exclusively a procedural due process argument."[33] The primary objection to the procedural interpretation is that the Eighth Amendment, of all the provisions in the Bill of Rights, is the most obviously substantive in its language. Constitutional scholar Raoul Berger has described the procedural approach as an "unwarranted manipulation of constitutional terms";[34] in his view, the Eighth Amendment clearly applies "only to the *nature* of the punishment, not to the *process* whereby it was decreed."[35]

On the other hand, another noted constitutional scholar, John Hart Ely, has argued that a procedural interpretation of the Eighth Amendment may actually be more legitimate than a textually based substantive interpretation.[36] According to Ely, the main purpose of the Eighth Amendment is to ensure that "cruel" punishments are not applied in "unusual" ways, in other words, against people who are politically unable to defend themselves, which in modern America means those who are economically disadvantaged or otherwise different from the politically active, generally white, middle to upper middle class. Ely contends that the three justices in *Furman* were on the right track, because it was the discretionary nature of the *Furman* statutes that allowed the "haves" to limit the use of the death penalty to the "have-nots," without fear that it might someday be imposed against them. Ely concludes, however, that no procedural reform can ever eliminate this discretion; thus, in his view, the death penalty itself must violate the Eighth Amendment: "It is so cruel that we know its imposition will be unusual."[37]

The state statutes upheld by the Court in *Gregg* tried to give more guidance in capital sentencing by providing lists of "aggravating" and "mitigating" factors for the sentencer's consideration. Contrary to Ely's contention that discretion was the primary evil to be eradicated, however, the Court, just two years after *Gregg*, reversed course and insisted, in *Lockett v. Ohio*,[38] that a capital sentencer have total discretion to consider absolutely anything that a defendant might offer in mitigation of a death sentence.

The Court's decision in *Lockett*, which increased sentencing discretion to ensure that the sentencer could mete out "individualized justice," was inconsistent with the basic thrust of *Furman* and *Gregg*, and the tension between the two lines of cases persists to this day. In the judicial tug-of-war between the pro-discretion and anti-discretion themes, many procedures used in death-penalty cases have been held unconstitutional. In some cases, the very same procedures have even been challenged as both allowing too much sentencing discretion to satisfy the Eighth Amendment and not allowing enough.

This unfortunate situation is why Justice Scalia recently declared, in *Walton v. Arizona*,[39] that he would no longer follow *Lockett* and its progeny. According to Justice Scalia, *Lockett* ignored the rationale of *Furman* and *Gregg* and should therefore be overruled. The battle cry has been issued for a revisitation of *Lockett*, and it seems likely that the Court soon will reconsider whether the states must insist that all mitigating factors be considered by a capital sentencer.

Another interesting procedural issue that has vexed the Court in recent years is whether a state may present to a capital sentencer evidence of the traumatic effect of the murder on the family and friends of the victim. The so-called victim-impact cases, beginning with the 1987 decision in *Booth v. Maryland*[40] and culminating in 1991 in *Payne v. Tennessee*,[41] reveal the Court's discomfort with the proposition that a defendant can be held morally accountable for harm that he or she causes but does not intend to cause nor realize will occur. In *Booth*, the Court held that such evidence violated the Eighth Amendment, because it would likely divert the sentencer's attention away from the "moral culpability" of the defendant. In *Payne*, however, the Court overruled *Booth*, finding "victim impact" to be within the scope of the defendant's "moral responsibility."

Lurking in the background of these victim-impact cases is the more troubling question whether a defendant, in tit-for-tat fashion, must constitutionally be allowed to argue that the death penalty should not be imposed because, for example, the victim was a loner who left no close friends or family members. The specter of such "mini-trials" of the victim has been raised by the Court's decision to permit the use of victim-impact evidence in capital sentencing; it is only a matter of time before the Court will have to decide whether a state can allow such evidence in aggravation, but not in mitigation.

Conclusion

The cruel and unusual punishment clause may well stand at a constitutional crossroads. It has enjoyed a brief period of prominence, although this prominence may have been achieved at some cost in terms of public perception of the legitimacy of the Court's decision-making process. In any event, the Court's recent concern with the clause is now seriously threatened by attempts to "roll back the clock" and adopt a more traditional, majoritarian approach toward interpreting the clause's language.

With the efforts by Justices Brennan and Marshall, in *Furman*, to find a principled basis for holding the death penalty unconstitutional per se having failed, the Court does not seem eager to entertain new challenges in this area. Regarding proportionality, Justice Scalia has undermined the historical basis for the entire doctrine, and the rest of the Court seems unable to reach a consensus about the proper method for analyzing the issue, let alone about the results of such an analysis. And the "super due process clause" death-penalty cases, although still numerous, seem increasingly likely to loosen, rather than tighten, the relevant constitutional procedural standards.

Will the cruel and unusual punishment clause, in the third century of the

Bill of Rights, prove to be a significant limit on the government's power to punish or will it become mere constitutional rhetoric? No one knows for sure. But the first 200 years of interpretation of the clause strongly suggest that, as a result of the clause's unique language and history, the Court may be unable to resist, at least for long, the inevitable pressure to adopt the majoritarian point of view.

Equal Protection and
Affirmative Action

Herman Belz

Liberty and equality, proclaimed as self-evident truths in the Declaration of Independence, are the fundamental principles of republican government in the United States. For almost a century after 1776, the existence of slavery denied liberty and mocked equality. The destruction of slavery during the Civil War, followed by the Reconstruction constitutional amendments, extended liberty to four million previously excluded black persons and established fundamental equality in civil rights. A century later the Civil Rights Act of 1964 repudiated the counterfeit equality of the separate but equal doctrine, adopted in the late nineteenth century as a constitutional expression of contemporary racial-group thinking. The culmination of decades of struggle for genuine equality of civil rights, this landmark legislation prohibited discrimination against any individual because of race, color, religion, and national origin in a wide range of public and private activities. The Civil Rights Act made equal rights for individuals the controlling principle of civil rights policy in the United States.

Before the 1960s the idea of equality rarely dominated debates on public policy.[1] The Civil Rights Act of 1964 altered the status of this basic principle, elevating it to ideological preeminence and making it a continuing preoccupation of American politics. Underlying the 1964 act was a national consensus that the Constitution extends its protection equally to every person as an independent individual. Since the late 1960s that consensus has disintegrated. In its place has arisen the radically different idea of equality among racial and ethnic groups, implemented through proportional representation, as the primary meaning of equal protection. Affirmative action is the vehicle of this new definition. The term refers to government policies that directly or indirectly award jobs, admission to colleges and professional schools, and other social goods to individuals on the basis of membership in designated protected groups. Its purpose is to compensate those groups for past discrimination caused by society as a whole. This essay will examine the contested meaning of equality in contemporary civil rights policy by focusing on equal employment opportunity and the emergence of affirmative action as a solution to the problem of employment discrimination.

Title VII and the Origins of Affirmative Action

Although the idea of group rights appears in many areas of civil rights policy, its use in employment raises peculiarly acute issues of broad significance for liberal democracy in the late twentieth century. Prior to the Civil Rights Act, national law permitted employers to select employees according to race or any other consideration, except for the National Labor Relations Act's restrictions on discrimination for labor union activity. Affirmative action in employment disregards the limitation on government power inherent in the prospective nature of the antidiscrimination principle of the Civil Rights Act. Reaching practices that were lawful when they occurred, it in effect declares them retrospectively unlawful in order to justify awarding economic benefits to members of groups designated as victims of societal discrimination. Unlike other civil rights issues, moreover, employment presents highly relevant questions about the qualifications of applicants that are in turn related to property rights and legitimate business considerations. In civil rights questions such as voting and desegregation of schools and public facilities there is an unlimited number of goods available—for instance, ballots to be cast or places to be occupied—but individuals compete for a limited number of jobs. Affirmative action in employment thus poses the issue of government regulation as an instrument of social redistribution and brings into conflict the civil rights both of employers and individuals who are members of protected and unprotected groups.

Because laws against racial discrimination in employment potentially threatened business freedom and the operation of the labor market, resistance to national legislation on equal employment opportunity was stronger than to other civil rights reforms. Although after World War II many states created fair employment practice commissions, the idea of a national ban on employment discrimination got nowhere from 1946, when President Roosevelt's wartime Fair Employment Practice Commission expired, until the early 1960s. The formation of a powerful national movement for civil rights reform made it possible in 1964 to include employment discrimination in the omnibus Civil Rights Act.[2]

Title VII of the Civil Rights Act prohibited discrimination in private employment in business firms and labor unions with twenty-five or more employees or members.[3] Congress declared it unlawful to fail or refuse to hire or to discharge any individual or to discriminate against an individual in the terms and conditions of employment on account of race, color, religion, national origin, or sex. Title VII made it an unlawful practice also to limit, segregate, or classify any individual or otherwise discriminate against or adversely affect an individual's status because of race. Although the law did not specify how to prove an unlawful practice, it defined discrimination as intentional unequal treatment of an individual because of race.

Judges could order relief under the act upon a finding that an employer intentionally engaged in an unlawful practice. As a remedy for discrimination, courts were authorized to stop the unlawful practice and order "affirmative action" as appropriate, including reinstatement with or without back pay. Employers could differentiate among employees in accordance with a bona fide seniority or merit system and could select employees by means of professionally developed ability tests, provided these devices were not designed, intended, or used to discriminate because of race. Title VII thus was aimed at preventing otherwise valid or nonracial practices from being used as a pretext for discrimination.

Title VII guaranteed an individual right to equal employment opportunity within the framework of the intentional disparate treatment theory of discrimination. In brief, the theory held that discrimination must stem from an intentional act that resulted in injury or denial of equal opportunity. This fact was underscored in the prohibition of preferential treatment on account of racial imbalance. Section 703(j) declared that nothing in the act shall be interpreted to require an employer or union to grant preferential treatment to any individual or group on account of racial imbalance that might exist between the number or percentage of persons of any race in the workforce and the number or percentage of persons of that race in any community or in the available workforce. This provision was intended to quiet fears that federal administrators and judges would regard statistics of racial imbalance as evidence of unlawful discrimination and force employers to use quotas to achieve racial balance. The ban on quotas also stood as the congressional response to the demand of many civil rights leaders in 1963–64 that racially preferential hiring practices be adopted as compensation for past discrimination.

It is important to note the guarantee of an individual right against racial discrimination in Title VII in view of subsequent Supreme Court decisions that the law's purpose was to open economic opportunities for blacks as a class. To be sure, Congress wanted to close the gap between the socioeconomic conditions of blacks and the white majority. The legal means of achieving this end, however, was the guarantee of equal employment opportunity for individuals, not enforcement of a group right to equal results for racial and ethnic classes.

Immediately after Title VII went into effect in 1965, federal judges and administrators and civil rights advocates advanced a new approach to employment discrimination. They argued that unlawful discrimination was the use of employment practices that had an unequal impact or adverse effect on blacks as a group. Under this disparate impact theory, discrimination was not intentional injury or denial of opportunity, but the sum of the unequal effects of employment procedures and business practices. A civil rights lawyer captured the essence of the new approach when he asked, "Why is intent any part of the process? Is not result the only relevant factor?"[4] Applying the disparate impact theory of discrimination, courts and administrative agencies introduced race-conscious affirmative action in the late 1960s.

In addition to Title VII, the federal contract program was a principal means of government intervention in the labor market to require racially preferential practices. Executive Order 10925, issued by President John F. Kennedy in 1961, imposed on government contractors an obligation to take "affirmative action" to ensure that individuals were treated without regard to race, creed, color, or national origin. Contractors had to post notices and make announcements of their nondiscrimination obligation and to furnish information and reports about their employment practices, including workforce statistics. This "outreach" approach to affirmative action was soon transformed into a "bottom line" approach aimed at increasing the number of minorities in the employer's workforce.

On the basis of workforce surveys showing low minority employment in industries or occupations, contract compliance officers tried to persuade employers to hire more blacks where they were "underrepresented." The policy became more clearly coercive when the Nixon administration in 1969 required contractors in the construction industry in Cleveland and Philadelphia to adopt specific goals and timetables for hiring minority employees. In 1970 the Office of Federal Contract Compliance in the Department of Labor extended the goals and timetables requirement to all nonconstruction contractors. It defined affirmative action as "a set of specific and result-oriented procedures to which a contractor commits himself to apply every good faith effort." OFCC regulations stated that "the objective of those procedures plus efforts is equal employment opportunity."[5]

In the contract compliance program, race-conscious affirmative action meant that companies wanting government business had to hire more minority employees. Under Title VII, by contrast, affirmative action was a remedy for unlawful discrimination. In order to establish this policy, the Equal Employment Opportunity Commission and the federal courts effectively rewrote Title VII to incorporate the disparate impact theory of discrimination. They transformed Title VII from a prospective law prohibiting intentional discrimination against individuals because of race into a retrospective measure aimed at societal discrimination against blacks as a class.

The first step in this process was to apply Title VII retrospectively to discrimination that occurred before passage of the act. According to the statute, practices occurring before the date it went into effect (July 2, 1965) were lawful and not subject to enforcement action. In a series of desegregation cases challenging the seniority system of hiring and promotion, courts circumvented this limitation by holding that racially neutral rules were illegal if they perpetuated the effects of past (lawful) discrimination and were not justified by business necessity. The second step in revising Title VII was to introduce the disparate impact concept. Courts decided that tests on which blacks scored lower than whites, resulting in their disproportionate exclusion, were unlawful unless the test could be shown to be job-related (i.e., predictive of job performance) and hence justified by business necessity. The third step in transforming Title VII was to nullify the ban on preferential treatment. The categorical statement that nothing in the law should be interpreted to require preferential treatment on account of racial imbalance was construed to mean only that an employer could not be charged with a violation for having a racially imbalanced workforce. This interpretation allowed courts to order quota relief after a finding of unlawful discrimination.[6]

In *Griggs v. Duke Power Co.* (1971) the Supreme Court affirmed these interpretive tendencies by reading the disparate impact theory of discrimination into Title VII. The case involved a claim by a class of black employees that the requirement of an aptitude test and high school diploma for departmental transfer was an unlawful practice because blacks scored lower than whites on these selection instruments. In a unanimous decision, the Court found the company in violation of Title VII. Although the company's practices were not intended to discriminate, intent was irrelevant. Congress directed Title VII at the consequences of employment practices, not simply their motivation. Practices that had a discriminatory effect were unlawful unless justified by "business necessity," described by Chief Justice Warren Burger as "the touchstone" of Title VII. He defined business necessity as having "a manifest relationship to the employment in question" or bearing "a demonstrable relationship to successful performance of the job in question."[7]

Although relatively unheralded, *Griggs* revolutionized employment law. The Court held the employer liable for societal discrimination that prevented blacks from receiving the education needed to enable them to compete equally with whites on the selection instruments in question.[8] As a result of *Griggs*, confusion existed concerning the meaning of discrimination. In a technical legal sense, disparate impact analysis could be viewed as a method of proving unlawful discrimination under Title VII. It could be seen as a strong form of enforcing the principle of nondiscrimination, a means of identifying employment practices not rationally related to the job in question or to legitimate business considerations. Such practices can fairly be regarded as arbitrary or a pretext for intentional discrimination, which is how most people think of it. In practical operation, however, the threat of liability under the disparate impact theory led irresistibly to the conclusion that racial imbalance is itself wrong and is a form of discrimination prohibited by Title VII. The impact of *Griggs* accordingly was to induce many employers to adopt racial hiring and promotion practices in order to create a racially balanced workforce and avoid charges of discrimination. In this sense disparate impact analysis became the engine that drove the affirmative action policymaking in public and private employment in the 1970s. It provided a vision of racially balanced or proportionate allocation of jobs and other public goods that could be expected to exist in the absence of intentional discrimination.

While accepting disparate impact analysis under Title VII, the Supreme Court, in *Washington v. Davis* (1976), responded to growing public apprehension about the spread of affirmative action by refusing to make the concept part of constitutional law.[9] Nevertheless, in the field of employment the Court permitted the federal judiciary and the Equal Employment Opportunity Commission to define business necessity narrowly, so as to place a heavy burden on employers to justify practices that had an adverse impact on minority groups. The government adopted testing guidelines that made it all but impossible to validate tests and other selection devices. Faced with the prospect of high litigation costs and expensive validation procedures, most employers abandoned objective tests. To avoid disparate impact liability, they hired "by the numbers," trying to achieve a satisfactory "bottom line" in terms of a racially balanced workforce.

From its beginning in the government contract program, affirmative action provoked objections that it constituted discrimination in reverse. As the policy became more systematic in the 1970s, white males filed discrimination charges that revealed the precarious legal position of employers seeking to comply with the conflicting demands of the nondiscrimination principle on the one hand and affirmative action on the other. Employers were subject to charges of unlawful practices from racial and ethnic minorities under the disparate impact theory of discrimination. If they adopted racially preferential affirmative action plans to avoid liability, they were subject to discrimination charges from white males under the disparate treatment theory of Title VII enforcement.

The Supreme Court tried to resolve the reverse discrimination problem in *Bakke v. Regents of the University of California* (1978), where it considered the legality of a medical school affirmative action plan that reserved a fixed number of places for minority group individuals. A 5–4 majority decided that the plan violated a white male applicant's right of nondiscrimination under Title VI of the Civil Rights Act.[10] The medical school did not practice discrimination in the past; the quota was therefore not remedial but was justified on social policy grounds as a way of providing minority physicians for minority communities. Offsetting the effect of the decision as a restriction on affirmative action was the fact that a majority of the Court expressed approval of race-conscious measures. Four justices voted to uphold the medical school quota, and Justice Lewis F. Powell expounded on the constitutionality of admission policies that considered race as a positive factor in promoting intellectual diversity under the First Amendment.

A year later the Supreme Court gave a major boost to affirmative action by approving racial quotas in private employment. In *Weber v. United Steelworkers of America* (1979) it rejected (5–4) the charge of a white employee that a 50 percent minority quota for admission to a training program violated the nondiscrimination requirement of Title VII. The quota was not a remedy for discrimination, for neither the labor union nor the company that jointly created the affirmative action plan was guilty of unlawful practices. Justice William Brennan for the Court said the quota was justified as a means of eliminating "manifest racial imbalances in traditionally segregated job categories."[11] This was a way of referring to societal discrimination.

The transformation of equal opportunity could be seen in *Weber* in judicial concern for the plight of the employer who was under pressure to adopt preferential policies while complying with the nondiscrimination requirement of Title VII. The law was intended to guarantee an individual right of equal employment opportunity, but the Court was looking for a way to protect employers. An employer could not be required to give preferential treatment because of racial imbalance, Justice Brennan said, but Title VII permitted the employer to take "private and voluntary" affirmative action if it wished.[12] *Weber* was the logical sequel to *Griggs*. It gave legal protection to employers who were forced to adopt racially preferential practices to avoid liability under the disparate impact theory of discrimination.[13]

A decade of affirmative action expansion climaxed in *Fullilove v. Klutznick* (1980), where the Supreme Court upheld a 10 percent quota for minority contractors under the Public Works Employment Act of 1977. The Court held, 6 to 3, that Congress under its commerce, spending, and Fourteenth Amendment enforcement powers could employ a racial classification for remedial purposes. This decision broadened the concept of remedy beyond its normal legal usage, for Congress in legislating the minority set-aside made no finding of unlawful discrimination in public contracting. It acted on the proposition, accepted by the Court, that racial preference was justified by the whole history of slavery, segregation, and societal discrimination. This generalized historical rationale was ultimately indistinguishable from the prospective justification of race-conscious measures on expedient, utilitarian grounds. After *Weber* and *Fullilove*, affirmative action was in essence a warrant for allocating public resources according to criteria of race, ethnicity, and gender in response to political and social pressures.

Affirmative Action in the 1980s

In the 1980s the Republican administrations of Presidents Ronald Reagan and George Bush questioned race-conscious affirmative action and tried to reestablish the principle of equal rights for individuals without regard to color. Although depicted by its critics as hostile to civil rights enforcement, the Reagan administration pursued a moderate course that accepted the disparate impact theory of discrimination and the substance of equal employment policy as it had developed by 1980. In two areas—the federal contract program and set-asides for minority contractors—the administration maintained race-conscious measures, adopting only minor changes to make affirmative action less administratively burdensome to employers. In sharp contrast, the Department of Justice and the Equal Employment Opportunity Commission opposed hiring and promotion quotas as unlawful under Title VII and the Constitution.

Leading the effort to stop the spread of quotas, Assistant Attorney General William Bradford Reynolds contended that the basic goal of civil rights policy had become equality of result for racial and ethnic groups, pursued through "separate but proportional" allocations in employment, school integration, and housing. Reynolds proposed to reform Title VII enforcement by basing it on three fundamental principles that he believed had been ignored in affirmative action policy. These were the individual right of nondiscrimination, the primacy of the free enterprise system, and the democratic basis of legitimate social reform.[14] Despite having his arguments against quotas rejected by the Supreme Court, Reynolds achieved a measure of success in refocusing the civil rights debate. It became harder for supporters of affirmative action to ignore the principle of individual rights and the idea of racially impartial equal protection. Drew S. Days III, assistant attorney general for civil rights in the Carter administration, conceded as much at the end of the Reagan era when he said that while he disagreed with the administration's policy, "its positions cannot be dismissed as inherently trivial."[15]

The Supreme Court rejected the Justice Department's anti-quota litigation policy in a series of decisions in the mid-1980s that rationalized and extended race-conscious affirmative action. After *Weber* and *Fullilove* two major unanswered questions concerned the legality of court-ordered quotas as a remedy for discrimination under Title VII and the validity of voluntary affirmative action by public employers. In *Local 28 Sheet Metal Workers v. EEOC* (1986), the Court approved a judicial quota order for 30 percent minority membership in a union that had a history of unlawful discrimination. The decision was a major victory for affirmative action insofar as it upheld a long line of remedial quota orders dating from 1969. Yet the Court's justification of quotas was more narrow than many civil rights lobbyists desired. Quota remedies were appropriate, Justice Brennan said for the 5–4 majority, where there was "persistent or egregious discrimination, or where necessary to dissipate the lingering effects of pervasive discrimination."[16]

In *Local 93 v. City of Cleveland* (1986), the Court approved a promotion quota in a consent decree agreed on by the city and a class of black firefighters. The district court that entered the consent decree did not violate its authority under Title VII because the decree was a form of voluntary affirmative action by the employer rather than a judicial order. In *U.S. v. Paradise* (1987) the Court affirmed a judicially imposed 50 percent promotion quota designed to rectify past discrimination by the Alabama state police and to achieve a 25 percent minority employment goal. Reviewing the criteria for establishing affirmative action programs, Justice Brennan said the quota order served a compelling governmental interest—to remedy past discrimination—and was "narrowly tailored." The quota order was flexible, temporary, and fair to white employees because it merely postponed their advancement rather than dismissed them in favor of minority employees.

Implicitly regarding preferential treatment as a departure from the equal protection concept, the Supreme Court's affirmative action decisions justified race-conscious measures by reference to past discrimination, either in the form of a specific finding of unlawful practices or generalized societal discrimination. In *Johnson v. Transportation Agency Santa Clara County* (1987) the Court dispensed with this limitation on affirmative action. The case concerned a Title VII discrimination charge by a male employee who was passed over for a slightly less qualified female employee under an affirmative action plan. The public agency had not discriminated, and the goal of the plan was to attain a workforce reflecting the percentage of women and minorities in the local area labor force.

In a 6–3 decision, the Supreme Court rejected the discrimination charge, thus approving voluntary affirmative action by a public employer. The chief significance of Justice Brennan's majority opinion was its justification of race- and gender-conscious measures as a means of correcting the underrepresentation of minorities and women in traditionally segregated job categories. Although Brennan referred to societal discrimination, his rationale for preferential treatment was clearly prospective rather than retrospective and remedial. The decision acknowledged that the true purpose and inner logic of affirmative action based on the disparate impact theory of discrimination was to achieve proportional racial, ethnic, and gender representation throughout society. Race and ethnicity were a legitimate and sound basis on which to allocate public goods and regulate the rights of individuals.

In two cases in the mid-1980s the Supreme Court invalidated judicial quota orders. In *Firefighters Local Union No. 1794 v. Stotts* (1984), the Court struck down a district court order modifying a Title VII consent decree in order to protect blacks hired under an affirmative action plan from being laid off in accordance with a seniority agreement. In *Wygant v. Jackson Board of Education* (1986), a 5–4 majority held that an affirmative action plan that protected minority employees against layoff, while laying off more senior white employees, violated the equal protection requirement of the Constitution. These decisions did not question the underlying logic of race-conscious measures by reasserting the rights of individuals under Title VII or the Constitution but rather affirmed the seniority rights of class members in a system of industrial relations.

Having protected quota remedies against the attack of the Reagan administration, the Supreme Court in 1988–89 attended to problems in the application of the disparate impact theory that exaggerated the tendency toward race-conscious practices. It revised the disparate impact concept by adapting it to or merging it with the disparate treatment theory of discrim-

ination. The intent of this revision was to balance the evidentiary burdens
between plaintiffs and employers and restore disparate impact analysis to
its original purpose of identifying pretextual discrimination.

Technical questions about the order and allocation of burdens of proof in
Title VII trials were related to substantive issues concerning the rights of
employers and employees and the meaning of equality. Plaintiffs' attorneys typically used the combination of disparate treatment and disparate
impact analysis as a one-two punch in proving a Title VII violation. The
plaintiff started with a charge of disparate treatment, and when the employer explained its rejection of a minority candidate by reference to some
measure of merit, the plaintiff charged disparate impact discrimination on
the criterion of merit.[17] By the 1980s it appeared that most employers had
stopped using objective aptitude tests because of the impossibility of vali-
dating them under the Uniform Guidelines for Employee Selection Procedures (1978). Increasingly employers relied on subjective devices, such as
interviews, which under the policies of the EEOC were not subject to disparate impact analysis. The civil rights lobby and the plaintiffs' bar wanted
to change this policy and expose subjective practices to the *Griggs* effects
test. Employers objected that it would be impossible to validate such practices; hence they would be forced further into adopting quotas and racial
preference.

In *Watson v. Fort Worth Bank* (1988) the Court unanimously decided that
subjective evaluation methods should be brought under the rules of disparate impact analysis. The justices split over the definition of business necessity as a defense to the *prima facie* charge. Pointing to a revised understanding of *Griggs,* a plurality held that the employer need only show that
the practice served a legitimate business purpose, as in a disparate treatment case.

In *Wards Cove v. Atonio* (1989), the Court went farther toward unifying
the disparate impact and disparate treatment concepts of discrimination. It
decided, 5 to 4, that a company with a high percentage of minorities in its
unskilled workforce and a low percentage of minorities in skilled jobs did
not violate Title VII. Clarifying basic procedures for proving unlawful discrimination under Title VII, the Court said a plaintiff could make a *prima
facie* disparate impact case by showing a discrepancy between the percentage of minorities in the workforce and the percentage of qualified minorities in the local labor market. The plaintiff had to point to a specific practice
or practices that caused the disparate impact, and the burden of proof remained on the plaintiff throughout the trial. As in a disparate treatment
case, the burden on the employer was to produce evidence that its practices were based on legitimate business reasons. Justice Byron White said
the employer's practices had to meet the *Griggs* business necessity standard, but this did not mean that they had to be shown to be "essential" or
"indispensable" to the enterprise.

Wards Cove tightened the rules of disparate impact analysis by making the burdens between plaintiff and defendant more equal. Although plainly a pro-employer decision, it was not viewed in the corporate EEO community as a defeat for affirmative action. Rather, it helped employers avoid the straitjacket of employment quotas by preserving their freedom to engage in nondiscriminatory practices and meaningful affirmative action.[18] Moreover, if employers did not have good records to respond to disparate impact charges, they might be found guilty of pretextual discrimination.[19]

The Supreme Court further modified the rules of affirmative action by making it easier for white employees to challenge racially preferential practices. In *Martin v. Wilks* (1989), a 5–4 majority held that white firefighters were entitled to their day in court and could question a consent decree that called for the promotion of less-qualified black employees. The purpose of the ruling was to assure that the claims of various interested parties be brought before the Court in negotiating an affirmative action settlement under Title VII.

The Court clarified the constitutional status of race-conscious practices in *City of Richmond v. Croson* (1989), a case dealing with set-asides for minority contractors. A 6–3 majority struck down a 30 percent quota for minority contractors as a violation of the equal protection clause of the Fourteenth Amendment. For the first time in an affirmative action case, a majority of the Court held that benign racial classifications were subject to strict judicial scrutiny. Under this standard, the 30 percent quota was unconstitutional because it was not predicated on a showing of identified past discrimination in public contracting in Richmond. Distinguishing *Fullilove*, Justice Sandra Day O'Connor said an assumption of generalized discrimination was an insufficient basis for racial quotas.

Affirmative Action and Congress

Civil rights organizations denounced the Supreme Court's 1989 decisions, and legislation was promptly introduced into Congress to reverse the statutory rulings by amending Title VII. Described as a measure to restore civil rights protections, the bill in fact expanded and strengthened disparate impact analysis to make racially preferential practices a functional requirement of Title VII jurisprudence.

The main point of the civil rights bill of 1990 was to reverse *Wards Cove*. It provided that a plaintiff could make a *prima facie* case under Title VII by showing that a group of employment practices had a disparate impact on a protected class. In other words, it was not necessary to identify a specific practice or practices that had an adverse impact on minorities. The bill placed the burden of proof on the employer to demonstrate that its practices were required by business necessity. Defined in *Griggs* as "having a manifest relationship to the employment in question," business necessity

was defined in the 1990 bill to mean "essential to effective job performance."[20]

The civil rights bill was drafted to overrule *Martin v. Wilks* by prohibiting
a challenge to a consent decree by any person who had notice of the proposed decree and an opportunity to object to it. It also proposed a major
change in Title VII policy by allowing a jury trial and the award of compensatory and punitive damages upon a finding of unlawful discrimination.[21]
The bill extended the filing time from 180 days to two years for a discrimination suit challenging a seniority system.[22] And it declared finally: "All
Federal laws protecting the civil rights of persons shall be broadly construed to effectuate the purpose of such laws to eliminate discrimination
and provide effective remedies."[23]

After letting judicial and executive officers lead the way in establishing
race-conscious policies for two decades, liberal lawmakers at last were in
the position of having to defend affirmative action. In the debate over the
civil rights bill of 1990, liberals claimed merely to restore *Griggs*, which they
said the Court had overruled in *Wards Cove*. Therefore they would put the
burden of proof on the employer, rather than on the plaintiff, and require
the employer to prove the business necessity of practices that had a disparate impact on minorities. In a practical sense the key issue was not whether
the burden on the employer was described as one of proof or production of
evidence; it was the meaning of business necessity. And on this point the
sponsors of the civil rights bill carefully avoided reliance on *Griggs*. Their
formulation of business necessity as "essential to effective job performance" is not found in *Griggs*.[24]

Although the federal courts had applied the *Griggs* effects test rigor-
ously, they never construed business necessity in a manner so antagonistic
to business freedom as the 1990 bill proposed. Courts recognized that employer practices could be tied to nonperformance factors, such as accident
rate, health and safety concerns, relocation or training expenses, and loss
of contracts. These and other legitimate business goals and considerations
would be excluded by the Title VII amendments from judicial evaluation of
business necessity.[25]

Accordingly, large corporate employers who had defended affirmative
action against the anti-quota policy of the Reagan administration opposed
the bill. They regarded it as a *de facto* quota measure that would eliminate
all employer defenses for practices that failed to assure proportionate hiring and promotion for minorities and women. William A. Kilberg, a leading EEO commentator, observed that the bill, "while defensively disclaim-
ing" any intent to mandate employment quotas, ". . . would force
employers surreptitiously to impose quotas or risk facing juries armed with
punitive damages trained at any and all statistical disparities."[26] Business
executives wanted protection against discrimination charges from both minority groups and white males and reasonable flexibility in operating affirmative action programs that were compatible with business purposes. Be-

cause the bill would disrupt the compromise achieved between business and government in the 1980s, corporate executives opposed it.

Responsive to business opinion, President Bush and Attorney General Richard Thornburgh criticized the civil rights bill as a quota bill. Congressional Democrats and the civil rights lobby denied the charge and accused the administration of playing racial politics. For political reasons both sides were reluctant to offer a precise academic definition of a quota, but the different concepts of equality and discrimination behind their arguments were clear.

Supporters of the civil rights bill defined a quota as a legal requirement by the government that an employer hire or promote an absolute or fixed number or percentage of persons from a protected class, regardless of qualifications or any other business considerations. Under this definition, liberals could honestly assert that the bill would not require or lead to quotas.[27] Opponents of the bill used the term "quotas" to refer to racially based employment practices that were intended to create a racially balanced or proportionately representative workforce, in order to avoid liability under the disparate impact theory of discrimination. For most people this was a reasonably accurate definition of a quota.

During the congressional debate, the managers of the bill amended it to refute the quota charge.[28] At the same time, acknowledging that the critical issue was the burden to be placed on the employer in responding to a *prima facie* charge of disparate impact, they continually revised the meaning of business necessity. Every time they needed a few more votes to answer the critics of quotas, the sponsors offered a new definition of business necessity and said the quota problem was solved.[29] Corporate EEO attorneys and testing experts said the definitions of business necessity were either too demanding, implying that formal validation was required, or too lenient with respect to qualifications, implying that only minimal performance standards could be used to select employees.[30]

Congress passed the civil rights bill in October 1990. Although agreeing with some of its provisions, President Bush vetoed the measure.[31] His veto message stated that "the bill actually employs a maze of highly legalistic language to introduce the destructive force of quotas into our nation's employment system."[32] The president pointed to rules of litigation in cases of unintentional discrimination that created powerful incentives for employers to adopt hiring and promotion quotas in order to avoid liability. He specifically criticized provisions allowing the plaintiff to make a *prima facie* case without identifying employer practices that caused a disparate impact and said the definition of business necessity was significantly more restrictive than that adopted in *Griggs*. President Bush also criticized the introduction into Title VII of a remedial approach based on tort damages in place of conciliation.

The Senate sustained the veto by a single vote. In the next session of Congress the civil rights bill was reintroduced in essentially the same form and passed the House of Representatives in June 1991. When it became clear that the president would again veto the bill, Republican moderates in the Senate led by John C. Danforth of Missouri proposed a compromise measure. After extensive negotiations among Senate Democrats, civil rights lobbyists, moderate Republicans, and the White House, the Senate passed the bill, 93 to 5. The House accepted the Senate bill and the president approved it in November 1991.

The Civil Rights Act of 1991 consolidated and protected race-conscious affirmative action in a variety of ways. Its most important provisions reversed *Martin v. Wilks* by making it much more difficult to challenge affirmative action plans established under consent decrees. It authorized compensatory and punitive damages under Title VII in cases of intentional discrimination, with limits on compensatory damage awards according to the size of the firm. It also permitted persons claiming injury from seniority systems to challenge them within a period starting at the time of the actual injury rather than a period after the adoption of the system, as the Supreme Court held in *Lorance v. A.T. & T. Technologies*. The act was appropriately equivocal concerning disparate impact discrimination charges, the burden of proof, and the business necessity defense. It reversed *Wards Cove* by placing the burden of proof in disparate impact cases on the employer. It did not expressly reject the definition of business necessity provided in *Wards Cove*, however, nor itself offer a definition of this key concept.

The 1991 act stated that its purpose was to codify the concepts of "business necessity" and "job related" enunciated by the Supreme Court in *Griggs* and other Title VII decisions prior to *Wards Cove*. It provided that disparate impact discrimination could be established when the plaintiff showed that a particular practice caused a disparate impact and the employer failed to prove that the practice was "job related for the position in question and consistent with business necessity." If the plaintiff could show that the employer's selection or employment process could not be separated into component parts for the purposes of analysis, the whole process could be challenged as a single practice causing disparate impact.

President Bush expressed satisfaction that the Civil Rights Act of 1991 would not lead to quotas. But the writing of the disparate impact theory of discrimination into Title VII had the effect of confirming the clear tendency toward race-conscious employment practices that forms the central historical meaning of affirmative action. Two important points in support of this conclusion emerge from a consideration of the act. First, employers were now statutorily required to prove the business necessity of any part or all of their employment decision-making process that had a disparate impact, as though racial imbalance per se is wrong. Second, Congress turned the problem of defining business necessity back to the courts. In theory the Supreme Court could define business necessity as it did in *Wards Cove*, concluding (again) that the definition arrived at in that decision is consistent with *Griggs* and its progeny. The obvious political meaning of the act, however, was that the courts should define business necessity more stringently than the Supreme Court did in *Wards Cove*. The policy envisioned in the act permits employers to establish only minimum qualifications, by which they will hire individuals by race, ethnicity, or sex according to their proportion of the applicant pool or their group's proportion of the qualified labor market.[33]

During the 1991 debate on the civil rights bill, public attention focused on a little-known feature of affirmative action policy that appeared to confirm the view of critics that the policy is aimed at proportional racial representation within a framework of minimal qualifications. This was the question of employment aptitude tests and "race norming."

Referred to by its defenders as "within-group scoring," race norming is a way of awarding points to minority applicants so they can compete better with whites who score higher on objective tests. Suppose, for example, that a black and a white candidate each score 300 on a test. Their scores are then adjusted according to their ranking within their racial group, so that the black's score is 79 and the white's 39. This adjusted score, rather than the raw score, is reported to the employer without explanation of the process used to reach it. In 1981 the Department of Labor adopted this method of within-group scoring in administering the General Aptitude Test Battery, used by many state employment agencies to refer unskilled and semi-skilled labor to employers. In 1986 the Department of Justice questioned the practice as a violation of the nondiscrimination requirement of Title VII. Rather than abandon race norming, the Department of Labor stopped using the GATB and asked the National Research Council (NRC), a committee of the National Academy of Sciences, to study and report on the matter.

The council concluded that the GATB was fair according to the definition of fairness used in industrial psychology. That is, the test accurately predicted job performance for persons of all racial groups. Nevertheless, the NRC said within-group scoring was justified because of the modest predictive accuracy of the GATB, reflected in a phenomenon called the "false negative" effect. This referred to the fact that some applicants who test low, if given the job, can perform above some minimal standard. Because proportionately more blacks than whites fall into this category, the GATB has a disparate impact. According to the NRC, race norming was needed in order to ensure equal referral chances for "able" minority and white applicants. Although the panel acknowledged that the problem was not race-based and affected persons in all groups, it proposed a race-based solution that would result in a less-productive workforce than one selected by pure rank ordering.[34]

Race norming made headlines when the debate on the civil rights bill resumed in 1991.[35] Critics attacked it as a flagrant illustration of the corruption of affirmative action and a gross violation of the equal rights principle. Unwilling to defend race norming publicly, Democrats agreed to a provision in the civil rights bill prohibiting the practice but also barring the use of tests that are not valid or fair. In final deliberations on the bill they agreed to stop the practice of race norming. Thus the Civil Rights Act of 1991 prohibited test score adjustment or the use of different cutoff scores on the basis of race, color, religion, sex, or national origin.

Support of race norming was consistent with the opposition that affirmative action supporters have often raised against the merit principle and the idea of individual equal rights. Professing to uphold equality of opportunity, they have assiduously pursued a conception of equality that regards membership in the group as the source of rights and that aims at proportional results for racial, ethnic, and gender groups. Objecting to the judicial elaboration of a moderate form of affirmative action acceptable to the business community, the civil rights lobby in the debate on the civil rights bills of 1990–91 confirmed that the logic of the disparate impact theory of discrimination is radically opposed to the principle of racially impartial individual rights.

Affirmative Action and the Transformation of Equal Rights

In concluding this account of affirmative action it is appropriate to reflect on the contested meaning of equality in American society in the 1990s. When the Civil Rights Act of 1964 proclaimed a national policy of equal employment opportunity, a presumption existed in constitutional law that racial classifications were inherently harmful and invidious. Race was a suspect classification, meaning that a measure based on race was presumably unconstitutional and valid only if it served a compelling governmental interest. In order to overcome this presumption, supporters of race-conscious affirmative action argued that remedying the effects of past discrimination was a legitimate social goal that satisfied the test of strict scrutiny and compelling governmental interest test. In this view the equality principle was served by recognizing the differences between racial groups, not their similarities. Justice Harry A. Blackmun summarized this revised, neo-racial approach to equal protection in a memorable dictum in the *Bakke* case: "In order to get beyond racism we must first take account of race. There is no other way. And in order to treat some persons equally, we must treat them differently."[36]

Against the background of slavery and racial discrimination and the not-so-distant memory of ghetto riots and burning cities, Justice Blackmun's dictum possessed a seeming logic that obscured its defiance of reason and common sense. Yet, as the political philosopher Douglas Rae points out, the idea of pursuing equality through inequality is as fallacious as killing for peace or lying in the name of truth.[37] Supporters of affirmative action have in effect acknowledged this fact by shifting from a remedial strategy to a prospective justification that defends racial-group preference on the ground of social utility and political expediency.

Although the remedial rationale provided legal justification for minority preferences, affirmative action theorists have long been convinced of the wisdom and legitimacy of racial classification as a prospective instrument of public policy. For example, Kenneth L. Karst and Harold W. Horowitz wrote in 1974 that the purpose of affirmative action was not to remedy discrimination but to serve contemporary social needs. While it was expedient for courts to invoke the concept of a remedy for unlawful discrimination to justify racial measures, judicial quota orders, properly understood, reflected a compelling governmental interest in creating an integrated society.[38] In the 1980s the appeal to race as a reasonable basis of social policy became more open and widespread, especially in view of judicial qualifications on the use of race-conscious measures as a remedy for discrimination. Rejecting the antidiscrimination principle as a legal rationale, Randall Kennedy expressed this outlook in stating that affirmative action rested on a rational calculation about the most socially beneficial use of limited resources.[39]

The Supreme Court offered just such a forward-looking rationale for race-conscious affirmative action in *Metro Broadcasting Inc. v. F.C.C.* (1990). At issue was the constitutionality of a congressional policy requiring the Federal Communications Commission to award an absolute quota to minorities in the sale of broadcast licenses that have been designated in distress and scheduled for a revocation hearing. In a 5–4 decision, the Court upheld the policy. Even though it was not remedial in the sense of being designed to compensate victims of past governmental or societal discrimination, Justice Brennan said the FCC policy was constitutionally permissible because it embodied a benign racial classification and served important governmental objectives.[40] In this instance the objective was programming diversity in the broadcasting industry, which the Court said benefited all Americans. Sensitive to the possible charge that its decision reflected racial stereotyping, the Court denied any assumption that minority ownership would necessarily express a "minority viewpoint" in a cultural sense.

Confident that a clear distinction can be drawn between benign and invidious or stigmatizing racial classifications, supporters of affirmative action propose a variety of measures to achieve equality defined in proportional racial group terms. In California a proposed law could require state colleges to grant degrees to ethnic and racial groups in direct proportion to their share of the state's high school graduates. Legislation has been introduced into Congress requiring the Department of Agriculture to establish a policy ensuring that black farmers sell their land only to other blacks. Reviving the old idea of reparations for slavery, black members of Congress propose a commission to study the impact of slavery and racial discrimination on living African Americans and make recommendations for appropriate remedies.[41] The farthest advance toward the prospective use of race in public policy is the interpretation of the Voting Rights Act of 1982 as requiring race-conscious electoral districting in order to produce election victories for minorities reasonably proportionate to their percentage of the relevant voting population.[42]

The use of benign racial classifications has drawbacks, however, not the least of which is the continuing perception that blacks are inferior to whites in their ability to compete. According to a black businessman testifying before the House Small Business Committee, "Successful minority businesses will never evolve until the public and private sectors stop viewing them as 'social causes' and start treating minorities in business as legitimate partners and competitors."[43] This reaction suggests that when blacks are selected on the ground that they will provide a role model for others of their race, a favorite justification of forward-looking affirmative action, the role they may illustrate is that of a patronized black whose qualifications are inferior to those of the best-qualified applicant.[44] A black writer confirms this perception in contending that to accept race norming, or to disparage tests of logical reasoning, is to accept the white supremacist idea that blacks lack the ability to reason objectively and methodically.[45]

If it was difficult to affirm the equality principle when there was general agreement about its meaning, as in the era of the civil rights movement, it is impossible to do so when there is fundamental disagreement about the meaning of equal protection. Yet this appears to be the situation American society finds itself in after two decades of controversy over affirmative action. Although at a high level of generality everyone involved in the debate affirms the principle of individual equality of opportunity, it is clear that this concept has taken on substantially different meanings for the critics and defenders of affirmative action. Critics of race-conscious measures define equal opportunity in procedural terms as equal treatment for individuals without regard to color. Underlying this approach is a theory of race relations that holds that blacks and whites are inherently or by nature the same and differ only in the superficial characteristic of race. Critics contend that enforcement of equal rights for individuals and the merit principle, as embodied in the Civil Rights Act of 1964, have been effective in removing barriers and enabling blacks and members of ethnic minority groups to enter the mainstream of society and achieve substantive equality.

Defenders of affirmative action, approaching civil rights policy under the disparate impact theory of discrimination, regard blacks as different from whites as a result of their historical and cultural conditioning under slavery and segregation. This circumstance is expressed in the assertion of Justice Thurgood Marshall in the *Bakke* decision that all blacks born in twentieth-century America have been victims of racial discrimination. Because blacks are different, tests and standards of merit cannot with fairness be used for blacks and whites equally. The merit principle is accordingly transformed or redefined as a function of social conditioning.

Affirmative action theory holds that since the life circumstances of individuals are fundamentally different because of the racial group into which they are born, what appears to be individual merit is really the result of social-historical conditions. Equality of opportunity in the traditional sense of equal treatment in procedures and rules of competition is therefore considered fraudulent or unrealistic. Unwilling or unable to reject the concept of equal opportunity, supporters of affirmative action insist that it can only be achieved by guaranteeing equal results for racial and ethnic groups. That is, proportional racial representation in the allocation of social goods, as the outcome of public policy, is taken as proof of the existence of equality of opportunity at the outset or throughout the social activity in question.[46] Equal opportunity is thus transformed into equality of achievement.

While the outcome of the affirmative action controversy remains unclear, from a historical point of view the most significant fact in the debate over civil rights is the acceptance by a substantial body of elite policymakers and opinion leaders of a collective group rights concept of equality. All blacks are held to be victims of discrimination and hence entitled to compensation. All whites are held to have benefited unjustly from the system of racial discrimination and are guilty.[47] These assumptions reflect primitive tribalistic concepts of collective and congenital blood guilt and blood virtue that historically have been the source of racial and ethnic violence.[48] They stand in fundamental opposition to the universal principle of individual natural rights that has been the moral and intellectual foundation of liberal democracy in the United States. The outcome of the affirmative action controversy will depend on, even as it reflects, the strength and vitality of the equal rights idea in the American political tradition.

PART THREE

Rights Remembered,
Revised, and Extended

A Ninth Amendment for Today's Constitution

Randy E. Barnett

On the first day of his Supreme Court confirmation testimony, Robert Bork described teaching a constitutional theory seminar at Yale law school in which he tried to justify what he called "a general right of freedom"[1] from the various provisions of the Constitution. He recalled that Alexander Bickel, with whom he taught the course, "fought me every step of the way; said it was not possible. At the end of six or seven years, I decided he was right."[2] The next day, Bork testified:

> I do not think you can use the Ninth Amendment unless you know something of what it means. For example, if you had an amendment that says Congress shall make no—and then there is an ink blot and you cannot read the rest of it and that is the only copy you have, I do not think the court can make up what might be under the ink blot if you cannot read it.[3]

In taking these two positions, former Judge Bork was, unfortunately, well within the mainstream of constitutional thought. For 200 years the Supreme Court of the United States has never seriously considered a general constitutional right to liberty; at the same time it has, with few exceptions, treated the Ninth Amendment as though it were an ink blot. This failure to find a "general right of freedom" in the Constitution is connected to a general inability to understand the Ninth Amendment's declaration that "The enumeration in the Constitution, of certain rights, shall not be construed to deny or disparage others retained by the people."

The bicentennial of the ratification of the Bill of Rights—including the Ninth Amendment—is an appropriate time to consider the important role that the Ninth Amendment can play in protecting our liberties under the Constitution. Indeed, this essay will explain how an interpretation ignoring the Ninth Amendment makes the Constitution look entirely different from one that takes the Ninth Amendment seriously. Any understanding of how the Ninth Amendment can work harmoniously with the rest of the Constitution, however, requires a brief examination of the origins of this intriguing and pregnant passage.

The Origins of the Ninth Amendment

The origins of the Ninth Amendment can be traced to the debate surrounding the ratification of the Constitution. The Anti-Federalists, who opposed ratification, concentrated much of their attack on the absence of a bill of rights. Although many Anti-Federalists were probably more concerned with defeating the Constitution than with obtaining a bill of rights, they repeatedly pressed this charge because it struck a responsive chord with the people. The Federalists who supported ratification, such as Alexander Hamilton and James Wilson, gave two answers to this complaint.

First, the Federalists said that a bill of rights was unnecessary. Because the federal government was one of enumerated and limited powers, it would have no power to violate the rights of the people. "Why, for instance," asked Hamilton, "should it be said that the liberty of the press shall not be restrained when no power is given by which restrictions may be imposed?"[4] Second, they argued that a bill of rights would be dangerous. Enumerating any rights might suggest to later interpreters of the Constitution that the rights not specified had been surrendered. An enumeration of rights could thereby lead to an unwarranted expansion of federal power and a corresponding erosion of individual rights.

Neither argument against a bill of rights carried the day. Anti-Federalists responded tellingly by turning these Federalist arguments against the Constitution itself. They noted that the Constitution already enumerated some of the rights of the people—such as the protections against *ex post facto* laws and bills of attainder in Article I, Section 9, and the right to a jury trial in criminal cases in Article III, Section 2. If an incomplete enumeration was as dangerous as the Federalists had so strenuously argued, then the severely incomplete list of rights already in the Constitution was dangerous indeed. No further harm could be done by expanding the list.

When it became clear that the Constitution was headed for defeat, the Federalists turned the political tide by promising to support a bill of rights after ratification. Several state conventions accompanied their ratification of the Constitution with lengthy lists of rights and other provisions they wanted added at the first opportunity. By this maneuver, the proponents of the Constitution deprived the Anti-Federalists of their principal argument against ratification.

However, getting Congress to consider a bill of rights turned out to be no easy feat. The congressional record shows Representative James Madison repeatedly urging the House to take up the matter only to be told by various congressmen that enacting the first tax bill was far more important than a bill of rights. Eventually, in a lengthy and revealing speech, Madison proposed a series of amendments to the Constitution. He explained that a bill of rights was needed, not only to quiet the fears and suspicions of those who still doubted the new Constitution and to induce those states who had not ratified the Constitution to do so, but also to better protect the liberties of the people. As Madison observed,

> If they are incorporated into the constitution, independent tribunals of justice will consider themselves in a peculiar manner the guardians of those rights; they will be an impenetrable bulwark against every assumption of power in the legislative or executive; they will naturally be led to resist every encroachment upon rights expressly stipulated for in the constitution by the declaration of rights.[5]

In his speech, Madison took up the Federalist argument he himself had made during the ratification debates that any effort to enumerate rights would be dangerous:

> It has been objected also against a bill of rights, that, by enumerating particular exceptions to the grant of power, it would disparage those rights which were not placed in the enumeration; and it might follow, by implication, that those rights which were not singled out were intended to be assigned into the hands of the General Government, and were consequently insecure. This is one of the most plausible arguments I have ever heard urged against the admission of a bill of rights into this system; but, I conceive, that it may be guarded against. I have attempted it, as gentlemen may see by turning to the last clause of the fourth resolution.[6]

The passage Madison referred to was the precursor of the Ninth Amendment, which read as follows:

> The exceptions here or elsewhere in the constitution, made in favor of particular rights, shall not be so construed as to diminish the just importance of other rights retained by the people, or as to enlarge the powers delegated by the constitution; but either as actual limitations of such powers, or as inserted merely for greater caution.[7]

Madison's proposals were referred to a Select Committee of the House, which was created to consider what amendments to the Constitution might be appropriate.

Although there is much that is controversial about the Ninth Amendment, the story of its enactment is not. In light of this history, the original meaning of the Ninth Amendment is clear: When forming a government the people retained rights in addition to those listed in the Bill of Rights. But while the meaning of the Ninth Amendment may be clear, its implications for constitutional adjudication are not. Are the unenumerated rights judicially enforceable as the enumerated rights have come to be? If so, what exactly are these rights? For most, the answer to the first of these questions hinges on our ability to answer the second. As Robert Bork observed at his confirmation hearing: "Senator, if anybody shows me historical evidence about what they meant, I would be delighted to do it. I just do not know."[8] Most commentators would agree with Bork that, if the uncertainty surrounding their content can be resolved, unenumerated rights should be enforceable. Otherwise, although the Congress and the president could be prevented from violating enumerated rights, both could violate the unenumerated rights with impunity. Surely this would disparage, if not entirely deny, the unenumerated rights.

There is little question that the rights retained by the people refer, at least in part, to what are called "natural rights"—that is, the rights people have independent of those they are granted by a government and by which the justice of governmental action is to be judged. Despite their many differences, the framers of the Constitution shared a common belief that although the people may delegate certain powers to their agents in government, they still retain their natural rights. This belief is illustrated by one provision of a recently discovered draft of a bill of rights written by Representative Roger Sherman, who served with Madison on the House Select Committee that drafted the Bill of Rights:

> The people have certain natural rights which are *retained* by them when they enter into Society. Such are the rights of Conscience in matters of religion; of acquiring property, and of pursuing happiness & Safety; of speaking, writing and publishing their Sentiments with decency and freedom; of peaceably assembling to consult their common good, and of applying to Government by petition or remonstrance for redress of grievances. Of these rights therefore they Shall not be deprived by the Government of the united States.[9]

This list, which was not intended to be exhaustive, includes some rights that were eventually enumerated in the Bill of Rights. Others, such as the rights to acquire property and pursue happiness and safety, were left unenumerated. The Ninth Amendment establishes that no one should conclude that, because some powers had been delegated to government and some rights had been singled out, the other unenumerated retained rights were, in Madison's words, "assigned into the hands of the general government, and were consequently insecure."

The problem with putting the Ninth Amendment into effect today is that many no longer appreciate the natural rights that the Constitution's framers took for granted. Yet if the framers had anticipated the modern philosophical skepticism about natural rights, they would never have settled for the few rights that were enumerated. Fortunately, there is a practical method of interpreting unenumerated rights that does not require us to agree about a list of unenumerated rights. Before considering this method, let me briefly describe what I have elsewhere called the "originalist method" of identifying unenumerated rights.[10]

The Originalist Method and Its Limits

We might begin, as Robert Bork suggested, by trying to discern those un-enumerated rights the framers had in mind by examining the written records of the period, including the numerous rights proposed by the rat-ification conventions and the theoretical writings of the framers. No ink blot prevents us from reading these materials. I have already mentioned the right to acquire property as one that the framers unquestionably be-lieved to be a natural and inalienable right that was retained by the people when forming a government. Freedom of conscience is another. Although a list of rights developed by using an originalist method of interpretation may be viewed as truncated—even from the framers' perspective—a trun-cated list is better than none.

The originalist method will hardly suffice, however. The framers be-lieved it was dangerous to enumerate any rights because the rights of the people are boundless. As James Wilson, a natural-rights theorist, ex-plained, "there are very few who understand the whole of these rights."[11] None of the classic political writers claim to provide "a complete enumer-ation of rights appertaining to the people as men and as citizens. . . . Enu-merate all the rights of men! I am sure, sirs, that no gentleman in the late Convention would have attempted such a thing."[12] This is the reason why Wilson and others thought any attempt to enumerate rights would be dan-gerous. "In all societies," Wilson observed,

> there are many powers and rights, which cannot be particularly enumerated. A bill of rights annexed to a constitution is an enumeration of the powers re-served. If we attempt an enumeration, everything that is not enumerated is presumed to be given. The consequence is, that an imperfect enumeration would throw all implied power into the scale of government; and the rights of the people would be rendered incomplete.[13]

It is important to understand exactly why rights cannot exhaustively be enumerated if we are to devise a way of protecting these retained rights without specifically enumerating each and every one. Rights are unenu-merable because rights define a private domain within which persons have a right to do as they wish, provided their conduct does not encroach upon the rightful domains of others. As long as their actions remain within this rightful domain, other persons—including the government—should not interfere. Because people have a right to do whatever they please within the boundaries defined by natural rights, this means that the rights re-tained by the people are *limited only by their imagination* and could never be completely specified or enumerated.

This open-ended conception of rights is illustrated by a fascinating exchange that occurred during the debate in the House over the wording of what eventually became the First Amendment proposed by the House Select Committee. At one juncture in the debate, Representative Theodore Sedgwick criticized the committee's inclusion of the right of assembly on the grounds that "it is a self-evident, unalienable right which the people possess; it is certainly a thing that never would be called into question; it is derogatory to the dignity of the House to descend to such minutiae."[14] Representative Egbert Benson replied to Sedgwick: "The committee who framed this report proceeded on the principle that these rights belonged to the people; they conceived them to be inherent; and all that they meant to provide against was their being infringed by the Government."[15] Sedgwick then responded that:

> if the committee were governed by that general principle, they might have gone into a very lengthy enumeration of rights; they might have declared that a man should have a right to wear his hat if he pleased; that he might get up when he pleased, and go to bed when he thought proper.[16]

Notice that Sedgwick was not denying that one had a right to wear one's hat or go to bed when one pleased. To the contrary, he equated these inherent rights with the right of assembly, which he characterized as "self-evident" and "unalienable." Indeed, Representative John Page's reply to Sedgwick made this explicit. "[L]et me observe to him," said Page,

> that such rights have been opposed, and a man has been obliged to pull off his hat when he appeared before the face of authority; people have also been prevented from assembling together on their lawful occasions, therefore it is well to guard against such stretches of authority, by inserting the privilege in the declaration of rights.[17]

Sedgwick's point was that the Constitution should not be cluttered with a potentially endless list of trifling rights that "would never be called in[to] question"[18] and were not "intended to be infringed."[19] Sedgwick's argument implicitly assumes that the "self-evident, unalienable," and inherent liberty rights retained by the people are unenumerable because the human imagination is limitless. It includes the right to wear a hat, to get up when one pleases and go to bed when one pleases, to scratch one's nose when it itches (and even when it doesn't), and to take a sip of Diet Coke when one is thirsty.

But this returns us to the most controversial aspect of the Ninth Amendment: How can such unenumerated rights find legal protection without empowering judges simply to make up whatever rights may appeal to them? Raoul Berger, for one, has charged that any effort to protect the unenumerated rights referred to in the Ninth Amendment would provide "a bottomless well in which the judiciary can dip for the formation of undreamed of 'rights' in their limitless discretion."[20] The answer to this concern lies in something like the "general right to liberty" that Robert Bork once searched for—only it is more accurate to call it a presumption of liberty.

The Presumption of Liberty

As long as they do not violate the rights of others (as defined by the common law of property, contract, and tort), persons are presumed to be "immune" from interference by government. This presumption means that citizens may challenge any governmental action that restricts their otherwise rightful conduct, and the burden is on the government to show that its action is within its proper powers or scope. At the national level, the government would bear the burden of showing that its acts were both "necessary and proper" to accomplish an enumerated function, rather than, as now, forcing the citizen to prove why it is he or she should be left alone. At the state level, the burden would fall upon state government to show that legislation infringing the liberty of its citizens was a necessary exercise of its "police power," that is, the state's power to protect the rights of its citizens.

Any society such as ours that purports to be based on a theory of limited government already assumes that legislation must be a proper exercise of government power. The presumption of liberty simply requires that when legislation or executive actions encroach upon the liberties of the people, they may be challenged on the grounds that they lack the requisite justification. And a neutral magistrate must decide the dispute. As Madison observed in *The Federalist*, Number 10:

> No man is allowed to be the judge in his own cause, because his interest would certainly bias his judgment, and, not improbably, corrupt his integrity. With equal, nay, with greater reason, a body of men are unfit to be both judges and parties at the same time; yet what are many of the most important acts of legislation but so many judicial determinations, not indeed concerning the rights of single persons, but concerning the rights of large bodies of citizens? And what are the different classes of legislators but advocates and parties to the causes which they determine? . . . Justice ought to hold the balance between them.[21]

When legislation encroaches upon the liberties of the people, only review by an impartial judiciary can ensure that the rights of citizens are protected and that justice holds the balance between the legislature or executive and the people.

Lest anyone think this point is obvious, let me hasten to note that today the presumption used by the Supreme Court is precisely the reverse. According to what the Court calls the "presumption of constitutionality," leg-

islation will be upheld if any "rational basis" for its passage can be imagined, unless it violates a "fundamental" right—and liberty has not been
deemed by the Court to be a fundamental right. As the Court stated in
United States v. Carolene Products Co. (1938): "There may be narrower scope
for operation of the presumption of constitutionality when legislation appears on its face to be within a specific prohibition of the Constitution, such
as those of the first ten amendments, which are deemed equally specific
when held to be embraced within the Fourteenth."[22] In other words, the
enumerated rights may narrow the presumption of constitutionality, but
one of the unenumerated rights retained by the people will have no such
power-limiting effect.

While the presumption of liberty is not the only implication of the Ninth
Amendment, it provides a practical and powerful method of protecting unenumerated rights. As lawyers well know, the outcome of legal disputes is
often determined by the burden of proof. For example, the First Amendment has been held to impose a serious burden on the government to justify any of its actions that restrict the natural right of free speech. In count-
less cases, this "presumption of free speech" has effectively protected this
retained but enumerated right. The Ninth Amendment simply extends the
same protective presumption to all other exercises of liberty.

Although originally the Ninth Amendment, like the rest of the Bill of
Rights, was most likely intended by the framers to be enforced only against
the federal government, this was not because it was thought that the people had surrendered all their rights to state governments—a suggestion be-
lied by the swift incorporation into most state constitutions of provisions
identical to the Ninth Amendment. Indeed many rights—such as the right
of conscience or the right to acquire property—were thought to be unalienable, which means that the people could not surrender them to any government even if they wanted to. Rather, the Congress and the federal
courts originally lacked jurisdiction to protect the retained "privileges or
immunities" of citizens from abuses by their states. As we all know, this
arrangement was fundamentally changed by the enactment of the Fourteenth Amendment after the Civil War. Today, if a state government infringes upon a right the people retained against their respective states,
there is no jurisdictional barrier preventing federal protection of this right.

Applying the Presumption of Liberty Today

To see how a presumption of liberty might operate today, consider Congress's power under Article I, Section 8, to "establish post offices." Having
exercised this establishment power, Congress is free under the necessary
and proper clause to regulate the operation of its post offices in any manner
it sees fit. However, what happens when Congress, allegedly pursuant to
its postal powers, goes beyond its power to administer its own offices and

claims the further power to establish a postal monopoly, as it has? According to the now prevailing presumption of constitutionality, Congress would be free to establish a monopoly unless either potential competitors or consumers of postal services could prove that this claimed government power violates a fundamental right. For example, competitors might allege a fundamental right to carry first-class mail, while recipients of mail could claim they had a fundamental right to send first-class mail by any means they chose. Because these rights sound trivial rather than fundamental they are easy to disparage—almost as easy to disparage as the trifling right to wear a hat or go to bed when one pleases. Consequently, courts have not barred the Congress from establishing its monopoly or even inquired very seriously as to whether such laws are truly necessary or proper. With judges lacking a proper view of the Ninth Amendment, today the outcome of such a lawsuit would be virtually predetermined: the government wins and the citizen loses.

A presumption of liberty, however, would shift the burden of proof from the citizen to the government. Instead of imposing the burden on the citizen to establish the violation of a "fundamental" right, a burden would be imposed on the government, in this case upon Congress, to show a compelling reason why it is both necessary and proper to grant its own post office a legal monopoly. In enacting the Constitution, the people retained their unenumerated right to establish their own private post offices if they so chose. They neither expressly nor implicitly surrendered this right up to the general government. The Ninth Amendment serves as an ever-present reminder that the mere fact that such a right is left out of the Bill of Rights ought not to suggest otherwise.

In a speech before the second House of Representatives, the author of the Ninth Amendment, James Madison, used it in a strikingly similar fashion to object to the pending bill to establish a single national bank on the grounds that the bill was unconstitutional. His usage also helps clarify the relationship between the Ninth Amendment's protection of the rights retained by the people and the Tenth Amendment's injunction that "The powers not delegated to the United States by the Constitution, nor prohibited by it to the States, are reserved to the States respectively, or to the people."

Madison examined the Constitution at length to see if the power to create such a bank could be found among any of those delegated to the government and he concluded that "it is not possible to discover in [the Constitution] the power to incorporate a Bank."[23] He then considered whether the proposed bank might be justified under the necessary and proper clause[24] as a means of executing the borrowing power.[25] "Whatever meaning this clause may have," Madison began,

> none can be admitted, that would give unlimited discretion to Congress. Its meaning must, according to the natural and obvious force of the terms and

the context, be limited to means necessary to the end, and incident to the nature of the specified powers.[26]

Madison's argument here reflects one of the reasons he had offered for adopting a bill of rights during his speech the year before to the first House of Representatives in which he proposed amendments to the Constitution:

> It is true, the powers of the General Government are circumscribed, they are directed to particular objects; but even if Government keeps within those limits, it has certain discretionary powers with respect to the means, which may admit of abuse to a certain extent, . . . because in the constitution of the United States, there is a clause granting to Congress the power to make all laws which shall be necessary and proper for carrying into execution the powers vested in the Government of the United States, or in any department thereof.[27]

Madison contended that a bill of rights was one way to police abuses of this lawmaking discretion.

In evaluating whether the necessary and proper clause justifies the claimed power to create a national bank, Madison contrasted the requirement of necessity with that of mere convenience or expediency. "But the proposed bank," he said,

> could not even be called necessary to the Government; at most it could be but convenient. Its uses to the Government could be supplied by keeping the taxes a little in advance; by loans from individuals; by the other Banks, over which the Government would have equal Command; nay greater, as it might grant or refuse to these the privilege (a free and irrevocable gift to the proposed Bank) of using their notes in the Federal revenues.[28]

Notice that Madison was not simply making what would now be called a "policy" choice. Earlier in his address to the House, Madison did address the policy issues raised by the proposal when he "began with a general review of the advantages and disadvantages of Banks."[29] However, "[i]n making these remarks on the merits of the bill, he had reserved to himself the right to deny the authority of Congress to pass it."[30] Rather, Madison is making the constitutional argument that these other means of accomplishing an enumerated object or end are superior precisely because they do not entail the violation of the rights retained by the people and are therefore to be preferred in principle. In particular, these measures do not involve the grant of a monopoly, "which," in Madison's words, "affects the equal rights of every citizen."[31]

In other words, there is a difference in principle between these alternative means; just as there is a difference in principle, not merely policy, between drafting citizens, and paying volunteers as the means of exercising the Congressional power "to raise and support Armies."[32] Although Article I, Section 8, delegates this power to Congress, when it chooses a means of accomplishing this end that intrudes upon the liberties of the people, as a military draft does, then it must justify this rights infringement by showing that its acts are genuinely necessary and proper. The government must show that it cannot accomplish its constitutionally delegated end by means that do not trespass upon the rights retained by the people.

Finally, in his bank speech Madison also questioned the proposed exercise of the necessary and proper clause on the grounds that the power claimed was highly remote from any enumerated power. "Mark the reasoning on which the validity of the bill depends," he observes:

> To borrow money is made the end, and the accumulation of capitals implied as the means. The accumulation of capitals is then the end, and a Bank implied as the means. The Bank is then the end, and a charter of incorporation, a monopoly, capital punishments, &c. implied as the means.
>
> If implications, thus remote and thus multiplied, can be linked together, a chain may be formed that will reach every object of legislation, every object within the whole compass of political economy.
>
> The *latitude of interpretation* required by the bill is condemned by the rule furnished by the Constitution itself.[33]

As authority for this "rule" of interpretation, Madison cited the Ninth Amendment:

> The explanatory amendments proposed by Congress themselves, at least, would be good authority with them; all these renunciations of power proceeded on a rule of construction, excluding the latitude now contended for. . . . He read several of the articles proposed, remarking particularly of the 11th [the Ninth Amendment] and 12th [the Tenth Amendment], the former, as guarding against a latitude of interpretation; the latter, as excluding every source of power not within the Constitution itself.[34]

Thus, Madison viewed the Ninth and Tenth Amendments as playing distinct roles. He viewed the Tenth Amendment ("The powers not delegated to the United States by the Constitution, nor prohibited by it to the States, are reserved to the States respectively, or to the people") as authority for the rule that Congress could only exercise a delegated power. For example, in the illustrations I have used, Congress could not establish a post office or raise and support armies without a delegation of power to pursue these ends. In contrast, Madison viewed the Ninth Amendment as providing authority for a rule against the loose construction of these powers—especially the necessary and proper clause—when legislation affects the rights retained by the people. As Madison concluded in his bank speech: "In fine, if the power were in the Constitution, the immediate exercise of it cannot be essential; if not there, the exercise of it involves the guilt of usurpation."[35]

In my examples, because a postal monopoly and a military draft infringe upon the rightful liberties of the people, these are suspect means for pursuing delegated ends. Those claiming that legislation restricting the rightful liberties of the people falls under a delegated power have the burden of showing that it is a genuinely necessary and proper exercise of such a power. As I have argued elsewhere, constitutional right—including unenumerated rights—operate both as "means constraints" and as "ends constraints."[36]

Once the Ninth Amendment is viewed as establishing a presumption of liberty, thereby placing a burden of justification on the government, every action of government that infringes upon the rightful liberties of the people can be called into question. Is it really necessary that persons—particularly poor persons—obtain licenses requiring extensive testing in such subjects as chemistry before they may work as beauticians? Is it really necessary that government limit the number of taxicabs it licenses so that the price of taxicab medallions in some cities ranges from $10,000 to $20,000 or even higher? Or are all these and other similar measures really ways by which a privileged few seek to eliminate lower-priced competition? Is it really necessary to criminalize the sale and use of intoxicating substances, or is a "drug-free" society better achieved in ways that do not infringe upon the liberties of the people—perhaps by the sort of education and social pressure that is currently being used so effectively to combat the use of nicotine in cigarettes and the abuse of alcohol. Even the current government restrictions that limit the practice of law to those who have attended three years of law school would not be beyond challenge and scrutiny.

None of these or any other Ninth Amendment claim can be decided in the abstract—by which I mean without taking into account the specifics of particular legislation and the factual context in which it is applied. What the Ninth Amendment requires, however, is that such claims as these be evaluated when liberty-restricting legislation is challenged by a citizen. Adopting the presumption of liberty would make this requirement effective.

This is not to say that the government would never be able to meet its burden. I fully expect that if a presumption of liberty is established, the courts would find that government has met its burden far more often than they should. We must never forget that the Supreme Court once upheld the government's power to imprison American citizens of Japanese descent in prison camps because of the threat to national security these citizens allegedly posed.[37] Judicial review is not a panacea for protecting liberty.

Nor does the presumption of liberty establish a license to do whatever one wishes. Liberal political theorist John Locke put the matter as follows:

> But though this be a State of Liberty, yet it is not a State of License. . . . The State of Nature has a Law of Nature to govern it, which obliges everyone: And Reason, which is that Law, teaches all Mankind, who will but consult it,

that being all equal and independent, no one ought to harm another in his Life, Health, Liberty, or Possessions.[38]

As I mentioned earlier, justice, which is to say rights, defines the boundaries within which one may do as one wishes. According to this conception of liberty, one cannot permissibly infringe upon the rightful domains of others. According to Locke, in the state of nature, "all Men may be restrained from invading other's Rights, and from doing hurt to one another."[39] The common law of property, contracts, and torts has traditionally defined the extent and nature of these boundaries. Tortious conduct is not a "rightful" exercise of one's liberty; one has no constitutional right to commit trespass upon the land of another. Provided that one is acting rightfully in this sense, however, a presumption of liberty would require government to justify any interference with such conduct.

Finally, a presumption of liberty does not authorize judges to usurp either legislative or executive functions. Protecting the rights of individuals and associations to act or refrain from acting in ways that do not violate the common-law rights of others neither empowers judges to create new "positive rights" nor authorizes them to enact taxes to pay for such rights. Judges may only strike down offending legislation—and judicial negation is not legislation. Assuming they have the political will, the other branches of government have more than enough power to defend themselves from judicial encroachment.

Conclusion

What is the future of the Ninth Amendment? In law, as in most areas of life, betting that the future is going to be pretty much like the past is usually the safest wager. If this turns out to be true, then the Ninth Amendment, which has been so tragically neglected by the Supreme Court over the past two centuries, is doomed to remain in a state of desuetude. But while betting against change may be the most conservative gamble, it is often a losing one. The past twenty years have witnessed a trend in the direction of a revived Ninth Amendment. In particular, a renewed interest in the views of the framers of the Constitution and of the Civil War amendments has caused those who favor an expansive judicial protection of fundamental rights to focus attention on the original intent of the Ninth Amendment. Moreover, the framers' concept of natural rights is no longer in dispute. If the Senate confirmation hearings of Judge Robert Bork to the Supreme Court was a watershed development in the legitimation of the Ninth Amendment, the confirmation hearings of Justice Clarence Thomas may prove to have a similar effect on the legitimacy of natural rights.

Although with the addition of Justices Scalia, Kennedy, Souter, and Thomas, conservatives appear now to be in firm control of the Supreme Court, the type of judicial conservatism that will emerge in the third century of the Bill of Rights is very much in doubt. Will it be a majoritarian conservatism of judicial deference to majority will as expressed in legislation? Or will it be a more libertarian conservatism that views the courts as neutral magistrates empowered to protect the individual from the state? Which of these conservative strains eventually prevails will depend, perhaps in principal part, upon whether a majority of the Court can be persuaded to take to heart James Madison's Ninth Amendment and its pivotal role in constitutional interpretation. However, it will also depend upon proponents of the Ninth Amendment to take a more principled position toward so-called fundamental liberties.

The liberties each person holds fundamental are imperiled when advocates of some liberties they hold dear are more willing to deprecate the liberties thought fundamental by others. For example, many if not most of those favoring a fundamental right of privacy that includes a woman's "right to choose" to terminate a pregnancy offer no support to and indeed would actively oppose those who favor a fundamental "right to choose" to engage in a lawful occupation—such as driving a taxicab—free from protectionist economic regulations. And few seem at all concerned with the fundamental "right to choose" whether or not to alter one's mental state by means of substances such as alcohol, nicotine, peyote, or heroin. According to this discriminatory methodology, if some choices are deemed fundamental, other rights-respecting choices are vilified and ridiculed.

By picking and choosing among all the unenumerated liberties of the people to determine which choices are fundamental and which are not, those who would limit judicial protection to those liberties deemed fundamental are putting courts in the difficult position of establishing a hierarchy of liberties. This contributes to the long-standing fear that any revival of the Ninth Amendment would place Courts in the role of a "super-legislature" usurping the functions of other branches. When interpreted as justifying a presumption of liberty, however, I think this fear of the Ninth Amendment is unfounded precisely because such a presumption provides a principled method of reaching a decision.

In sum, adopting the presumption of liberty would enable us finally to acknowledge the Ninth Amendment's unique constitutional function by resisting legislative or executive usurpation of the unenumerated rights "retained by the people" while, at the same time, avoiding unfettered judicial discretion. The presumption of liberty would permit us finally to remove the ink blot from the Ninth Amendment. I can think of no better way to celebrate its two hundredth birthday.

Of Floors and Ceilings
The New Federalism and State Bills of Rights

Kermit L. Hall

A worldwide renaissance in federalism and individual rights has gathered momentum during the past twenty years. Constitutional reformers in Canada, India, Nigeria, Switzerland, Australia, and, most recently, Eastern Europe and the Soviet Union have demanded increased autonomy for the major subunits (the states and provinces) of their national governments as a way of promoting greater individual liberty.[1] At least as measured by constitutional creation and amendment, judicial decisions, scholarly publications, and official reports, these advocates of reform have concluded that in order for liberty to be genuinely secure the states as well as the nation must guard it. These recent developments, of course, draw strength from a classical tradition of constitutionalism: local responsibility for liberty offers the best check on the tyranny of a centralized government.

Federalism Old and New

The American phase of this reform movement has been labeled the "New Federalism" or simply the state-law revolution. The "old" federalism began in the era of the New Deal, when Franklin D. Roosevelt's appointees to the Supreme Court relied on the due process clause of the Fourteenth Amendment to nationalize selected portions of the Bill of Rights. This process reached a crescendo during the chief justiceship of Earl Warren (1953–1969), when the Supreme Court expansively interpreted federal authority with regard to racial equality, freedom of speech, press, and conscience, and the rights of the accused. By the 1970s, however, the state-law revolution was under way, as judges of the highest state appellate courts invoked their own constitutions and bills of rights to protect individual rights. In the architecture of the New Federalism, the Supreme Court, interpreting the Bill of Rights, sets the minimum floor for rights, while state supreme courts, interpreting their state's bills of rights, fix the ceiling.[2]

The "New Federalism" has had significant impact and broad support. Ronald K. L. Collins, a leading authority on state constitutional law, has counted more than 600 opinions by the highest courts of the states that have gone "beyond the federal minimum standards on individual rights issues" since 1970.[3] Former Supreme Court Justice William J. Brennan, Jr., and Judge Hans Linde of the Oregon Supreme Court have done more than any other jurisprudential figures to spark this reassertion of state-based constitutional rights.[4] As early as 1961, Justice Brennan urged state supreme courts to apply their bills and declarations of rights in ways that go "beyond that required of the national government by the corresponding federal guarantee."[5] In 1977 Justice Brennan went even further by warning that "our liberties cannot survive if the states betray the trust the Court has put in them."[6] California Supreme Court Justice Stanley Mosk, another pioneer in the state-law revolution, has ironically concluded that the new enthusiasm for state bills of rights is justified since, unlike the era of George Wallace, "[t]oday states' rights are associated with increased, not lessened individual guarantees."[7] Even the press has seized on the "New Federalism," with the *New York Times* pronouncing on its front page that "On Rights, New York Looks to State, Not U. S. Law."[8]

The Politics of the State-Law Revolution

Since the 1960s the pulse of the "New Federalism" has quickened appreciably with both liberals and conservatives seeking to arrest the further centralization of authority in the nation's capital. Republican Presidents Richard M. Nixon, Ronald Reagan, and George Bush, for example, have insisted that the best way to curb the national government generally and the Supreme Court specifically is to return power—and responsibilities—to the states, especially state legislatures. This vision of the state-law revolution stresses the popular and majoritarian aspects of state constitutions instead of their value as charters of fundamental law and minority rights. It stems from the historic belief that popular consent and control form the basis of state constitutions. That tradition is sufficiently strong in state government today that most appellate judges are elected by one means or another and hold limited terms of office; most state constitutions are susceptible to amendment by initiative; and most legislatures are the engines of state government. The stress laid on popular consent and control also affirms the historic role of state constitutions in filling the gaps in the "incomplete" federal Constitution.[9] The federal document cannot be understood or activated without reference to state constitutions. Through their police powers, state legislatures have defined and implemented many provisions of the U. S. Constitution while structuring the potentially vast powers reserved to them and to the people by that organic law.

Former Chief Justice Warren Burger, an appointee of President Nixon, added judicial support to this position by insisting that the tension in state constitutions between popular will and fundamental law should be resolved in favor of the former. Burger agreed that greater authority should be returned to the states but he also worried that state court judges might actually interpret their respective state constitutions in ways that would "require *more* than the Federal Constitution."[10] Burger insisted that the states, especially when the rights of criminal defendants were involved, should conform their bills of rights with federal constitutional requirements through the amending process rather than relying on what he denounced as judicial lawmaking. The specter of judicially expanded state-based constitutional freedoms raised Burger's hackles because it threatened popular consent and control as the touchstones of state government.

At the same time, political liberals and advocates of civil liberties, such as Justice Brennan, have deemphasized the tradition of popular consent and control and stressed instead the importance of state constitutions as fundamental law. When properly interpreted by state high court judges, Brennan and others argue, state bills of rights promise not only to check the centralizing tendencies of the national government but to protect minority rights by limiting state legislative discretion. Political liberals, who once praised the virtues of centralized authority and federal judicial review of state actions, have pragmatically adapted their views to suit the new political realities. After all, the liberal discovery of state courts and state bills of rights coincided with the ideological transformation wrought by Presidents Nixon, Reagan, and Bush in the membership of the U.S. Supreme Court. More than their counterparts during the heyday of the Warren Court, the new Republican appointees to the high bench have displayed considerable sympathy for state legislative initiatives. Confronted with a Supreme Court unwilling to sustain the due process revolution, Brennan and others have turned to state courts and state constitutions. Viewed from this angle, the "New Federalism" promises through state judicial review to empower groups otherwise neglected by the Burger and Rehnquist Courts.

Whatever one's political views, this new attention to state constitution law is welcome, if for no other reason than it has been for so long neglected. The story of our *federal* constitutional history has been explained from the top down rather than the bottom up, a perspective encouraged by the stability of the national government and the difficulty of generalizing about constitutional developments in fifty different states. The United States, after all, has had only one constitutional convention (in Philadelphia in 1787); the states have had more than 230 separate conventions. Since the beginning of the republic there has never been a three-year period in which at least one state constitutional convention has not met. The fifty states have operated under no fewer than 146 different constitutions, with most states having had two or more. Through 1988 more than 8,000 amendments have been proposed and more than 5,000 of these have actually been added to the organic laws of the states.

State Bills of Right, the Supreme Court, and Nineteenth-Century Federalism

In one sense, the state-law revolution is no revolution at all, since from the beginning of the nation state bills of rights have figured prominently in the history of liberty. Even as they wrote a constitution designed to strengthen the central government, most of the delegates to the Philadelphia Convention in 1787 turned to state constitutions and bills of rights for models. The Massachusetts Constitution of 1780 is the world's oldest written democratic constitution still in force. Vermont drafted a written declaration of rights fourteen years before it was admitted to the Union in 1791. The drafters of the federal Bill of Rights, moreover, borrowed extensively from their state experiences, which in turn derived from the strong conventual tradition in the colonies. That tradition included the Mayflower Compact of 1620, the charters of the original colonies, and later town covenants of the early American frontier. All of the rights eventually recognized in the federal Bill of Rights had previously been spelled out in one or more of these early documents. The legacy of rights runs deep in the states.

State bills of rights retained their importance throughout the nineteenth century despite the presence of the first ten amendments in the new federal Constitution. The vitality of state-based rights was due, at least in part, to the frailty of the federal government, described by Alexander Hamilton as "at a distance and out of sight."[11] During the Philadelphia Convention, for example, Oliver Ellsworth, a future chief justice of the Supreme Court, expressed the views of most of his contemporaries when he concluded that it was from state governments "alone [that] he could derive the greatest happiness he expects in this life" and to state constitutions that he expected to turn "for the preservation of his rights."[12] Roger Sherman, of Connecticut, argued that the new Constitution did no harm to the state documents; if anything, it gave them greater currency. He insisted that "The State Declarations of Rights are not replead by this Constitution; and being in force are sufficient."[13]

The members of the First Congress in 1789–90 reinforced this commitment to state bills of rights during the debate over the federal Bill of Rights. Given the opportunity to do otherwise, they chose to apply the first ten amendments only against the federal government, not the states. James Madison, the architect of both the Constitution and the Bill of Rights, believed so strongly that popularly based state constitutions would be inadequate to protect minority rights that he urged that most of the federal Bill of Rights should apply against the states as well as the national government. Accordingly, his proposed Bill of Rights provided that "No State shall infringe the right of trial by Jury in criminal cases, nor the right of conscience, nor the freedom of speech or of the press."[14]

The Senate rejected Madison's wording, in part because the senators were jealous for the prerogatives of their states. This action, however, also expressed a tradition of constitutional government that equated liberty with popular consent and control and individual happiness with a close relationship between the people and their government. Bills of rights, in this regard, were more important as means of protecting majorities against abuse by government than protecting minorities from the excesses of popular majorities. Most senators either did not understand or rejected as unfounded Madison's concern with majority tyranny.[15]

Throughout the nineteenth century the Supreme Court applied the Bill of Rights only against the national government, even though a handful of radical lawyers and judges argued that it was intended to limit the states as well. Chief Justice John Marshall seemingly erased any doubts with his opinion in *Barron v. Baltimore* (1833). That case raised the question of whether John Barron might recover damages under the takings clause of the Fifth Amendment when improvements made by the city of Baltimore rendered a wharf he owned unusable. Marshall rebuffed Barron's claim and directed him to seek relief based on the Maryland constitution.

Marshall's opinion was nonetheless controversial in some quarters. On one level, of course, it confirmed the wishes of the framers by preserving the state-centered scheme of protecting rights. In doing so, however, the opinion also raised portentous consequences about the disposition of another form of property, slavery—the abolition of it in the South, the control of it in the new territories, and the ability of the Northern states, under their own constitutional authority, to free fugitive slaves from their masters. Antislavery advocates, such as Lysander Spooner of Boston, mocked the notion that state bills of right, subject as they were to popular consent and control, could ever provide adequate grounds to end the peculiar institution or keep fugitive slaves from their masters' clutches. Instead, Spooner pleaded for the federal judiciary to apply the Bill of Rights directly against the states.

The pro-slavery forces frustrated this line of development because of the control they exercised over the federal courts. Chief Justice Roger B. Taney's opinions in *Dred Scott v. Sanford* (1857) and *Ableman v. Booth* (1859) drove home this political truth. His opinion in *Dred Scott* affirmed the property rights of masters in their slaves and held that Congress could do nothing that would disturb those rights. In effect, Taney had nationalized the Fifth Amendment provision against the taking of property, in this instance slave property.

Taney's opinion in *Booth* was important because it called into question the concept of state-based rights that Marshall had seemingly approved in

Barron. Sherman Booth, a Wisconsin abolitionist editor, was charged with violating the Fugitive Slave Act of 1850 by aiding a runaway Negro. While technically held by federal authorities, Booth was actually placed in a local jail. From there he secured a writ of *habeas corpus* under Wisconsin law from a state judge who also declared the federal fugitive slave act unconstitutional. The Wisconsin Supreme Court affirmed both actions only to have Taney and his brethren overturn its decision. The Chief Justice not only ridiculed the idea that state courts could declare a federal law unconstitutional, but he dismissed as well the notion that state courts, where fugitive slaves were involved, were free to interpret their constitutions without regard to the federal document.

As Paul Finkelman has observed, taken together these decisions meant that as a matter of both federal *and* state constitutional law, slavery, fugitive slaves, and those persons who aided them were beyond the pale of both state and federal bills of rights. Masters, on the other hand, could claim an apparently nationalized protection for their property free from state constitutional control.[16]

The Post–Civil War Revolution in Federalism and the Doctrine of Adequate and Independent State Grounds

The adoption of the Fourteenth Amendment in 1868 raised anew the question supposedly answered in *Barron* about whether the Bill of Rights applied against the states. Along with it came the equally tangled problem of when state courts alone could rely on their own bills of rights to determine the constitutionality of executive and legislative acts.

The Fourteenth Amendment granted significant new authority to the national government to prevent the states from interfering with due process of law, equal protection of the law, and privileges and immunities. The Supreme Court initially held that the state action provision of the amendment did not incorporate (that is, bring under the scope of the amendment) the various guarantees of the Bill of Rights. By the 1890s, however, the states were again turning to their own police powers to deal with a major policy issue, in this instance the social and economic costs associated with massive industrialization. Once again the justices rebuked state legislative action. In the landmark case of *Chicago, Burlington & Quincy Railroad v. Chicago* (1897), the justices, as the earlier Taney court had done with fugitive slavery, proscribed state legislative authority. Brushing aside Marshall's opinion in *Barron*, they held that the due process clause of the Fourteenth Amendment applied to a state's taking of private property. Over the course of the next seventy-five years the justices selectively incorporated most of the Bill of Rights against the states.

The Fourteenth Amendment and the subsequent adoption of the doctrine of selective incorporation threatened the traditional scheme of federalism in which the states had primary responsibility for protecting rights. The justices addressed this matter for the first time in *Murdock v. Memphis* (1874). They held that short of explicit congressional authorization, the Court would not overturn state decisions reached on separate state grounds, as long as those decisions did not conflict with the federal Constitution. The Court in *Murdock* developed the doctrine of "adequate and independent state grounds." Under it a state court's interpretation of a state law or a state constitution is adequate if this interpretation is sufficient to support the judgment and does not violate the federal Constitution. It is independent if the result is reached on the basis of state interpretation that is not dependent on federal constitutional law. In essence, the Court in *Murdock* gave to state judges the power to expand liberties within their jurisdiction well beyond the standards required by the United States Supreme Court under the federal Constitution and federal laws. These same state judges were prohibited under *Murdock* from restricting rights to such a degree that doing so would violate federally protected rights.

Demand and Response in Nineteenth-Century State Constitutions

Nineteenth-century state bills of rights developed independently of the Supreme Court, responding as they did to social, economic, and political demands. Any generalization about their development is subject to alteration because of the great variety of state experience. Still, patterns do emerge, and those patterns cast the state-law revolution in a somewhat more sober light than do its more enthusiastic proponents.

Popular consent and control tended to override principles of fundamental law in nineteenth-century state constitutions. Throughout the century, these documents and their accompanying bills of rights grew longer and longer, filled with seemingly endless details that diminished their value as organic, fundamental laws. With each passing decade they came increasingly to resemble super-legislation. For example, the decision by Wyoming constitution-makers in 1890 to proscribe certain school textbooks affirmed that whoever controlled the course of constitutional change could also mold constitutionally mandated rights. Politicians frustrated by the regular legislative process turned to constitutional conventions and the amending process as ways of securing otherwise unattainable social and economic objectives. As the girth of state constitutions swelled, they became more like codes of law than fundamental frames of government, a process that diluted the substantive content of bills of rights by adding more and more provisions while diminishing their rhetorical power by promising more than they could deliver.

The comparative brevity of the federal Constitution has been a source of its strength. It is composed of approximately 7,300 words; only the Vermont constitution among the states is today shorter at an estimated 6,600 words. In 1776 the average length of state constitutions was 7,150 words; by 1900 it had ballooned to approximately 29,000 words, somewhat greater than the 27,000-word average today. Nineteenth-century state constitutions became remarkably pliable documents of modest age that increasingly paled before the federal Constitution as stable representations of fundamental principles and timeless structures designed to distribute and protect rights fairly.

The emphasis on popular consent and control also eroded the independence of nineteenth-century state supreme courts, the major interpreters of state constitutions. The justices of the federal Supreme Court were appointed for good behavior; their independence enabled them to found the institution of judicial review and promote the idea that they alone could conclusively interpret the federal Bill of Rights. The state appellate judiciary developed in exactly the other way. Beginning in the 1840s, state constitutional reformers succeeded in making most of the highest judgeships elective offices filled for limited terms rather than appointive positions held during good behavior. Local majorities were able to shape the meaning of state bills of rights through pressure brought at the ballot box on elected judges as well as through constitutional conventions and the amending process.

The result was variety in the rights enumerated in the state documents, often differing interpretations of the scope of those rights from state to state, and even instances when rights that were enumerated, such as freedom of speech and press, were not enforced, or even litigated. Not until 1931, in *Near v. Minnesota*, did the United States Supreme Court incorporate the First Amendment through the due process clause of the Fourteenth Amendment. Until then constitutional protection of speech fell exclusively under state bills of rights. Even though every state constitution enumerated it as a right, there are only a handful of reported cases dealing with freedom of speech during the entire century.[17] The one right that we consider the most fundamental to democratic self-governance today was barely enforced as a matter of nineteenth-century state constitutional law. In the pre-Civil War era, moreover, several state courts (both North and South) interpreted the speech and press clauses of their constitutions in ways that muzzled abolitionist and antislavery advocates.

The status of religious freedom during the nineteenth century offers another example of the way in which state bills of right often yielded before majority social pressures. As G. Alan Tarr has explained, the new American states did not so much guarantee freedom of religion as they regularized the relationship between church and state within their borders.[18] While state-established churches persisted, early constitution-makers framed bills of rights that repudiated the colonial practices of government, either infringing worship by faiths other than the established church or lending support to collect taxes for that church. As Tarr reminds us, the liberal Pennsylvania Constitution of 1776 set the standard for the nineteenth century, although some states adopted it sooner than others. The Pennsylvania document guaranteed that "all men have a natural and indefeasible right of worship Almighty Good according to the dictates of their own conscience; that no man can of right be compelled to attend, erect, or support any place of worship, or to maintain any ministry, against his consent."[19]

Nineteenth-century constitution-makers also recognized the existence of God and the dependence of the state on God's favor. The New Jersey Constitution of 1844, for example, attributed both the civil and religious liberty of the state directly to the guiding hand of God. This provision, however, offered scant protection to nonbelievers, which is exactly what its framers intended. The prevailing assumption was that government protected religion generally and Protestant Christianity in particular. Religion clauses in state constitutions reinforced the impact of religion on society and government while simultaneously blunting the intrusion by government into the religious sphere. Prevailing interpretations of state bills of rights, therefore, permitted government officials to prosecute individual blasphemers of the Protestant church and store merchants who insisted on doing business on Sunday.

By the 1850s the ethnic and religious upheavals generated by increasing foreign immigration inspired state constitution-makers to reformulate bill of rights provisions dealing with religion. The leaders of the emerging Roman Catholic church in New York City and Boston, for example, insisted that public education indoctrinated students in the Protestant ethic to the exclusion of other religious beliefs. Even more important, they complained that public revenues should not be used exclusively for schools that preached Protestant learning. The Protestant majorities in state constitutional conventions and legislatures did not respond to these demands by redistributing funds; instead, they reformulated the religion and education provisions of their constitutions to take account of the newcomers while maintaining Protestant hegemony. In almost every instance, eastern states adopted constitutional language that made it a matter of right that public funds could not be diverted for denominational purposes and prohibited schools that received those funds from carrying out any religious practices.

Where the impact of immigration was less direct, traditional practices continued. The constitution of post–Civil War Mississippi, for example, retained a requirement for Bible reading in schools. Constitution-makers in other Southern states embraced language that either permitted or required this practice. The decision to include such an item in their bills of rights suggests that without them the practices would probably have been prohibited.

Settlers in the trans-Mississippi West carried much of their constitutional baggage with them, including attitudes toward religious freedom. Initially, they simply mimicked their experiences from back East. The Oregon Constitution of 1859, for example, closely paralleled its Indiana counterpart, including in almost exact form the latter's approach to religious freedom. As the West matured, however, forces of popular consent and control began to leave their own often unique imprint on state bills of rights. The Washington Constitution of 1889 affirmed the independence of the West by declaring that public schools "shall be forever free from sectarian control or influence" and forbidding the expenditure of public money on any "religious worship, exercise or institution" or the "support of any religious establishment."[20]

Constitution-makers in the West innovated in other ways as well. Even as a territory, Wyoming in 1869 extended the right to vote to women; when the nation adopted the Nineteenth Amendment to the U.S. Constitution in 1920, seventeen states west of the Mississippi River had already authorized female suffrage. One by one, the arid states of the far West followed the example of Colorado in 1879, when that state's constitution-makers elevated the use of water to the status of a public property right to be distributed in the best interests of the state. Taken together, these developments in the West underscore the pragmatic tradition bequeathed by the architects of nineteenth-century bills of rights to the twentieth century.

Popular consent and control also limited the rights guaranteed to racial minorities. Constitutions drawn in the Southern states, for example, included provisions that enslaved African Americans before the Civil War and segregated them after Reconstruction. A similar fate befell Chinese Americans in the West, where state governments systematically denied them basic political, social, and economic rights. Popularly elected state supreme court justices in both sections often turned a blind eye to such discrimination.

In matters of racial equality, the post–Civil War protection of liberty was at best mixed. In nearly half of the twenty cases J. Morgan Kousser studied in Kansas and Louisiana, blacks won when they raised issues of equal protection of the laws under various provisions of state constitutions and the Fourteenth Amendment to the federal Constitution.[21] In *Board of Education of Ottawa, Kansas v. Leslie Tinnon* (1881), for example, Justice Daniel M. Valentine of the Kansas Supreme Court rejected an effort by a school board to segregate children on the basis of race because the "tendency of the times is . . . to abolish all distinctions on account of race, or color, or previous condition of servitude, and to make all persons absolutely equal before the law."[22] Judge Valentine, however, despite arguments by counsel, did not rest his reasoning on either the equal protection clause of the Fourteenth Amendment or the guarantees to equality outlined in the Kansas Constitution; instead, he addressed only the relatively narrow ground of whether the legislature had authorized such a classification and, since it had not, whether the school board could rely on its general power to regulate the schools as a basis upon which to segregate the schools.

In Louisiana, explicit state constitutional prohibitions against segregation had little effect on judges willing to ignore them. Article 135 of the Louisiana Constitution required the legislature to integrate the schools, but the state supreme court in *Paul Trevigne v. School Board and William O. Rogers* (1879) refused on disingenuous technical grounds to order such integration.[23]

Despite the somewhat different political and legal climates in Kansas and

Louisiana, by the end of the nineteenth century public officials had embraced segregation as lawful under their constitutions, a development confirmed by the Supreme Court's famous "separate but equal" ruling in *Plessy v. Ferguson* (1896). As Kousser notes, "in the end in both states, blacks lost out because a new set of racist judges took office and emasculated [state] constitutional guarantees."[24]

The heritage of nineteenth-century discrimination died hard, even when state bills of right appeared to affirm unequivocally the equal protection and due process of law. That is one reason why in the early twentieth century such groups as the American Civil Liberties Union, the International Labor Defense, and the National Association for the Advancement of Colored People undertook organized litigation in the federal courts. These groups invoked the Fourteenth Amendment and the Bill of Rights before federal judges as a way of sidestepping bloated and populistic state constitutions and elected appellate court judges.

State Constitutional Rights in the Twentieth Century

Since World War II efforts to streamline and modernize state constitutions have actually reduced them to the point where they are on average about three times as long as the federal Constitution. Yet the substantive provisions of state bills of rights have expanded well beyond the federal Bill of Rights. As was true in the nineteenth-century, the states have been creative laboratories for testing rights. Many state constitutions, for example, explicitly guarantee the right to privacy, protection of and the right to enjoy natural resources and environmental health, a right to education, and equal protection of the laws regardless of gender.

The development of the right of privacy exemplifies the way constitutional revision, amendment, and judicial review have combined to expand the scope of liberty in this century. The federal Bill of Rights contains no explicit guarantee of privacy, either in the sense of controlling government access to and dissemination of personal information or in the autonomy of individuals to make fundamental and intimate decisions in such matters as childbearing, personal appearance, medical care, sexuality, and living arrangements. The right to privacy in the federal Constitution has been implied from the "penumbra" of other fundamental rights that protect privacy interest, notably the First, Third, Fourth, Fifth, and Ninth Amendments. Some states have also relied on judicial interpretation to establish such a right. The New Jersey Supreme Court has interpreted Article I, Section 1, of that state's constitution to find a right of privacy as one of the general "rights of personality" guaranteed by that article. In Massachusetts, the judiciary has concluded that privacy is implicit in the due process safeguards outlined in Article X of that state's constitution.

Eleven states, however, have framed the right of privacy directly in their bills of rights. Constitution-makers in California, for example, added the word "privacy" to that state's declaration of fundamental rights; Florida adopted a specific amendment that provides that "Every natural person has the right to be let alone and free from governmental intrusion into his [p]rivate life. . . ."[25]

While the federal Supreme Court has been reluctant to construe the right of privacy broadly, especially where sexual acts such as sodomy and prostitution are involved, the states have acted with greater boldness. The New Jersey Supreme Court has struck down on privacy grounds state statutes prohibiting fornication and consensual sodomy. The Pennsylvania Supreme Court in 1980 voided that state's "voluntary deviate sexual intercourse" statute on the grounds that "[s]piritual leadership, not the government, has the responsibility for striving to improve the morality of individuals."[26] Moreover, several states, most notably California, have interpreted their privacy provisions to impose an obligation of neutrality on state governments in dealing with matters of procreation. The California Supreme Court, in *The Committee to Defend Reproductive Rights v. Myers* (1981), overturned a statute that excluded abortion coverage from the medical assistance programs for the indigent.[27]

Freedom of expression has also benefited from greater state constitutional protection in this century. Take for example New York, which has long been a center of the press and the arts. Its bill of rights provides that "[e]very citizen may freely speak, write and publish his sentiments on all subjects, being responsible for the abuse of that right; and no law shall be passed to restrain or abridge that liberty of speech or of the press."[28] The New York Court of Appeals has construed these words to give protections well beyond those afforded by the U.S. Supreme Court's interpretation of the First Amendment. Under existing federal constitution law, a state can shut down a bookstore if its patrons are engaging in illegal acts, even though the store owner may be innocent of any wrongdoing. New York judges, however, have taken a broader view. In that state, as Chief Judge Sol Wachtler of the Court of Appeals has written, the question is not "who is aimed at but who is hit."[29] Because the closing will affect the bookstore, which is entitled to constitutional protection, the state has to show that no other measures, such as prosecution of the offending patrons, will eliminate the nuisance before it can order the store closed.

The Limits of State Bills of Rights

As these examples demonstrate, the "New Federalism" has through the doctrine of adequate and independent state grounds expanded liberty. Not only do state constitutions contain a greater number of rights, but state appellate court judges have recently interpreted them in ways that raise the ceiling of rights above the minimum floor established by the Burger and

Rehnquist Courts. Yet, skepticism about the state-law revolution is in order, a skepticism rooted in not only the checkered history of state-based liberty in the nineteenth century but the realities of modern federalism. Indeed, there is reason to question whether the "New Federalism," at least from the perspective of liberal advocates such as Brennan and Linde, can shoulder the burden they have placed on it.

The rights of criminal defendants is one area of the "New Federalism" where the states seem on first impression to have pushed well beyond the Burger and Rehnquist courts. Recent studies have shown that state courts in hundreds of decisions have gone beyond the federal requirements and that more than one-third of all rulings in this area by the Supreme Court are subsequently liberalized by the states.

New York offers a good example. Its constitution makes the same guarantee of the assistance of counsel to a person charged with a crime as does the Sixth Amendment to the United States Constitution. The most important recent issue involving this right has not been whether it exists, but when it attaches before formal charges have been made. That is, at what point can it be invoked? Arguably, individuals may be most vulnerable to police questioning during the early phases of the investigation process, usually well before formal charges have been made. Under the famous Warren Court decision in *Miranda v. Arizona* (1966), the police are required only to advise the defendant of the right to counsel before questioning begins. The New York Court of Appeals, however, has read the guarantee to counsel in that state's constitution more expansively. Once an attorney appears to represent a person, the person cannot subsequently be questioned unless the attorney is also present. The court has interpreted this rule to mean that, once an individual has requested counsel, questioning cannot proceed without a lawyer present at any stage in the process. The New York standard not only exceeds the federal constitutional requirement, but it is probably the toughest in the country.[30] In New York a person put in a lineup has a right to counsel; under the Sixth Amendment the same person, unless formally charged, would not have that same right.

Relying on this and similar examples from other states is somewhat misleading. If one out of three Supreme Court rulings involving the rights of criminal defendants have been rejected by state high courts since the 1960s, two-thirds have been adopted. As Barry Latzer has argued, the "New Federalism" contains much of the same "hidden conservatism" associated with nineteenth-century state constitutional law.[31]

These developments are summarized in Tables 1 and 2. The first presents the ten states that have been most active in relying on state bill of rights' provisions involving defendants' rights and the ten least active. As Latzer persuasively argues, not only have state high courts adopted most of the significant changes brought about by the Burger and Rehnquist Courts in the area of rights of criminal defendants, but the high courts of Connecticut and New Hampshire have done so even though they are usually portrayed as pioneers of the state-law revolution. As Table 2 suggests, more than two-fifths (44%) of all state courts have readily adopted federal constitutional guidelines, while less than one-tenth (8%) have routinely gone beyond the federal mandates. Even those states that actively interpret their bill of rights provisions covering criminal defendants are likely to fall between these two extremes.

In the two states—California and Florida—with the highest crime rates in the country and the highest rates of rejecting federal guidelines, the tradition of popular consent and control has nonetheless shaped defendants' rights. Constitutional initiatives in both states in 1982 resulted in the addition of anti-exclusionary rule amendments to their respective constitutions. The exclusionary rule provides that evidence illegally seized can be excluded from the prosecution of a criminal defendant. The California and Florida amendments require that search and seizure provisions of these states' constitutions be construed in accordance with the interpretation given the Fourth Amendment by an increasingly conservative federal Supreme Court.

These figures suggest that a more critical and realistic assessment of the supposed revolution in state constitutional rights of criminal defendants is in order. The "New Federalism" is not nearly as liberal as it is often portrayed, since in two cases out of three the highest courts of the states have followed the path already marked out by the "conservative" Burger and Rehnquist Courts. The movement toward independent state constitutional doctrine, something strongly urged by former Justice Brennan and Judge Linde, is unlikely to succeed, at least in the highly touted area of the rights of criminal defendants. That result is likely in part because these courts are clearly susceptible to public concern over violent crime, a fact of life driven home in 1986 when California voters recalled Chief Justice Rose Bird and two other justices because they were widely perceived as being soft on criminals.

Moreover, state court judges invariably end up, at least in the area of criminal procedure, dealing with issues that the Supreme Court has already treated. Since state courts must always consider the federal floor provided by rights, they necessarily must take account of federal constitutional requirements. Those guidelines leave state courts vulnerable to second-guessing on supremacy clause issues.

The repeated refrain that "separate state grounds" can free state courts from control by the Supreme Court is also questionable. In theory, at least, state supreme courts can immunize their decisions by resting them squarely on state law. The Supreme Court in *Michigan v. Long* (1988), as Latzer reminds us, exacted a price for this independence by requiring that the states sharply differentiate their state and federal law decisions in such a way as to conform any use of federal law to applicable Supreme Court rulings. Under *Long*, if any part of a decision rests on federal constitutional law then the Supreme Court may review the entire case. Most students of the constitutional system believe that the relationship between federal and state constitutional protections is too symbiotic to leave state courts much more authority than they already have. Only the sheer volume of state-based cases and the inability of the Supreme Court to hear more than a few of them prevents the justices from reviewing more state court actions taken where federal and state constitutional principles become mixed.

Of Floors and Ceilings

The lessons to be drawn from the history of judicially enforced state bills of rights are twofold. The first is that an important tradition of rights has existed in the states and that tradition serves as an inspiration today. Despite the majoritarian forces of consent and control and despite the degeneration of state constitutions into law codes filled with supra-legislation and overblown promises of rights that cannot be met, these documents have and will continue in some instances to raise the ceiling of rights above the federal floor. It is a tribute to our federal system that state bills of rights remain a bulwark of individual liberty.

While the states have been, from time to time, creative constitutional laboratories, their history is as much one of limitations as possibilities. Because state constitutions rest so heavily on popular consent and control, only the judicially interpreted federal Bill of Rights has commanded sufficient authority in this century to protect local minorities in each of the states from politically dominant majorities. We should not, of course, ignore state constitutional law. Justice Brennan is right: "federal preservation of civil liberties is a minimum, which the states may surpass. . . ."[32] This proposition is nonetheless disturbing in both its optimism and its simplicity.[33] It is too optimistic because it ignores the power of the Supreme Court, as was true with slavery and industrialization, to limit on federal grounds the authority of the states to invoke successfully their own constitutions. It is too simplistic in that it underestimates the grip that the tradition of popular consent and control exercises over state constitutions generally and state-based fundamental rights in particular.

There seems little doubt that the decade of the 1990s will see an even greater output of state constitutional law rulings, but whatever gains are made in favor of liberty will depend as well on a supportive federal bench. We cannot hope to raise the ceiling of state constitutional rights if, at the same time, the Supreme Court lowers the federal floor.

Table 1
The Ten Most and Least Active State High Courts
in Relying on State Bills of Rights, 1968–1989*

Most Active		Least Active	
	Cases		**Cases**
California	43	South Carolina	0
New Hampshire	41	Arkansas	1
Oregon	28	Nevada	2
Florida	27	Alabama	3
Pennsylvania	27	Indiana	3
Montana	26	Minnesota	3
West Virginia	25	New Mexico	3
Connecticut	24	Virginia	3
Alaska	22	Georgia	5
New Jersey	22	North Dakota	5

* The data in these tables come from Latzer, "The Hidden Conservatism of the State Court 'Revolution,'" 192–93.

Table 2
State High Courts with the Highest and Lowest
Incidence of Adopting[1] U.S. Supreme Court Rulings, 1968–1989

Rejection of 75% or more (4)	*Adoption of 75% or more (22)*	
California (83%)	IL (100%)	OH (86%)
Alaska (82%)	NE (100%)	FL (after '83 amd.) (82%)[2]
Florida (before '83 amd.)[3] (80%)	IA (94%)	TX (81%)
Massachusetts (75%)	WN (95%)	KY (80%)
	NC (93%)	NH (80%)
	CT (92%)	ND (80%)
	MD (92%)	MI (79%)
	DL (89%)	SD (77%)
	WY (88%)	UT (77%)
	MO (87%)	ID (75%)
	KN (86%)	ME (75%)

[1] Latzer arbitrarily set a cutoff of 75 percent to place states in either the rejectionist or adoptionist categories.

[2] Florida in 1982 adopted a constitutional amendment designed to reduce the exclusion of evidence on state law grounds. The amendment limited the ability of the state supreme court to reject federal Fourth Amendment guidelines in favor of a state constitutional rule.

[3] California, like Florida, in 1982 adopted a constitutional amendment requiring that the state supreme court conform its exclusionary rule findings to standards set by the U. S. Supreme Court. The impact was clearly less in California, since, unlike Florida, it did not appear after 1982 on the list of states with a high rate of adoption.

Notes

Rights Consciousness in American History

1. Oscar and Mary Handlin, eds., *The Popular Sources of Political Authority: Documents on the Massachusetts Constitution of 1780* (Cambridge, Mass., 1966), 65.
2. *The Works of John Adams*, ed. Charles Francis Adams (3 vols., Boston, 1850–56), III, 465.
3. Bernard Bailyn, *The Ideological Origins of the American Revolution* (Cambridge, Mass., 1967), 188; Adams, *Works*, III, 463.
4. Gordon S. Wood, *The Creation of the American Republic, 1776–1787* (Chapel Hill, N.C., 1969), 63.
5. Edward Dumbauld, *The Bill of Rights and What It Means Today* (Norman, Okla., 1957), 170–72.
6. Handlin, *Popular Sources of Political Authority*, 202–379.
7. Marvin Meyers, ed., *The Mind of the Founder: Sources of the Political Thought of James Madison* (Indianapolis, 1973), 204, 206, 224.
8. Helen E. Veit, et al., eds., *Creating the Bill of Rights: The Documentary Record from the First Congress* (Baltimore, 1991), 300.
9. Meyers, *Mind of the Founder*, 207.
10. Eric Foner, *Tom Paine and Revolutionary America* (New York, 1976), 133.
11. John R. Commons, et al., eds., *A Documentary History of American Industrial Society* (6 vols., Cleveland, 1910–11), V, 86; VI, 94.
12. John L. Thomas, *The Liberator: William Lloyd Garrison* (Boston, 1963), 173.
13. Mary Jo Buhle and Paul Buhle, eds., *The Concise History of Woman Suffrage* (Urbana, Ill., 1978), 94–95; Angelina E. Grimke, *Letters to Catherine E. Beecher* (Boston, 1838), 108.
14. *Slaughter-House Cases*, 16 Wallace 110 (1873); *Adkins v. Children's Hospital*, 261 U.S. 561 (1923).
15. Arnold M. Paul, *Conservative Crisis and the Rule of Law: Attitudes of Bar and Bench, 1887–1895* (Ithaca, N.Y., 1960), 81.
16. Woodrow Wilson, *Mere Literature and Other Essays* (Boston, 1896), 198; A. Lawrence Lowell, *Essays on Government* (Boston, 1889), 193, 183.
17. Robert S. Lynd and Helen Merrell Lynd, *Middletown* (New York, 1956), 198.
18. Charles A. Beard, *Politics* (New York, 1908), 31; Woodrow Wilson, *Congressional Government* (Boston, 1913), 5; Henry S. Commager, *The American Mind: An Interpretation of American Thought and Character Since the 1880s* (New Haven, Conn., 1950), 375.
19. Donald B. Johnson, ed., *National Party Platforms* (2 vols., Urbana, Ill., 1978), I, 175–82, 360–63.
20. *The Public Papers and Addresses of Franklin D. Roosevelt*, ed. Samuel I. Rosenman (13 vols., New York, 1938–50), XIII, 41–42.
21. Francis L. Broderick and August Meier, eds., *Negro Protest Thought in the Twentieth Century* (Indianapolis, 1965), 48–52.
22. *Karl Marx: The Essential Writings*, ed. Frederick L. Bender (2nd ed., Boulder, Col., 1986), 62–63.

The Explosion and Erosion of Rights

1. Jacob Cooke, ed., *The Federalist*, No. 2 (Middleton, Conn., 1961), 8.
2. *The Federalist*, No. 78, 525.
3. *The Federalist*, No. 84, 581.
4. *Barron v. Baltimore*, 32 U.S. (7 Pet.) 243, 247, 250 (1833).
5. *The Federalist*, No. 78, 525.
6. *Palko v. Connecticut*, 302 U.S. 319 (1937).
7. The *Gitlow* decision was no sleeper; its radical implications were immediately clear. Writing in the *Harvard Law Review*, Charles Warren put it this way: "[I]f the doctrine of the *Gitlow* case is to be carried to its logical and inevitable conclusion . . . the simple word 'liberty' will have become a tremendous engine for attack on State legislation—an engine which could not have been conceived possible by the framers of the first Ten Amendments or by the framers of the Fourteenth Amendment itself. And the foreboding of Chief Justice Taney, in 1849, will have justified itself, when he said: 'If in this court we are at liberty to give old words new meanings when we find them in the Constitution, there is no power which may not, by this mode of construction, be conferred on the general government and denied to the States.'" Charles Warren, "The New 'Liberty' Under the Fourteenth Amendment," *Harvard Law Review* 39 (1926), 460–63 (quoting Taney's dissent in *The Passenger Cases*, 48 U.S. 478 (1849).
8. *Palko v. Connecticut*, 302 U.S. 319 (1937).
9. *United States v. Carolene Products Co.*, 304 U.S. 144 (1938).
10. See Raoul Berger, *Government by Judiciary: The Transformation of the Fourteenth Amendment* (Cambridge, Mass., 1977).
11. William O. Douglas, "The Bill of Rights Is Not Enough," *New York University Law Review* 38 (1963), 207.
12. Thomas Grey, "Do We Have an Unwritten Constitution?" *Stanford Law Review* 27 (1975), 715.
13. *Meyers v. Nebraska*, 262 U.S. 390 (1923).
14. *Pierce v. Society of Sisters*, 268 U.S. 512 (1925).
15. *Meyers v. Nebraska*, 399.
16. *Ibid.*, 400.
17. *Pierce v. Society of Sisters*, 535.
18. *Ibid.*, 536.
19. *Ibid.*, 535.
20. *Skinner v. Oklahoma*, 316 U.S. 536 (1942).
21. *Ibid.*, 545.
22. *Ibid.*, 546.
23. *Poe v. Ullman*, 367 U.S. 501 (1961).

Symbolic Speech and the First Amendment

1. Minneapolis *Star Tribune*, June 11, 1991, p. 1.
2. Minneapolis *Star Tribune*, June 11, 1991, p. 16A.
3. *Ibid.*
4. *Minnesota Civil Liberties Union News*, No. 185, July 1991, p. 1.
5. *R.A.V., Petitioner v. St. Paul, Minnesota*, 1992 U.S. Lexis 3863; 60 U.S.L.W. 4667 (1992) at 4691.
6. *Ibid.*, 4701.

7. *Gilbert v. Minnesota*, 254 U.S. 325, 343 (1920).

8. *Stromberg v. California*, 283 U.S. 359 (1931).

9. *Ibid.*, 369.

10. *Collin v. Smith*, 447 F. Supp. 767 (N.D. Ill. 1978); affirmed by the Court of Appeals, 478 F. 2d 1197 (7th Cir. 1978); denied review, 439 U.S. 916 (1978).

11. *Minersville School District v. Gobitis*, 310 U.S. 586, 596 (1940).

12. Oliver Wendell Holmes, Jr., *Speeches* (Boston, 1913), 87.

13. *West Virginia State Board of Education v. Barnette*, 319 U.S. 624, 633 (1943).

14. *Ibid.*, 642.

15. *Wooley v. Maynard*, 430 U.S. 715 (1977).

16. *Cox v. Louisiana*, 379 U.S. 536, 559 (1965).

17. *U.S. v. O'Brien*, 391 U.S. 367, 376 (1968).

18. *Ibid.*, 376–77.

19. *Tinker v. Des Moines School District*, 393 U.S. 503, 505 (1969).

20. *Ibid.*, 526.

21. *Cohen v. California*, 403 U.S. 15 (1971).

22. *Clark v. Community for Creative Non-Violence*, 468 U.S. 288, 304 (1984).

23. *Cantwell v. Connecticut*, 310 U.S. 296 (1940).

24. *Wayte v. U.S.*, 470 U.S. 598 (1985).

25. *U.S. v. Albertini*, 472 U.S. 675 (1985).

26. *Street v. New York*, 394 U.S. 576 (1969).

27. *Cowgill v. California*, 420 U.S. 930 (1974).

28. *Radich v. New York*, 401 U.S. 531 (1971); *U.S. ex rel. Radich v. Criminal Court of New York*, 385 U.S. F. Supp. 165 (1974).

29. *Smith v. Goguen*, 415 U.S. 566 (1974).

30. *Spence v. Washington*, 418 U.S. 405 (1974).

31. *Schacht v. U.S.*, 398 U.S. 58 (1970).

32. *Texas v. Johnson*, 491 U.S. 397 (1989).

33. *Ibid.*, 419.

34. *Ibid.*, 421.

35. *Ibid.*, 429.

36. American Bar Association, "Flag Desecration Amendment Opposed," Press Release, Sept. 3, 1989.

37. Flag Protection Act, Pub. L. No. 101–131, 103 *Stat.* 777 (1989).

38. St. Paul *Pioneer Press Dispatch*, October 13, 1989, p. 2A.

39. *U.S. v. Eichman, U.S. v. Haggerty*, 110 S.Ct. 2404 (1990).

40. *Ibid.*, 2408.

41. *Ibid.*, 2412.

42. Minneapolis *Star Tribune*, June 22, 1991, pp. 1, 9A.

Church and State

1. *Everson v. Board of Education*, 330 U.S. 15–16 (1947).

2. *Ibid.*, 18.

3. *Ibid.*, 19.

4. *Ibid.*, 44–45.

5. *McCollum v. Board of Education*, 333 U.S. 203 (1948).

6. *Zorach v. Clauson*, 343 U.S. 306, 313 (1952).

7. *Engel v. Vitale*, 370 U.S. 421 (1962).

8. *Abington School District v. Schempp*, 374 U.S. 203 (1963). In a companion case, *Murray v. Curlett*, the noted atheist Madelaine Murray and her son challenged a lo-

cal Baltimore school rule that each school day begin with the "reading, without comment, of a chapter in the Holy Bible and/or use of the Lord's Prayer." The schools did permit children to be excused at the request of parents.

9. *Ibid.*

10. *Epperson v. Arkansas*, 393 U.S. 97 (1968).

11. *Edwards v. Aquillard*, 107 S.Ct. 2573 (1987).

12. See, for example, *Lovell v. Griffin*, 303 U.S. 444 (1938); *Martin v. Struthers*, 319 U.S. 141 (1943); and *Kunz v. New York*, 340 U.S. 290 (1951), and the discussion in chap. 3 of Richard E. Morgan, *The Supreme Court and Religion* (New York, 1972).

13. *Reynolds v. United States*, 98 U.S. 145 (1879).

14. *Cantwell v. Connecticut*, 310 U.S. 296 (1940).

15. *McGowan v. Maryland*, 366 U.S. 420 (1961).

16. *Braunfeld v. Brown*, 366 U.S. 599 (1961).

17. *Ibid.*

18. *Sherbert v. Verner*, 374 U.S. 398 (1963).

19. Philip B. Kurland, "Of Church and State and the Supreme Court," *University of Chicago Law Review*, 29 (1961), 1.

20. Dissenting in *Plessy v. Ferguson*, 163 U.S. 539 (1896).

21. *Everson v. Board of Education*, 16.

22. Edwin L. Meese, Jr., "Construing the Constitution," *University of California at Davis Law Review* 19 (1985), 22–23.

23. *Board of Education v. Allen*, 392 U.S. 236 (1968).

24. *Walz v. Tax Commission*, 397 U.S. 664 (1970). For a discussion of religious tax exemption, see Dean M. Kelley, "The Supreme Court Redefines Tax Exemption," in Thomas Robbins and Roland Robertson, eds., *Church-State Relations: Tensions and Transitions* (1987).

25. *Lemon v. Kurtzman*, 403 U.S. 602 (1971).

26. *Marsh v. Chambers*, 463 U.S. 783 (1983).

27. Norman Redlich, "The Separation of Church and State: The Burger Court's Tortuous Journey," *Notre Dame Law Review* 60 (1985), 1094, 1122–26.

28. *Lynch v. Donnelly*, 465 U.S. 668 (1984).

29. Leonard W. Levy, *The Establishment Clause and the First Amendment* (New York, 1986), 157.

30. The full prayer read: "Almighty God, You alone are our God. We acknowledge you as the Creator and Supreme judge of the world. May Your justice, Your truth, and Your peace abound this day in the hearts of our countrymen, in the counsels of our government, in the sanctity of our homes and in the classrooms of our schools in the name of our Lord. Amen."

31. *Grand Rapids School District v. Ball*, 473 U.S. 373 (1985).

32. *Aguilar v. Felton*, 473 U.S. 402 (1985).

33. *Wisconsin v. Yoder*, 406 U.S. 205 (1972).

34. Jesse H. Choper, "The Free Exercise Clause: A Structural Overview and an Appraisal of Recent Developments," *William and Mary Law Review*, 27 (1986), 947–48.

35. *Employment Division, Oregon Department of Human Resources v. Smith*, 110 S.Ct. 1595 (1990).

Public Safety and the Right to Bear Arms

1. Bernard Bailyn, *The Ideological Origins of the American Revolution* (New York, 1967).

2. See generally Joyce Lee Malcolm, "The Right to Keep and Bear Arms: The Common Law Tradition," *Hastings Constitutional Law Quarterly*, 10 (1983), 285.

3. 1 Wm and Mary Sess. 2 c.2 (1689).

4. William Blackstone, *Commentaries on the Laws of England*, Vol. I, *Of the Rights of Persons* (4 vols., London, 1765–69; 1979 repr.), 139.

5. C. M. Kenyon, ed., *The Anti-Federalists* (New York, 1966), 228.

6. *The Federalist*, No. 46 (rev. ed., New York, 1961), 299.

7. 1 *Statutes at Large* 271 (May 1792).

8. Joseph Story, *Commentaries on the Constitution of the United States* (2 vols., Boston, 1858; 1987 repr.), I, 708.

9. See *Nunn v. State*, 1 Georgia 243 (1846).

10. Walter L. Fleming, ed., *Documentary History of Reconstruction: Political, Military, Social, Religious, Educational, and Industrial, 1865–1906* (New York, 1909; 1966 repr.), 290.

11. For a good discussion of the incorporation question, see Michael Kent Curtis, *No State Shall Abridge: The Fourteenth Amendment and the Bill of Rights* (New York, 1986). For the 39th Congress's views concerning the Second Amendment and its applicability to the states through the Fourteenth Amendment, see Stephen P. Holbrook, *That Every Man Be Armed: The Evolution of a Constitutional Right* (Albuquerque, N.M., 1984), 107–23.

12. *United States v. Cruikshank*, 92 U.S. 542 (1876).

13. *Presser v. Illinois*, 116 U.S. 252 (1886).

14. Don B. Kates, "Towards a History of Handgun Prohibition in the United States," in Don B. Kates, ed., *Restricting Handguns: The Liberal Skeptics Speak Out* (Croton-on-Hudson, N.Y., 1979), 7–30; Lee Kennett and James La Verne Anderson, *The Gun in America: The Origins of a National Dilemma* (Westport, Conn., 1975), 174–80.

15. *United States v. Miller*, 307 U.S. 178 (1935).

16. *Ibid.*

17. *Quilici v. Village of Morton Grove*, 695 F. 2d 261 (1982).

18. "Oh That Annoying Second Amendment: It Shows No Signs of Going Away Yet," *Philadelphia Inquirer*, March 22, 1991.

The Enigmatic Place of Property Rights in Modern Constitutional Thought

1. Max Farrand, ed., *The Records of the Federal Constitution of 1787*, rev. ed. (5 vols., New Haven, Conn., 1937), I, 534.

2. James W. Ely, Jr., *The Guardian of Every Other Right: A Constitutional History of Property Rights* (New York, 1992), 133–34, 139–40.

3. James L. Oakes, "'Property Rights' in Constitutional Analysis Today," *Washington Law Review* 56 (1981), 583.

4. David L. Callies, "Property Rights: Are There Any Left?" *Urban Lawyer* 20 (1988), 597.

5. Bernard Schwartz, *The New Right and the Constitution: Turning Back the Legal Clock* (Boston, 1990), 256.

6. Charles H. Clarke, "Rent Control and the Constitutional Ghosts and Goblins of Laissez-Faire Past," *University of Dayton Law Review* 14 (1988), 115, 146.

7. Ely, *The Guardian of Every Other Right*, 88–91.

8. Geoffrey P. Miller, "The True Story of Carolene Products," *Supreme Court Review 1987* (1988), 397–426.

9. William H. Riker, "Civil Rights and Property Rights," in Ellen Frankel Paul

and Howard Dickman, eds., *Liberty, Property and the Future of Constitutional Development* (Albany, N.Y., 1990), 49–64.

10. Henry Summer Maine, *Popular Government* (London, 1885), 247–48.

11. *Home Building and Loan Association v. Blaisdell*, 290 U.S. 398, 428 (1934).

12. E.g., *State of Nevada Employees Association v. Keating*, 903 F.2d 1223 (9th Cir. 1990), cert. den. 111 S.Ct. 558 (1990).

13. *Association of Surrogates and Supreme Court Reporters v. New York*, 940 F.2d 766 (2nd Cir. 1991), cert. den. 117 L Ed 2d 107 (1992).

14. *General Motors Corporation v. Romein*, 112 S. Ct. 1105 (1992).

15. James W. Ely, Jr., " 'That due satisfaction may be made': The Fifth Amendment and the Origins of the Compensation Principle," *American Journal of Legal History* 36 (Jan. 1992), 1.

16. *Chicago, Burlington and Quincy Railroad Company v. Chicago*, 166 U.S. 226 (1897).

17. *Hall v. City of Santa Barbara*, 833 F.2d 1270, 1278 (9th Cir. 1986), cert. den. 485 U.S. 940 (1988). See also *Azul Pacifico, Inc. v. City of Los Angeles*, 948 F.2d 575 (9th Cir. 1991).

18. *Yee v. City of Escondido*, 112 S. Ct. 1522, 1529 (1992).

19. *Pennsylvania Coal Co. v. Mahon*, 260 U.S. 393, 415 (1922).

20. A presidential advisory commission has recently concluded that the web of zoning laws and environmental regulations significantly increases the cost of housing and inhibits the construction of moderately priced homes. "Not in My Back Yard: Regulatory Barriers to Affordable Housing," Advisory Commission on Regulatory Barriers to Affordable Housing, July 8, 1991.

21. *Agins v. City of Tiburon*, 447 U.S. 255, 260 (1980).

22. *Nollan v. California Coastal Commission*, 483 U.S. 825, 841 (1987).

23. Executive Order No. 12630, March 15, 1988, 53 FR 8859.

24. 1991 S. 553.

25. *Whitney Benefits, Inc. v. United States*, 926 F.2d 1169 (Fed. Cir. 1991), cert. den. 112 Sup.Ct. 406 (1991).

26. Carol M. Rose, "Property Rights, Regulatory Regimes and the New Takings Jurisprudence—An Evolutionary Approach," *Tennessee Law Review* 57 (1990), 579.

27. *Lucas v. South Carolina Coastal Commission*, No. 91-453, 1992 U.S. LEXIS 4537 (June 29, 1992).

28. For a discussion of the *Midkiff* decision and the public use limitation see Richard A. Epstein, *Takings: Private Property and the Power of Eminent Domain* (Cambridge, Mass., 1985), 161–81.

29. *Duquesne Light Co. v. Barasch*, 488 U.S. 299 (1989).

30. *Nordlinger v. Hahn*, 60 U.S.L.W. 4563 (1992).

31. Antonin Scalia, "Economic Affairs as Human Affairs," in James A. Dorn and Henry G. Manne, eds., *Economic Liberties and the Judiciary* (Fairfax, Va., 1987), 31.

Reversing the Revolution

1. Stephen J. Markham, "Foreword: The 'Truth in Criminal Justice' Series," *Journal of Law Reform* 22 (1989), 425.

2. Prefatory statement of Meese, unpublished reports.

3. Markham, "Foreword," 428.

4. Quotations from David J. Bodenhamer, *Fair Trial: Rights of the Accused in American History* (New York, 1992), 127, 129.

5. Chief Justice John Fortescue of the Court of King's Bench in the mid-fifteenth century wrote, "Indeed, one would much rather that twenty guilty persons should

escape the punishment of death, than one innocent person should be condemned and suffer capitally." Quoted in Bradley Chapin, *Criminal Justice in Colonial America, 1606–1660* (Athens, Ga., 1983), 3.

6. *Palko v. Connecticut*, 302 U.S. 319, 325–26.

7. *Breithaupt v. Abram*, 352 U.S. 432 (1957), 442.

8. *Ohio ex rel. Eaton v. Price*, 364 U.S. 274 (1960).

9. Earl Warren, *The Memoirs of Earl Warren* (New York, 1977), 332.

10. As quoted in Richard C. Cortner, *The Supreme Court and the Second Bill of Rights: The Fourteenth Amendment and the Nationalization of Civil Liberties* (Madison, Wisc., 1981), 196.

11. The theory of selective incorporation, accepted in *Malloy v. Hogan* (1964), held that the due process clause of the Fourteenth Amendment incorporated many of the rights of the first eight amendments, thus restraining state discretion to adopt different criminal procedures.

12. *Mapp v. Ohio*, 367 U.S. 656 (1961).

13. The rule of automatic reversal has governed coerced confession cases since *Malinski v. New York*, 324 U.S. 401 (1945).

14. *Miranda v. Arizona*, 384 U.S. 457 (1966).

15. *Ibid.*, 470–75.

16. Anthony Lewis, "A Talk with Warren on Crime, the Court, and the Country," *New York Times Magazine* (Oct. 19, 1969), 126.

17. *Miranda v. Arizona*, 572.

18. *Ibid.*, 508.

19. *Chapman v. California*, 386 U.S. 24 (1967).

20. *Duncan v. Louisiana*, 391 U.S. 150 (1968).

21. *New York Times*, July 4, 1971, p. 1A.

22. *United States v. Harris*, 403 U.S. 582 (1971).

23. *United States v. Calandra*, 414 U.S. 348, 354 (1974).

24. Only in cases involving the death penalty did the Court move beyond the Warren Court's conception of defendants' rights. See Bodenhamer, *Fair Trial*, 132–36.

25. Four years later, the Court declined 6 to 2 to weaken Miranda further by holding that once the suspect requested counsel all questioning must stop until a lawyer was present, whether or not the accused had consulted with an attorney. *Minnick v. Mississippi*, 59 L.W. 4037 (1990).

26. *Arizona v. Fulminante*, 111 S.Ct. 1266 (1991).

27. *Ibid.*, 1266. Rehnquist quoted with approval from an earlier case that the harmless-error doctrine is essential to preserve "the principle that the central purpose of a criminal trial is to decide the factual question of the defendant's guilt or innocence, and promotes public respect for the criminal process by focusing on the underlying fairness of the trial rather than on the virtually inevitable presence of immaterial error."

28. *Powers v. Ohio*, 111 S.Ct. 1381 (1991).

29. *Schad v. Arizona*, 111 S.Ct. 2503 (1991).

30. *Ibid.*, 2507.

31. Earl Warren, "The Law and the Future," *Fortune* (Nov. 1955), 106, 226.

32. *Coleman v. Thompson*, 111 S.Ct. 2552, 2559, 2565 (1991). In a 1992 case, however, Justice O'Connor took great exception to Justice Clarence Thomas's opinion for the Court, which sought to foreclose any collateral review by federal courts of state decisions on mixed constitutional questions. She challenged Thomas's recounting of federal habeas law and caustically noted that Congress had rejected the view Thomas endorsed on thirteen occasions during the past thirty-seven years. See *Wright v. West*, 60 L.W. 4639 (1992).

33. *Ibid.*, 2569, 2572.

34. *Payne v. Tennessee*, 111 S.Ct. 2601–2602, 2607–2609 (1991).

35. *Ibid.*, 2619.

36. *Ibid.*, 2616.

37. *Malinski v. New York*, 324 U.S. 414 (1941).

Police Practices and the Bill of Rights

1. Edward S. Corwin, *Liberty against Government: The Rise, Flowering and Decline of a Famous Judicial Concept* (Baton Rouge, La., 1948), 7.

2. Leonard W. Levy, *Origins of the Fifth Amendment: The Right Against Self-Incrimination* (New York, 1968), 432.

3. Justice Brandeis, dissenting in *Olmstead v. United States*, 277 U.S. 438 (1928).

4. Nelson Lasson, *The History and Development of the Fourth Amendment to the United States Constitution* (Baltimore, 1937), 13–20.

5. Lasson, *History and Development*, 35–36; Matthew Hale, *History of the Pleas of the Crown* (3 vols., Philadelphia, 1847), I, II.

6. Lasson, *History and Development*, 20–39.

7. *Entick v. Carrington*, 19 Howell's State Trials 1029 (1765).

8. Lasson, *History and Development*, 51–72.

9. John Adams's abstract of James Otis's argument, in L. Kevin Wroth and Hiller B. Zobel, eds., *The Legal Papers of John Adams* (3 vols., Cambridge, Mass., 1965), I, 142, 144.

10. *Ibid.*, 107 (spelling modernized).

11. *Annals of Congress*, 1st Cong., 1st Session, 452.

12. See Osmand K. Frankel, "Concerning Searches and Seizures," *Harvard Law Review* 34 (1921), 361, n. 30.

13. *Terry v. Ohio*, 392 U.S. 1 (1968).

14. *United States v. Martinez-Fuerte*, 428 U.S. 543 (1976).

15. *O'Connor v. Ortega*, 480 U.S. 709 (1987).

16. *Skinner v. Railway Labor Executives' Association*, 489 U.S. 602 (1989).

17. *National Treasury Employees Union v. Von Raab*, 489 U.S 656 (1989).

18. "So You Smoke? Eat Junk Food? Sorry, You're Fired," *San Diego Union*, April 6, 1991.

19. "Newsman Says He Was Target of Probe," *San Diego Union*, December 21, 1990.

20. *Michigan Dept. of State Police v. Sitz*, 110 S.Ct. 2481, 2490 (1990) [quoting *Alameida-Sanchez v. United States*, 413 U.S. 266, 273 (1973)].

21. *Boyd v. United States*, 116 U.S. 616 (1886).

22. *Weeks v. United States*, 232 U.S. 393–94 (1913).

23. Roger B. Traynor, "*Mapp v. Ohio* at Large in the Fifty States," *Duke Law Journal* (1962), 321–22.

24. *Mapp v. Ohio*, 367 U.S. 660 (1961).

25. Peter F. Nardulli, "The Societal Cost of the Exclusionary Rule: An Empirical Assessment," *American Bar Foundation Research Journal* (1983), 585; and "The Societal Costs of the Exclusionary Rule Revisited," *University of Illinois Law Review* (1987), 223–39.

26. Office of Legal Policy, United States Department of Justice, *Report to the Attorney General on the Search and Seizure Exclusionary Rule: Report No. 2 in the Truth in Criminal Justice Series*, reprinted in *University of Michigan Journal of Law Reform* 22 (1989), 573–659.

27. Yale Kamisar, "Remembering the 'Old World' of Criminal Procedure," *University of Michigan Journal of Law Reform* 23 (1990), 568.

28. Daniel Webster, *The Writing and Speeches of Daniel Webster* (10 vols., Boston, 1903), VII, 122.

29. Acts 22: 24–30.

30. *Escobedo v. Illinois*, 378 U.S. 478 (1964). The Sixth Amendment basis for the right to counsel has subsequently been disavowed by the Court in *Moran v. Burbine*, 475 U.S. 412 (1986).

31. *Escobedo v. Illinois*, 488–89.

32. *Miranda v. Arizona*, 384 U.S. 436 (1966).

33. Yale Kamisar, Prepared Remarks at the U.S. Law Week's Constitutional Law Conference, September 17, 1987, Washington, D.C., on file in the law libraries of California Western School of Law and the University of Michigan.

34. Stephen J. Schulhofer, "Reconsidering Miranda," *University of Chicago Law Review* 54 (1987), 435–61; Special Commission of Criminal Justice in a Free Society, Criminal Justice Section, American Bar Association, *Criminal Justice in Crisis* (Chicago, 1988), 28–29.

35. See Herbert L. Packer, "Two Models of the Criminal Process," *University of Pennsylvania Law Review* 113 (1964), 1–23.

36. *Olmstead v. United States*, 277 U.S. 479 (1928) (dissenting opinion).

The "Cruel and Unusual Punishment" Clause

1. The Eighth Amendment reads, in full: "Excessive bail shall not be required, nor excessive fines imposed, nor cruel and unusual punishments inflicted." This essay addresses only the amendment's "cruel and unusual punishment" clause.

2. Joseph Story, *Commentaries on the Constitution of the United States* (2 vols., Boston, 1833), II, sec. 1903.

3. *Furman v. Georgia*, 408 U.S. 382 (1972) (Burger, C.J., dissenting).

4. *Trop v. Dulles*, 356 U.S. 101 (1958).

5. *Furman v. Georgia*, 408 U.S. 375–76 (1972).

6. The issues and cases discussed in this essay are by no means a complete compilation of those that are included within the scope of the Eighth Amendment's cruel and unusual punishment clause. For instance, there is a significant line of cases dealing with whether inadequate prison conditions can constitute "cruel and unusual punishment"; see, e.g., *Wilson v. Seiter*, 59 *U.S.L.W.* 4671 (June 17, 1991) (conditions of confinement do not violate Eighth Amendment unless they result from the "deliberate indifference" of responsible prison officials). Such cases, however, generally do not involve judicial review of legislatively enacted punishments, and they are therefore omitted from this essay.

7. *Harmelin v. Michigan*, 59 U.S.L.W. 4839, 4844 (June 25, 1991) (opinion of Scalia, J., announcing the judgment of the Court).

8. 1 *Journals of the House of Lords* 367 (May 31, 1689), quoted in *Second Trial of Titus Oates*, 10 How. St. Tr. 1227, 1325 (K.B. 1685).

9. *Ibid.*, 1316.

10. 1 *Journals of the House of Lords* 367 (May 31, 1689).

11. *Weems v. United States*, 217 U.S. 349 (1910).

12. *Trop v. Dulles*, 356 U.S. 86 (1958).

13. The two cases were *Furman v. Georgia*, 408 U.S. 238 (1972), and *Gregg v. Georgia*, 428 U.S. 153 (1976). In several other cases, the Court was presented with a facial Eighth Amendment challenge to the death penalty but declined to address the subject. See, e.g., *McGautha v. California*, 402 U.S. 183 (1971).

14. *Furman v. Georgia*, 408 U.S. 238 (1972).

15. *Furman v. Georgia*, 408 U.S. 362–63, 369 (1972).

16. *Ibid.*, 309.

17. *Gregg v. Georgia*, 428 U.S. 153 (1976).

18. The states that have abolished the death penalty are Alaska, Hawaii, Iowa, Kansas, Maine, Massachusetts, Michigan, Minnesota, New York, North Dakota, Rhode Island, Vermont, West Virginia, and Wisconsin. In addition, the District of Columbia has abolished the death penalty.

19. These statistics about death sentences, executions, and death row populations are taken from *Death Row, U.S.A.*, a quarterly publication of the NAACP Legal Defense and Education Fund, Inc.

20. See, e.g., William Bowers and Margaret Vandiver, "New Yorkers Want an Alternative to the Death Penalty," Executive Summary of a New York State Survey Conducted March 1–4, 1991 (reporting that less than 20 percent of New York residents surveyed preferred the death penalty for convicted murderers if presented with the alternative of life imprisonment without parole plus restitution for the victims' families).

21. *Wilkerson v. Utah*, 99 U.S. 130 (1879).

22. *In re Kemmler*, 136 U.S. 436 (1890).

23. *Glass v. Louisiana*, 471 U.S. 1080 (1985).

24. 59 *U.S.L.W.* 4839 (June 25, 1991).

25. *Ibid.*, 4844.

26. In *Robinson v. California*, 370 U.S. 660 (1962), the first case to apply the Eighth Amendment to the states, the Court rejected a ninety-day prison sentence for the crime of being addicted to narcotics. Since the sentence could not possibly have been "cruel and unusual" in the abstract, *Robinson* can plausibly be characterized as another proportionality case. Conversely, the Court seemed more concerned about the criminalization of addiction than about the amount of punishment imposed, suggesting that *Robinson* may concern "due process" more than proportionality.

27. *Solem v. Helm*, 463 U.S. 277 (1983).

28. *Ibid.*, 284.

29. See *Harmelin v. Michigan*, 59 *U.S.L.W.* 4839, 4850–51 (June 25, 1991).

30. See *Stanford v. Kentucky*, 492 U.S. 361, 377–80 (1989).

31. *Ibid.*, 389–90.

32. See *Coker v. Georgia*, 433 U.S. 584 (1977).

33. *Furman v. Georgia*, 408 U.S. 399.

34. Raoul Berger, *Selected Writings on the Constitution* (Cumberland, Ky., 1987), 272.

35. *Ibid.*, 273.

36. John Hart Ely, *Democracy and Distrust* (Cambridge, Mass., 1980), 173–77.

37. *Ibid.*, 176. Reaching a similar conclusion, although by a different route, is David A. J. Richards. Richards is highly critical of what he sees as Raoul Berger's overly narrow reliance on the history behind the "cruel and unusual punishment" clause. Richards aligns himself, however, with the substantive approach taken by Justices Brennan and Marshall in *Furman*, finding support for their views in a broadly contextual historical analysis of the origins of the Eighth Amendment. See David A. J. Richards, "Constitutional Interpretation, History, and the Death Penalty: A Book Review," *California Law Review* 71 (1983), 1372–98.

38. *Lockett v. Ohio*, 438 U.S. 586 (1978).

39. *Walton v. Arizona*, 110 S.Ct. (1990).

40. *Booth v. Maryland*, 482 U.S. 496 (1987).

41. *Payne v. Tennessee*, 59 *U.S.L.W.* 4814 (June 25, 1991).

Equal Protection and Affirmative Action

1. J. R. Pole, *The Pursuit of Equality in American History* (Berkeley, 1978), ix.

2. Hugh Davis Graham, *The Civil Rights Era: Origins and Development of National Policy 1960–1972* (New York, 1990), 3–152.

3. Discrimination in public employment was arguably unconstitutional under the Fifth and Fourteenth Amendments and was not covered by Title VII. In 1972 the law was amended to apply to public employment in state and local governments.

4. Carl Rachlin, "Title VII: Limitations and Qualifications," *Boston College Industrial and Commercial Law Review* 7 (Spring 1966), 488.

5. 41 C.F.R. (1971) Sect. 60–2.10.

6. It should be noted of course that under the disparate impact theory of discrimination, racial imbalance was in fact regarded as constituting an unlawful practice if any employer's selection methods could not be validated or shown to be specifically job-related.

7. *Griggs v. Duke Power Co.*, 401 U.S. 431–32 (1971).

8. Not until 1973, in *McDonnell Douglas v. Green*, did the Court decide that Title VII also prohibited intentional disparate treatment discrimination.

9. Recognizing the sweeping potential of the *Griggs* disparate impact concept for challenging the operation of state governments, the Supreme Court in *Washington v. Davis* rejected it as an interpretation of the equal protection clause.

10. Title VI prohibits racial discrimination in federally funded activities.

11. *Weber v. United Steelworkers of America*, 443 U.S. 197 (1979).

12. *Ibid.*, 204.

13. The affirmative action plan in *Weber* was in part also a response to pressure applied by the Office of Federal Contract Compliance for preferential treatment under E.O. 11246.

14. William Bradford Reynolds, "The Reagan Administration's Civil Rights Policy: The Challenge for the Future," *Vanderbilt Law Review* 42 (May 1989), 994–95.

15. Drew S. Days III, "The Court's Response to the Reagan Civil Rights Agenda," *Vanderbilt Law Review* 42 (May 1989), 1009.

16. *Local 28 Sheet Metal Workers v. EEOC*, 106 S.Ct. 3034 (1986).

17. Douglas Laycock, "Statistical Proof and Theories of Discrimination," *Law and Contemporary Problems* 49 (Autumn 1986), 97.

18. William J. Kilberg, "From the Editor," *Employment Relations Law Journal* 15 (Autumn 1989), 172.

19. Alfred W. Blumrosen, "The 1989 Supreme Court Rulings Concerning Employment Discrimination and Affirmative Action: A Minefield for Employers and a Gold Mine for Their Lawyers," *Employment Relations Law Journal* 15 (Autumn 1989), 177.

20. S. 2104, sec. 3, 101st Congress, 2d Session, Feb. 7, 1990.

21. This provision was designed to make remedies for discrimination against women under Title VII comparable to those available to racial minorities under Section 1981 of the U.S. Code.

22. This provision overruled *Lorance v. A.T. & T. Technologies* (1989), which upheld the 180-day filing period.

23. S. 2104, sec. 11.

24. Douglas S. McDowell, " 'Disparate Impact' and 'Business Necessity' — An Assessment and Guidelines for the Civil Rights Debate," Policy Paper, Employment Policy Foundation (Washington, 1991), I.

25. *Ibid.*, 41, 47.

26. William A. Kilberg, "The Civil Rights Act of 1990," *Employment Relations Law Journal* 16 (Summer 1990), 1. The sponsors of the bill added a provision stating that quotas were prohibited under Title VII. See below, note 28.

27. Representative Don Edwards, letter to the editor, *Washington Post*, March 3, 1990, p. A-24.

28. The bill stated: "Nothing in these amendments made by this Act shall be construed to require or encourage an employer to adopt hiring or promotion quotas on the basis of race, color, religion, or national origin: *Provided, however*, that nothing in the amendments made by this Act shall be construed to affect court-ordered remedies, affirmative action, or conciliation agreements that are otherwise in accordance with the law." This meant that while ostensibly prohibited, quotas could be required as a remedy for discrimination, as the Supreme Court decisions of the mid-1980s held.

29. McDowell, " 'Disparate Impact' and 'Business Necessity,' " 39. Some of the definitions of business necessity were: "bears a substantial and demonstrable relationship to effective job performance"; "significant relationship to significant business objective of the employer"; "significant relationship to successful performance of the job"; "significant relationship to a manifest business objective of the employer." *Ibid.*, 59–65.

30. *Ibid.*, 68.

31. The administration supported a provision extending Section 1981 to the performance as well as the making of a contract. This was intended to overrule the Supreme Court decision in *Patterson v. McLean Credit Union* (1989). The White House also agreed that the period within which an employee could challenge a seniority system should begin when the plaintiff experiences harm from the system, not the date of the establishment of the seniority system as the Supreme Court held in *Lorance v. A.T. & T. Technologies* (1989).

32. Memorandum of Disapproval of President Bush on S. 2104, *Congressional Quarterly Weekly Report* (Oct. 27, 1990), 3654.

33. Statement of Kingsley R. Browne on the Civil Rights Act of 1991 (S. 1745), Sept. 28, 1991, Senate Committee on the Judiciary.

34. John Hartigan and Alexandra Wigdor, letter to the editor, *Science*, July 7, 1989, Vol. 245, p. 14; Constance Holden, letter to the editor, *ibid*.

35. Race norming was also included in the 1990 bill. The report of the Senate Committee on Labor and Human Resources stated that race norming, which it referred to as "performance-based score adjustment," was an alternative procedure to a selection device that is valid (i.e., it accurately predicts job performance), yet has a disparate impact. The committee report was intended to provide legislative history to guide judicial interpretation of the act. Race norming was intended as a means of promoting preferential treatment independent of the procedural requirements concerning a *prima facie* case and burden of proof that dominated the discussion on the civil rights bill. Linda S. Gottfredson, "When Job-Testing 'Fairness' Is Nothing but a Quota," *Wall St. Journal*, Dec. 6, 1990.

36. *Regents of the University of California v. Bakke*, 438 U.S. 407 (1978).

37. Douglas Rae et al., *Inequalities* (Cambridge, Mass., 1981), 56.

38. Kenneth L. Karst and Harold W. Horowitz, "Affirmative Action and Equal Protection," *Virginia Law Review* 60 (October 1974), 956, 964–65.

39. Randall Kennedy, "Persuasion and Distrust: A Comment on the Affirmative Action Debate," *Harvard Law Review* 99 (March 1986), 1335–36.

40. In other words, the racially preferential policy was not subject to the strict scrutiny review that the Court in *Croson* said was required of measures resting on race as a suspect classification.

41. *Washington Times*, June 19, 1991, p. G3; *Washington Times*, June 17, 1991, p. A6; H.R. 3745, 101st Congress, 1st Session, Nov. 20, 1989.

42. See the Supreme Court decision in *Chisom v. Roemer* (1992).

43. *Washington Times*, June 13, 1991, p. C3.

44. Russell Nieli, "Ethnic Tribalism and Human Personhood," in Russell Nieli, ed., *Racial Preferences and Racial Justice: The New Affirmative Action Controversy* (Washington: Ethics and Public Policy Center, 1991), 88–89.

45. Colbert I. King, "Buying into White Supremacy," *Washington Post*, May 31, 1991, p. A19.

46. Aaron Wildavsky, "The 'Reverse Sequence' in Civil Liberties," *The Public Interest* 78 (Winter 1985), 32–42.

47. Thomas Ross, "Innocence and Affirmative Action," *Vanderbilt Law Review* 43 (March 1990), 297–316.

48. Nieli, "Ethnic Tribalism and Human Personhood," 61–103.

A Ninth Amendment for Today's Constitution

1. *Nomination of Robert H. Bork to be Associate Justice of the Supreme Court of the United States: Hearings before the Senate Committee on the Judiciary* [hereinafter "Nomination Hearings"], I (Washington, D.C., 1989), 117.

2. *Ibid.*

3. *Ibid.*, 249.

4. *The Federalist* No. 84 (New York, 1961), 513–14.

5. Joseph Gales, *The Debates and Proceedings in the Congress of the United States*, (Washington, D.C., 1834), I, 457.

6. *Ibid.*, 456.

7. *Ibid.*, 452.

8. "Nomination Hearings," 249.

9. "Roger Sherman's Draft of the Bill of Rights," in Randy E. Barnett, ed., *The Rights Retained by the People: The History and Meaning of the Ninth Amendment* (Fairfax, Va., 1989), 351 (emphasis added). Along the same lines, Madison had proposed to Congress that the following be added as a prefix to the Constitution:

> That Government is instituted and ought to be exercised for the benefit of the people; which consists in the enjoyment of life and liberty, with the right of acquiring and using property, and generally pursuing and obtaining happiness and safety. (*Annals of Congress*, I, 451)

10. See Randy E. Barnett, "Reconceiving the Ninth Amendment," *Cornell Law Review* 74 (1988), 30–32.

11. Jonathon Elliot, ed., *The Debates in the Several State Conventions on the Adoption of the Federal Constitution*, II (2d ed. 1836) (Philadelphia, 1937), 454.

12. *Ibid.*

13. Merrell Jensen, ed., *The Documentary History of the Ratification of the Constitution* (Madison, Wisc., 1976), II, 388 (statement of James Wilson to the Pennsylvania Ratifying Convention, Nov. 28, 1787).

14. *Annals of Congress*, I, 731.

15. *Ibid.*, 731–32.

16. *Ibid.*, 732.

17. *Ibid.*

18. *Ibid.*, 731.

19. *Ibid.*, 732.

20. Raoul Berger, "The Ninth Amendment," *Cornell Law Review* 66 (1980), 2.

21. *The Federalist*, No. 10, 79–80.

22. *United States v. Carolene Products Co.*, 304 U.S. 152, n.4 (1938). In this case, the Court also suggested that the presumption may be rebutted by showing that discrete and insular minorities are adversely affected or that the political process is being impeded.

23. *Annals of Congress*, II, 1836.

24. See U.S. Constitution., Art I, Sec. 8 ("The Congress shall have Power . . . To make all Laws which shall be necessary and proper for carrying into Execution the foregoing powers.").

25. *Ibid.* ("The Congress shall have Power . . . To borrow Money on the credit of the United States. . . .").

26. *Ibid.*, II, 1947.

27. *Ibid.*, I, 455.

28. *Ibid.*, II, 1950.

29. *Ibid.*, 1944.

30. *Ibid.*, 1945.

31. *Ibid.*, 1950.

32. U.S. Constitution, Art. I, Sec. 8.

33. *Annals of Congress*, II, 1948–49 (statement of Rep. Madison) (emphasis added).

34. *Ibid.*, 1951. The number of the amendments changed because the first two amendments proposed by Congress were not ratified by the states. At the time Madison spoke, this outcome was not yet known.

35. *Ibid.*

36. See Barnett, "Reconceiving the Ninth Amendment," 11–16.

37. *Korematsu v. United States*, 323 U.S. 214 (1944).

38. John Locke, *Two Treatises of Government* (New York, 1967 repr. of 3d ed., 1689), 311.

39. *Ibid.*, 312.

Of Floors and Ceilings

1. James A. Thomson, "State Constitutional Law: The Quiet Revolution," *University of Western Australia Law Review* 20 (1990 Special Issue), 311–22.

2. William F. Swindler, "Minimum Standards of Constitutional Justice: Federal Floor and State Ceiling," *Missouri Law Review* 49 (Winter 1984), 1–15.

3. As quoted in Barry Latzer, "The Hidden Conservatism of the State Court 'Revolution,'" *Judicature* 74 (Dec.-Jan. 1991), 190–97.

4. William J. Brennan, Jr., "State Constitutions and the Protection of Individual Rights," *Harvard Law Review*, 90 (Jan. 1977), 489–504; Hans Linde, "Due Process of Lawmaking," *Nebraska Law Review* 55 (1976), 197–237.

5. William J. Brennan, Jr., *The Bill of Rights and the States* (Santa Barbara, 1961), 20.

6. Brennan, "State Constitutions and the Protection of Individual Rights," 503.

7. Stanley Mosk, "The Power of State Constitutions in Protecting Individual Liberty," *Northern Illinois University Law Journal*, 8 (1988), 662.

8. *New York Times*, Jan. 8, 1990, p. A1.

9. Donald Lutz, "The Purposes of American State Constitutions," *Publius: The Journal of Federalism* 12 (Winter 1982), 27.

10. *Florida v. Casal*, 462 U.S. 637, 639 (1983).

11. Alexander Hamilton, John Jay, and James Madison, *The Federalist Papers* (New York, 1961), 176.

12. Max Farrand, ed., *Records of the Federal Convention* (5 vols., New Haven, 1966), I, 492.

13. *Records of the Federal Convention*, II, 618.

14. As quoted in Kermit L. Hall, ed., *"By and for the People": The Bill of Rights in American History* (Arlington Heights, Ill., 1991), 20.

15. Paul Finkelman and Steven E. Gottlieb, eds., *Toward a Usable Past: An Examination of the Origins and Implications of State Protections of Liberty* (Athens, Ga., 1991), 4.

16. Paul Finkelman, *An Imperfect Union: Slavery, Federalism, and Comity* (Chapel Hill, N. C., 1981), 223–36.

17. We know much more about the fate of the press than of speech in the nineteenth century. See Timothy W. Gleason, *The Watchdog Concept; The Press and the Courts in Nineteenth-Century America* (Ames, Iowa, 1990).

18. G. Alan Tarr, "Religion under State Constitutions," *Annals of the American Academy of Political and Social Sciences* 496 (March 1988), 65–75.

19. *Ibid.*, 66.

20. *Constitution of the State of Washington, 1889*, Art. 9, Sec. 4.

21. J. Morgan Kousser, "Before *Plessy*, Before *Brown*: The Development of the Law of Racial Integration in Louisiana and Kansas," in Finkelman and Gottlieb, eds., *Toward a Usable Past*, 212–40.

22. 28 Kansas 1, 18–19 (1881).

23. As cited in *ibid.*, 231.

24. *Ibid.*, 238.

25. Florida Constitution, Article I, Sec. 12.

26. *Commonwealth v. Bonadio*, 490 Pa. 91, 415 A.2d 47, 50 (1980).

27. 29 Ca.3d 252, 172 (1981).

28. *Constitution of the State of New York*, Art. 1, Sec. 8.

29. Sol Wachtler, "Constitutional Rights: Resuming the States' Role," *Intergovernmental Perspective* 15 (Summer 1989), 24.

30. Wachtler, "Constitutional Rights," 24.

31. Latzer, "The Hidden Conservatism of the State Court 'Revolution,' " 190.

32. Brennan, *The Bill of Rights and the States*, 266.

33. Kousser, "Before *Plessy*, Before *Brown*," 231.

Bibliographic Essays

Rights Consciousness in American History

The arguments of this essay are more fully elaborated in Daniel T. Rodgers, *Contested Truths: Keywords in American Politics since Independence* (New York, 1987). Alternative readings of the language and ideas of American politics are, of course, many. Among the most rewarding are Louis Hartz, *The Liberal Tradition in America* (New York, 1955); Yehoshua Arieli, *Individualism and Nationalism in American Ideology* (Cambridge, Mass., 1964); John P. Diggins, *The Lost Soul of American Politics* (New York, 1984); Willmoore Kendall and George W. Carey, *The Basic Symbols of the American Political Tradition* (Baton Rouge, La., 1970); and Samuel P. Huntington, *American Politics: The Promise of Disharmony* (Cambridge, Mass., 1981).

The place of natural rights language in the American Revolution is discussed in Clinton Rossiter, *Seedtime of the Republic* (New York, 1953); Bernard Bailyn, *The Ideological Origins of the American Revolution* (Cambridge, Mass., 1967); Staughton Lynd, *The Intellectual Origins of American Radicalism* (New York, 1968); Eric Foner, *Tom Paine and Revolutionary America* (New York, 1976); Garry Wills, *Inventing America: Jefferson's Declaration of Independence* (Garden City, N.Y., 1978); David Brion Davis, *The Problem of Slavery in the Age of Revolution, 1770–1823* (Ithaca, N.Y., 1975); and John Phillip Reid, *The Authority of Rights* (Madison, Wisc., 1986). There is no better starting place, however, than Thomas Paine, *The Rights of Man* (1791–92).

On the background to the Bill of Rights, see Gordon S. Wood, *The Creation of the American Republic, 1776–1787* (Chapel Hill, N.C., 1969), and Bernard Schwartz, ed., *The Bill of Rights: A Documentary History* (New York, 1971).

On the second wave of natural rights invention, see Edward Pessen, *Most Uncommon Jacksonians: The Radical Leaders of the Early Labor Movement* (Albany, N.Y., 1967); Sean Wilentz, *Chants Democratic: New York City and the Rise of the American Working Class, 1788–1850* (New York, 1984); Aileen S. Kraditor, *Means and Ends in American Abolitionism* (New York, 1969); Robert M. Cover, *Justice Accused: Antislavery and the Judicial Process* (New Haven, Conn., 1975); and Philip S. Foner, ed., *We, the Other People: Alternative Declarations of Independence by Labor Groups, Farmers, Woman's Rights Advocates, Socialists, and Blacks, 1829–1975* (Urbana, Ill., 1976).

The rise of judicial activism is analyzed in Morton J. Horwitz, "The Rise of Legal Formalism," *American Journal of Legal History* 19 (1975), 251–64; William E. Nelson, "The Impact of the Antislavery Movement upon Styles of Judicial Reasoning in Nineteenth Century America," *Harvard Law Review* 87 (1974), 513–66; Arnold M. Paul, *Conservative Crisis and the Rule of Law* (Ithaca, N.Y., 1960); Michael Les Benedict, "Laissez-Faire and Liberty: A Re-Evaluation of the Meaning and Origins of Laissez-Faire Constitutionalism," *Law and History Review* 3 (1985), 293–331; and Robert W. Gordon, "Legal Thought and Legal Practice in the Age of American Enterprise, 1870–1920," in *Professions and Professional Ideologies in America*, ed. Gerald L. Geison (Chapel Hill, N.C., 1983).

The clearest guide to the anti-rights animus of progressive and New Deal reformers is to be found in their own writings. Among the best are Herbert Croly, *The Promise of American Life* (New York, 1909); Frank J. Goodnow, *Social Reform and the Constitution* (New York, 1911); Charles G. Haines, *The Revival of Natural Law Concepts*

(Cambridge, Mass., 1930); Jerome Frank, *Law and the Modern Mind* (New York, 1930); and Thurman W. Arnold, *The Symbols of Government* (New Haven, Conn., 1935).

The shifting ideological mood of the 1940s is captured in Richard H. Pells, *The Liberal Mind in a Conservative Age* (New York, 1985), and Edward A. Purcell, Jr., *The Crisis of Democratic Theory* (Lexington, Ky., 1973). Samuel Walker's *In Defense of American Liberties: A History of the ACLU* (New York, 1990) is a fine introduction to the modern rights revolution. The critical literature that revolution spawned is vast and ever growing, but a useful entry to the rival points of view can be made through Alexander M. Bickel, *The Supreme Court and the Idea of Progress* (New York, 1970); Stuart A. Scheingold, *The Politics of Rights* (New Haven, 1974); and Mark Tushnet, et al., "Symposium: A Critique of Rights," *Texas Law Review* 62, no. 2 (1984).

The literature on rights violations is—like the subject itself—large. An introduction to its historical aspects can be made through Leonard Levy, *Jefferson and Civil Liberties: The Darker Side* (Cambridge, Mass., 1963), and *The Emergence of a Free Press* (New York, 1985); Leon F. Litwak, *North of Slavery: The Negro in the Free States, 1790–1860* (Chicago, 1961); Paul L. Murphy, *World War I and the Origins of Civil Liberties in the United States* (New York, 1979); and David Caute, *The Great Fear* (New York, 1978).

The Explosion and Erosion of Rights

The literature on the history and transformation of our conception of rights is, to put it simply, voluminous. There are several general works that merit special mention, however. For the best account of the creation of the Bill of Rights there is Robert A. Rutland's classic history, *The Birth of the Bill of Rights* (Chapel Hill, N.C., 1955; Bicentennial ed., 1991); few works offer as much in such small compass. The evolution of the Bill of Rights in the Supreme Court is best sought in Henry J. Abraham's sound account of these matters, *Freedom and the Court: Civil Rights and Liberties in the United States* (5th ed., New York, 1988).

The history of the incorporation doctrine, which is also covered in Abraham's *Freedom and the Court*, is covered in detail by Raoul Berger in *The Fourteenth Amendment and the Bill of Rights* (Norman, Okla., 1989). The related theme of the transformation of the Fourteenth Amendment itself is neatly—and provocatively—assessed by Berger in his *Government by Judiciary: The Transformation of the Fourteenth Amendment* (Cambridge, Mass., 1977). But it is also well to start at the beginning: Charles Warren's seminal essay "The New Liberty under the Fourteenth Amendment, *Harvard Law Review* 39 (1926), 431–65, written in the wake of *Gitlow v. New York* (1925), is not to be missed.

On the contemporary debate over the nature and extent of rights, Ronald Dworkin's *Taking Rights Seriously* (Cambridge, Mass., 1977) and Michael J. Perry's *The Constitution, the Court and Human Rights* (New Haven, Conn., 1981) lay out the case for an activist judicial approach to expanding old and creating new rights. The other side is best found in Walter Berns's "Judicial Review and the Rights and Laws of Nature," in *The Supreme Court Review* (1982), 49–83; this responds in particular to Thomas Grey's influential article in the *Stanford Law Review* 30 (1978), 843–91, "Origins of the Unwritten Constitution: Fundamental Law in American Revolutionary Thought."

Judge Robert Bork's important work *The Tempting of America: The Political Seduction of the Law* (New York, 1989) merits attention not merely because it makes a strong case against liberal experimentation with the Bill of Rights but because he sounds the alarm over activism from the right as well. In regard to the political ramifications of the contemporary obsession with rights, one should read with care Mary Ann Glendon's *Rights Talk: The Impoverishment of Political Discourse* (New York, 1991); Glendon's insights are compelling.

Symbolic Speech and the First Amendment

A number of general studies of free speech include sections dealing with symbolic expression. See especially Thomas Emerson, *The System of Freedom of Expression* (New York, 1970), and Franklyn Haiman, *Speech and Law in a Free Society* (Chicago, 1981). Also see Haiman's valuable article "Non-Verbal Communication and the First Amendment: The Rhetoric of the Streets, Revisited," *Quarterly Journal of Speech* 68 (Nov., 1982), 371–83. Jerome Barron and C. Thomas Dienes's *Handbook of Free Speech and Free Press* (Boston, 1979) contains a useful section on symbolic speech. See also Louis Henkin, "The Supreme Court, 1967 Term—Foreword: On Drawing Lines," *Harvard Law Review* 82 (1968), 63–75. Insightful is Thomas Scanlon, "Freedom of Expression and Categories of Expression," *University of Pittsburgh Law Review* 40 (1979), 519–50.

More explicit studies include Nelville Nimmer, "The Meaning of Symbolic Speech under the First Amendment," *U.C.L.A. Law Review* 21 (1973), 29–62; and Note, "Symbolic Conduct," *Columbia Law Review* 68 (1968), 1091–1126. Vincent Blasi, "The Checking Value in First Amendment Theory," *American Bar Foundation Research Journal* (1977), 521–649, sets forth a valuable conception. Also see C. Edwin Baker, "Scope of the First Amendment Freedom of Speech," *U.C.L.A. Law Review* 25 (1978), 964–1040. John Hart Ely, "Flag Desecration: A Case Study in the Roles of Categorization and Balancing in First Amendment Analysis," *Harvard Law Review* 88 (1975), 1481–1508, raises different dimensions of the issue. Dean Alfange, Jr., "Free Speech and Symbolic Conduct: The Draft-Card Burning Case," *Supreme Court Review* (1968), 1–52, is a useful exploration of the limits of symbolic expression. Thomas Scanlon, "A Theory of Freedom of Expression," *Philosophy and Public Affairs* 1 (1972), 204–26, is a readable popular view. A good casebook assessment of the leading cases is Harold Chase and Craig Ducat, *Constitutional Interpretation* (4th ed., St. Paul, Minn., 1988), 1198–1297.

Church and State

Leonard W. Levy, *The Establishment Clause and the First Amendment* (New York, 1986), is the best single overview of problems arising under the establishment clause but is written from a definite absolutist position. Thomas J. Curry, *The First Freedoms: Church and State in America to the Passage of the First Amendment* (New York, 1986), discusses the different ties and tensions between religion and authority during the colonial era and the first years of independence and raises serious questions about whether any "original intent" attached to the religion clauses can ever be discerned. Another balanced look at the complex relations between religion and authority in early America is William Lee Miller, *The First Liberty: Religion and the American Republic* (New York, 1986).

A good overview of the cases and issues involved in the prayer controversy, as well as the conflicting constitutional positions, is Rodney K. Smith, *Public Prayer and the Constitution* (Wilmington, Del., 1987). Two fine case studies that go well beyond the issues of the particular cases are David Manwaring, *Render unto Caesar: The Flag Salute Controversy* (Chicago, 1962), and Wayne R. Swanson, *The Christ Child Goes to Court* (Philadelphia, 1989), an examination of *Lynch v. Donnelly*.

Public Safety and the Right to Bear Arms

The legal and historical bibliography of the Second Amendment and gun control is one that until recently has escaped the attention of academic legal scholars. Not until Sanford Levinson published "The Embarrassing Second Amendment," *Yale Law Journal* 99 (1989) 637–59, did legal scholars enter the debate on the Second Amendment. Since Levinson's article, which supported the amendment as an individual right, other scholars have published on the subject, all supporting the individual-rights view to one extent or another: David C. Williams, "Civic Republicanism and the Citizen Militia: The Terrifying Second Amendment," *Yale Law Journal* 101 (1991), 551–615; Robert J. Cottrol and Raymond T. Diamond, "The Second Amendment: Towards an Afro-Americanist Reconsideration," *Georgetown Law Journal* 80 (1991), 309–61; and Akhil R. Amar, "The Bill of Rights as a Constitution," *Yale Law Journal* 100 (1991), 1131–1210.

Historians had earlier undertaken the Second Amendment as a field of inquiry. The work of Lee Kennett and James LaVergne Anderson, *The Gun in America: The Origins of a National Dilemma* (Westport, Conn., 1975), describes the history of firearms and gun control in America but does not take a normative view of the Second Amendment right as collective or not. Works that support the individual-rights view of the amendment are Robert E. Shalhope, "The Ideological Origins of the Second Amendment," *Journal of American History* 69 (1982), 599–614, and Joyce Lee Malcolm, "The Right of the People to Keep and Bear Arms: The Common Law Tradition," *Hastings Constitutional Law Quarterly* 10 (1983), 285–314. Arguing in support of the collective rights theory of the Second Amendment is Lawrence Delbert Cress, "An Armed Community: The Origins and Meaning of the Right to Bear Arms," *Journal of American History* 71 (1984), 22–42.

Because until recently legal academicians have been reluctant to enter the field, debate with respect to the Second Amendment and gun control has been left to and dominated by independent scholars. Influential among advocates of the individual-rights view of the Second Amendment have been Don B. Kates, Jr., and Stephen P. Halbrook. Halbrook has authored *That Every Man Be Armed: The Evolution of a Constitutional Right* (Albuquerque, N.M., 1984); Kates is the author of "Handgun Prohibition and the Original Meaning of the Second Amendment," *Michigan Law Review* 82 (1983), 204.

Two scholars who are concerned with the criminological aspects of gun control and who support the collective rights theory of the Second Amendment are Franklin E. Zimring and Gordon Hawkins, who have authored *The Citizen's Guide to Gun Control* (New York, 1987). Representative of nonacademic legal scholars who argue the collective rights view of the Second Amendment and support the case in favor of gun control are Warren Freedman, *The Privilege to Keep and Bear Arms: The Second Amendment and Its Interpretation* (New York, 1989); Keith A. Ehrman and Dennis A. Hennigan, "The Second Amendment in the Twentieth Century: Have You Seen Your Militia Lately?," *University of Dayton Law Review* 15 (1989), 5–58; and Maynard H. Jackson, Jr., "Handgun Control: Constitutional and Critically Needed," *North Carolina Central Law Journal* 8 (1977), 189.

The preeminent sociological and criminological writings on issues related to gun control are Gary Kleck, *Point Blank: Guns and Violence in America* (New York, 1991); James D. Wright and Peter H. Rossi, *Armed and Considered Dangerous: A Survey of Felons and Their Firearms* (New York, 1986); and James D. Wright, Peter H. Rossi, and Kathleen Daly, *Under the Gun: Weapons, Crime and Violence in America* (New York, 1983).

Paxton Quigley, *Armed and Female* (New York, 1989), presents a feminist perspective on the merits of bearing firearms, and Robert Sherrill, *The Saturday Night Special* (New York, 1973), presents an evenhanded journalist's view of the gun control debate. Useful anthologies of scholars and commentators from various disciplines are Don B. Kates, Jr., ed., *Restricting Handguns: The Liberal Skeptics Speak Out* (Croton-on-Hudson, N.Y., 1979), and Don B. Kates, Jr., ed., *Firearms and Violence: Issues of Public Policy* (San Francisco, 1984), both of which are supportive of the case against gun control; and Robert Emmet Long, ed., *Gun Control* (New York, 1989), which presents legal, historical, and policy arguments on both sides of the issue.

The Enigmatic Place of Property Rights in Modern Constitutional Thought

Perhaps the best survey of property rights over the course of American history is James W. Ely, Jr., *The Guardian of Every Other Right: A Constitutional History of Property Rights* (New York, 1992). There are several comprehensive studies of constitutional and legal history that address issues relating to property rights. See Alfred H. Kelly, Winfred A. Harbison, and Herman Belz, *The American Constitution: Its Origins and Development* (7th ed., New York, 1991); Kermit L. Hall, *The Magic Mirror: Law in American History* (New York, 1989). Another important work, Kermit L. Hall, James W. Ely, Jr., Joel Grossman, and William Wiecek, eds., *The Oxford Companion to the Supreme Court of the United States* (New York, 1992), contains numerous essays dealing with the Supreme Court and economic liberty. Fine collections of essays edited by Ellen Frankel Paul and Howard Dickman, *Liberty, Property, and Government: Constitutional Interpretation Before the New Deal* (Albany, N.Y., 1989) and *Liberty, Property, and the Future of Constitutional Development* (Albany, N.Y., 1990) offer a good introduction to thinking about property rights.

Many excellent studies examine particular subjects pertaining to the constitutional protection of property rights. For the importance of property in Revolutionary thought see John Phillip Reid, *Constitutional History of the American Revolution: The Authority of Rights* (Madison, Wisc., 1986). Several works give attention to property rights in the constitution-drafting process. See Willi Paul Adams, *The First American Constitutions: Republican Ideology and the Making of the State Constitutions in the Revolutionary Era* (Chapel Hill, N.C., 1980); James W. Ely, Jr., " 'that due satisfaction be made': The Fifth Amendment and the Origins of the Compensation Principle," *American Journal of Legal History* 36 (1992), 1–18. Important insights regarding the concept of economic due process are provided in Michael Les Benedict, "Laissez-Faire and Liberty: A Re-Evaluation of the Meaning and Origins of Laissez-Faire Constitutionalism," *Law and History Review* 3 (1985), 292–331, and Herbert Hovenkamp, "The Political Economy of Substantive Due Process," *Stanford Law Review* 40 (1988), 379–447. Paul Kens's *Judicial Power and Reform Politics: The Anatomy of Lochner v. New York* (Lawrence, Kans., 1990) is a rewarding account of a famous decision. For the subordination of property rights by the New Deal, see Geoffrey P. Miller, "The True Story of Carolene Products," *Supreme Court Review 1987* (1988), 397–428; Richard A. Epstein, "The Mistakes of 1937," *George Mason University of Law Review*

11 (1988), 5–20; and Jonathan R. Macey, "Some Causes and Consequences of the Bifurcated Treatment of Economic Rights under the United States Constitution," *Social Philosophy and Policy* 9 (1992), 141–70.

Calls for reinvigorated constitutional protection of economic interests have fueled the current debate. See Bernard H. Siegan, *Economic Liberties and the Constitution* (Chicago, 1980); Richard A. Epstein, *Takings: Private Property and the Power of Eminent Domain* (Cambridge, Mass., 1985); Stephen Macedo, *The New Right v. The Constitution* (Washington, D.C., 1986); James A. Dorn and Henry G. Manne, eds., *Economic Liberties and the Judiciary* (Fairfax, Va., 1987); and Note, "Resurrecting Economic Rights: The Doctrine of Economic Due Process Reconsidered," *Harvard Law Review* 103 (1990), 1363–83. Other scholars have criticized this renewed interest in property rights. See Bernard Schwartz, *The New Right and the Constitution: Turning Back the Legal Clock* (Boston, 1990); Thomas C. Grey, "The Malthusian Constitution," *University of Miami Law Review* 41 (1986), 21–48. For a thoughtful assessment of the controversy over land use regulations see Carol M. Rose, "Property Rights, Regulatory Regimes and the New Takings Jurisprudence—An Evolutionary Approach," *Tennessee Law Review* 57 (1990), 577–94.

Reversing the Revolution

There are surprisingly few surveys of the due process revolution of the last several decades, at least as it affected criminal defendants. Readers should start with the appropriate chapters in David J. Bodenhamer, *Fair Trial: Rights of the Accused in American History* (New York, 1992), a work that may be supplemented by Melvin I. Urofsky, *The Continuity of Change: The Supreme Court and Individual Liberties, 1953–1986* (New York, 1989). The story of how the Bill of Rights' guarantees came to be incorporated into the Fourteenth Amendment as a restriction on state criminal process is found in Richard C. Cortner, *The Supreme Court and the Second Bill of Rights: The Fourteenth Amendment and the Nationalization of Civil Liberties* (Madison, Wisc., 1981). David Fellman, *The Defendant's Rights Today* (Madison, Wisc., 1975), serves as a useful guide to changes of the 1960s and early 1970s, while several essays in Herman Schwartz, ed., *The Burger Years: Rights and Wrongs in the Supreme Court, 1969–1986* (New York, 1987), extend the discussion to the mid-1980s.

Judicial biographies often serve as a good introduction to issues before the Supreme Court. James Simon, *The Antagonists: Hugo Black, Felix Frankfurter and Civil Liberties in Modern America* (New York, 1989), details the momentous clash of these two personalities over the meaning and extent of due process protections. There are two able biographies of Earl Warren, under whose leadership the due process revolution occurred: G. Edward White, *Earl Warren: A Public Life* (New York, 1982) and Bernard Schwartz, *Super Chief: Earl Warren and His Supreme Court* (New York, 1983). Sue Davis, *Justice Rehnquist and the Constitution* (Princeton, N.J., 1989), provides a good understanding of the current Chief Justice's legal philosophy.

Studies of landmark and other important cases offer another fruitful way to learn about rights of the accused in these transitional decades. Among the more useful works are Dan T. Carter, *Scottsboro: A Tragedy of the American South* (rev. ed., Baton Rouge, 1979), a study of *Powell v. Alabama* (1932); Anthony Lewis, *Gideon's Trumpet* (New York, 1964), the story of *Gideon v. Wainwright* (1963), the famous right to counsel case; and Lisa Baker, *Miranda: Crime, Law, and Politics* (New York, 1983), which provides a detailed look at *Miranda v. Arizona* (1966). Both Carter's and Lewis's books served as the basis for interesting television movies in the 1980s.

Police Practices and the Bill of Rights

The best introduction to the constitutional law of police practices is Shelvin Singer and Marshall J. Hartman, *Constitutional Criminal Procedure Handbook* (New York, 1986). Chapters 8 through 10 and chapter 12 of this book provide an extremely readable analysis of all the major Supreme Court cases on the Fourth and Fifth Amendments. More theoretical are Herbert L. Packer's "Two Models of the Criminal Process," *University of Pennsylvania Law Review* 113 (1964), 1–68, and *The Limits of the Criminal Sanction* (Stanford, Calif., 1968), which outline contrasting philosophical approaches to criminal procedure and explain why it matters whether a given criminal justice system places greater emphasis on crime control or on due process. Students interested in the history of those Bill of Rights provisions that regulate police practices should begin their reading with David Bodenhamer, *Fair Trial: Rights of the Accused in American History* (New York, 1992). For development of the attitudes underlying these and other constitutional limitations on governmental power, see Edward S. Corwin, *Liberty against Government: The Rise, Flowering and Decline of a Famous Judicial Concept* (Baton Rouge, La., 1948).

The best historical work on the privilege against self-incrimination is Leonard W. Levy's Pulitzer Prize-winning classic, *Origins of the Fifth Amendment: The Right against Self-Incrimination* (New York, 1968). Laurence A. Benner, "Requiem for *Miranda*: The Rehnquist Court's Voluntariness Doctrine in Historical Perspective," *Washington University Law Quarterly* 67 (1989), 59–163, critiques the Rehnquist Court rulings undermining the *Miranda* decision. In "Reconsidering *Miranda*," *University of Chicago Law Review* 54 (1987), 435–61, Stephen J. Schulhoffer provides an excellent analysis of the Supreme Court's ruling in that case and also summarizes a number of studies that assess its impact on law enforcement. For further information on the latter subject, as well as a discussion of the judicial decisions leading up to *Miranda*, see Otis H. Stephens, Jr., *The Supreme Court and Confessions of Guilt* (Lexington, Ky., 1973). A far more insightful examination of how the law concerning police interrogations developed is Yale Kamisar's *Police Interrogation and Confessions* (Ann Arbor, Mich., 1980).

Readers particularly interested in the Fourth Amendment should consult Anthony G. Amsterdam's "Perspectives on the Fourth Amendment," *Minnesota Law Review* 58 (1974), 349–477, regarded as a classic in the literature on that subject. Although somewhat dated, Nelson Lasson's *The History and Development of the Fourth Amendment* (Baltimore, 1937) remains useful, because it details the historical origins of the concepts embodied in the Fourth Amendment from Roman times through the American Revolution and also analyzes early judicial interpretation of that constitutional provision. For those seeking insights into the values protected by the Fourth Amendment, a good place to start is Ferdinand D. Schoeman, *Philosophical Dimensions of Privacy: An Anthology* (Cambridge, 1984), a book that collects essays by political scientists, lawyers, philosophers, and anthropologists, representative of the diversity of attitudes on privacy, and introduces them with a thoughtful interpretive essay critiquing the literature on the subject. Laurence A. Benner's "Diminishing Expectations of Privacy in the Rehnquist Court," *John Marshall Law Review* 22 (1989), 825–76, focuses on recent Supreme Court rulings that have employed the concept of "a reasonable expectation of privacy" to restrict the protection afforded by the Fourth Amendment.

The controversial exclusionary rule, which the Court uses to enforce constitutional limitations on police practices, has received the attention of a number of scholars. Particularly useful are two detailed studies by Peter F. Nardulli of the impact of that rule on conviction rates, "Societal Cost of the Exclusionary Rule: An Empirical Assessment," *American Bar Foundation Research Journal* (1983), 585–609, and "The Societal Costs of the Exclusionary Rule Revisited," *University of Illinois Law Review* (1987), 223–39. Also informative is Thomas Y. Davies, "A Hard Look at What We Know (and Still Need to Learn) about the 'Costs' of the Exclusionary Rule: The NIJ Study and Other Studies of Lost Arrests," *American Bar Foundation Research Journal* (1983), 611–90, which critiques previous research on the subject and reports the findings of a California study. Steven F. Schlesinger presents a vigorous critique of the rule in *Exclusionary Injustice: The Problem of Illegally Obtained Evidence* (New York, 1977).

The "Cruel and Unusual Punishment" Clause

Unlike most of the provisions of the Bill of Rights, few scholarly works deal with the full range of textual, historical, philosophical, and political concerns surrounding the interpretation of the Eighth Amendment. Perhaps this is because most modern Eighth Amendment cases to reach the Supreme Court have involved the death penalty, a scholarly subspecialty of little interest to most general constitutional scholars, legal historians, and even criminal law professors. Nevertheless, there are some important works of general constitutional scholarship that address, at least in passing, the Eighth Amendment. These include Raoul Berger, *Selected Writings on the Constitution* (Cumberland, Md., 1987); John Hart Ely, *Democracy and Distrust* (Cambridge, Mass., 1980); and Bernard Schwartz, *A Commentary on the Constitution of the United States* (New York, 1968). Two prominent general constitutional scholars have written books specifically about the death penalty: Raoul Berger, *Death Penalties: The Supreme Court's Obstacle Course* (Cambridge, Mass., 1982), and Charles Black, Jr., *Capital Punishment: The Inevitability of Caprice and Mistake* (New York, 1981). An excellent short essay is David A. J. Richards, "Constitutional Interpretation, History, and the Death Penalty: A Book Review," *California Law Review* 71 (1983), 1372–98.

A useful general reference that includes material about the Eighth Amendment is Philip Kurland and Ralph Lerner, eds., *The Founders' Constitution* (Chicago, 1987). Many of the original historical documents are compiled and reproduced in Richard Perry and John Cooper, eds., *The Sources of Our Liberties: Documentary Origins of Individual Liberties in the United States Constitution and Bill of Rights* (New York, 1959). Two influential articles that focus specifically on the history of the Eighth Amendment are Anthony Granucci, " 'Nor Cruel and Unusual Punishments Inflicted': The Original Meaning," *California Law Review* 57 (1969), 839–65, and Charles Schwartz, "Eighth Amendment Proportionality Analysis and the Compelling Case of William Rummel," *Journal of Criminal Law and Criminology* 71 (1980), 378–420.

Many of the difficult questions that the Supreme Court struggles with in deciding modern Eighth Amendment cases can best be described as involving "moral reasoning," or "moral philosophy." Two helpful collections of essays on wide-ranging topics of moral philosophy are Gertrude Ezorsky, ed., *Philosophical Perspectives on Punishment* (Albany, N.Y., 1972), and H. L. A. Hart, *Punishment and Responsibility: Essays in the Philosophy of Law* (New York, 1968). Further insight into these (and other) interesting moral questions can be found in Jeffrie Murphy and Jean Hampton, *Forgiveness and Mercy* (Cambridge, Mass., 1988) and Judith Shklar, *Ordinary Vices* (Cambridge, Mass., 1984).

The death penalty has provided the Supreme Court with its most significant and controversial Eighth Amendment cases. Not surprisingly, therefore, much of the recent scholarly writing about the Eighth Amendment has dealt specifically with the death-penalty cases. The best recent books on the law of the death penalty include David Baldus, George Woodworth, and Charles Pulaski, Jr., *Equal Justice and the Death Penalty: A Legal and Empirical Analysis* (Boston, 1990); Hugo Adam Bedau, *Death Is Different: Studies in the Morality, Law, and Politics of Capital Punishment* (Boston, 1987); William Bowers, *Legal Homicide: Death as Punishment in America, 1864–1982* (Boston, 1984); Stephen Nathanson, *An Eye for an Eye? The Morality of Punishing by Death* (Totowa, N.J., 1987); Ernest van den Haag and John Conrad, *The Death Penalty: A Debate* (New York, 1983); and Welsh White, *Life in the Balance: Procedural Safeguards in Capital Cases* (Ann Arbor, Mich., 1984). Important shorter works on the subject include: Samuel Gross and Robert Mauro, "Patterns of Death: An Analysis of Racial Disparities in Capital Sentencing and Homicide Victimization," *Stanford Law Review* 37 (1984), 27–153; Joseph Hoffmann, "On the Perils of Line-Drawing: Juveniles and the Death Penalty," *Hastings Law Journal* 40 (1989), 229–84; Margaret Jane Radin, "Cruel Punishment and Respect for Persons: Super Due Process for Death," *Southern California Law Review* 53 (1980), 1143–85; Eric Schnapper, "The Capital Punishment Conundrum," *Michigan Law Review* 84 (1986), 715–36; and Robert Weisberg, "Deregulating Death," *The Supreme Court Review 1983* (1984), 305–95.

Equal Protection and Affirmative Action

General works on equality that provide necessary background for understanding the affirmative action controversy include J. R. Pole, *The Pursuit of Equality in American History* (Berkeley, Calif., 1978); Terry Eastland and William J. Bennett, *Counting by Race: Equality from the Founding Fathers to Bakke and Weber* (New York, 1979); Charles Redenius, *The American Ideal of Equality: From Jefferson's Declaration to the Burger Court* (Port Washington, N.Y., 1981); Judith N. Shklar, *American Citizenship: The Quest for Inclusion* (Cambridge, Mass., 1991); Aaron Wildavsky, "The 'Reverse Sequence' in Civil Liberties," *The Public Interest* 78 (Winter 1985), 32–42.

An early study of affirmative action that retains its analytical acuity and relevance is Nathan Glazer, *Affirmative Discrimination: Ethnic Inequality and Public Policy* (New York, 1975). *Racial Preferences and Racial Justice: The New Affirmative Action Controversy* (Washington, 1991), ed. Russell Nieli, is a valuable anthology of writings on affirmative action, including key judicial opinions. An authoritative recent study of voting rights and affirmative action is Abigail M. Thernstrom, *Whose Votes Count? Affirmative Action and Minority Rights* (Cambridge, Mass., 1987). Contrasting evaluations of affirmative action are presented by black writers Shelby Steele, *The Content of Our Character* (New York, 1990), and Roy L. Brooks, *Rethinking the American Race Problem* (Berkeley, Calif., 1990). Worthwhile studies of affirmative action from a philosophical perspective include Barry R. Gross, *Discrimination in Reverse: Is Turnabout Fair Play?* (New York, 1978); Alan H. Goldman, *Justice and Reverse Discrimination* (Princeton, N.J., 1979); Robert K. Fullinwider, *The Reverse Discrimination Controversy: A Moral and Legal Analysis* (Totowa, N.J., 1980); Michael W. Combs and John Gruhl, eds., *Affirmative Action: Theory, Analysis, and Prospects* (Jefferson, N.C., 1986); Michel Rosenfeld, *Affirmative Action and Justice: A Philosophical and Constitutional Inquiry* (New Haven, Conn., 1991).

Affirmative action in employment discrimination is treated in Herman Belz, *Equality Transformed: A Quarter Century of Affirmative Action* (New Brunswick, N.J., 1991). Hugh Davis Graham, *The Civil Rights Era: Origins and Development of National Policy 1960–1972* (New York, 1990), discusses the origins of affirmative action in employment, voting, and school desegregation. Alfred W. Blumrosen, *Black Employ-*

ment and the Law (New Brunswick, N.J., 1971), and William B. Gould, *Black Workers in White Unions: Job Discrimination in the United States* (Ithaca, N.Y., 1977), provide legal accounts of affirmative action by former lawyer-participants in the civil rights bureaucracy. Perceptive legal analyses of affirmative action in employment are Michael Evan Gold, "*Griggs'* Folly: An Essay on the Theory, Problems, and Origin of the Adverse Impact Definition of Employment Discrimination and a Recommendation for Reform," *Industrial Relations Law Journal* 7 (1985), 429–598; George Rutherglen, "Disparate Impact under Title VII: An Objective Theory of Discrimination," *Virginia Law Review* 73 (Oct. 1987), 1297–1345; Joel W. Friedman, "Redefining Equality, Discrimination, and Affirmative Action under Title VII: The Access Principle," *Texas Law Review* 65 (Nov. 1986), 41–99. Mary H. Cooper, "Racial Quotas," *CQ Researcher* 1 (May 17, 1991), surveys recent developments in the field of employment discrimination.

A Ninth Amendment for Today's Constitution

The Ninth Amendment has been discussed in a number of recent articles and books. The most significant of these can be found in two anthologies. The first, Randy E. Barnett, ed., *The Rights Retained by the People, Volume One: The History and Meaning of the Ninth Amendment* (Fairfax, Va., 1989), contains the most influential essays that preceded the current rush of interest in the Ninth Amendment. These essays focus primarily on the history and original intent of the Ninth Amendment and include the writings of James Madison, Raoul Berger, Charles Black, Russell Caplan, John Hart Ely, Calvin Massey, and Norman Redlich. Also included are several useful appendices—including Roger Sherman's draft of a bill of rights and all the amendments originally proposed by state ratification conventions—as well as a detailed bibliography of Ninth Amendment scholarship. The second, Randy E. Barnett, ed., *The Rights Retained by the People, Volume Two: The Ninth Amendment and Constitutional Interpretation* (Fairfax, Va., 1992), contains recent essays discussing the implications of the Ninth Amendment for how the Constitution should be interpreted by the courts. They include writings by Sotirios Barber, Thomas Grey, Sanford Levinson, Steven Macedo, Earl Maltz, Thomas McAffee, Michael McConnell, Andrzej Rapaczynsky, Lawrence Sager, and Suzanna Sherry. Also included is the complete text of James Madison's speech concerning the proposed national bank.

Of Floors and Ceilings

Scholars have much work to do before state constitutions and bills of rights make their way from the archives into the legal and historical literature. The broad outline of their development is treated in Kermit L. Hall, *The Magic Mirror: Law in American History* (New York, 1989), and in J. Willard Hurst, *The Growth of American Law: The Law Makers* (Boston, 1950), but there is no overall history of these documents. The best general collection of materials relating to them is Robert F. Williams, ed., *State Constitutional Law: Cases and Materials* (Washington, D.C., 1988). Williams has collected materials that shed light not only on legal developments but on the history and political science underlying state constitutions. Phylis S. Bamberger, ed., *Recent Developments in State Constitutional Law* (New York, 1985), contains additional valuable material. The documents themselves, including their bills of rights, can be found in William F. Swindler, ed., *Sources and Documents of U.S. Constitutions*, 11 vols. (Dobbs Ferry, N.Y., 1973–1979). The best treatment of issues in state constitutional law can be found in "Symposium on the Arizona Constitution," *Arizona State Law Journal* 20 (Spring 1988). Although the symposium concentrated on the Arizona document, the general lessons it draws are applicable to almost every other state. The case for the importance of state constitutions is most cogently made by William F. Swindler, "Minimum Standards of Constitutional Justice: Federal Floor and State Ceiling," *Missouri Law Review* 49 (Winter 1984), 1–15.

No student on state-based rights can ignore the fine work of Donald Lutz, who has done a great deal to link the state and federal documents. In addition to *Origins of American Constitutionalism* (Baton Rouge, La., 1988), Lutz has also published two widely influential essays: "The Purposes of American State Constitutions," *Publius: The Journal of Federalism* 12 (Winter 1982), 27–40, and "The United States Constitution as an Incomplete Document," *Annals of the American Academy of Political and Social Science* 496 (March 1988), 21–32. The best study of the impact of the state documents on the federal Constitution is Willi Paul Adams, *The First American Constitutions: Republican Ideology and the Making of the State Constitutions of the Revolutionary Era* (Chapel Hill, N.C., 1980). The nineteenth- and twentieth-century developments are treated in broad compass by Kermit L. Hall, "'Mostly Anchor and Little Sail': State Constitutions in American History," in *Toward a Usable Past: Liberty under State Constitutions,* ed. Paul L. Finkelman and Steven Gottlieb (Athens, Ga., 1991), 221–45, a book that contains several excellent essays on various aspects of state-based liberty, including an especially fine piece by James Henretta. Equally valuable as an overview is Daniel J. Elazar, "State Constitutional Design in the United States and Other Systems," *Publius: A Journal of Federalism* 12 (Winter 1982), 1–10. Frank P. Grad, "The State Constitution: Its Function and Form for Our Time," *Virginia Law Review* 54 (June 1968), 928–73, is also a valuable introduction to current problems in state constitutional rights.

The recent surge in importance of state bills of rights as documents of liberty has been the subject of an extensive body of writing, only a small part of which can be covered here. In addition to the literature cited in the notes, readers should also consult Hans A. Linde, "Without 'Due Process' of Law: Unconstitutional Law in Oregon," *Oregon Law Review* 49 (Feb. 1970), 133–56, which applauds the possibilities of an activist state judiciary broadly interpreting state bills of rights, and Earl Maltz, "The Dark Side of State Court Activism," *Texas Law Review* 63 (March/April 1985), 995–1023, which raises substantial doubts about such activism. That there may not be quite the revolution in state constitutional law that many commentators believed is the subject of Barry Latzer, "The Hidden Conservatism of the State Court 'Revolution,' " *Judicature: The Journal of the American Judicature Society* 74 (Dec.-Jan. 1991), 190–97.

Contributors

Randy E. Barnett is Professor of Law at Chicago-Kent College of Law. He is the author of several books including *Assessing the Criminal: Restitution, Retribution and the Legal Process* (1977) and *The Rights Retained by the People: The History and Meaning of the Ninth Amendment* (1989). Professor Barnett has also written and lectured widely on the meaning of the Ninth Amendment.

Michal R. Belknap is Professor of Law and History at California Western School of Law. In addition to more than thirty articles, essays in books, and encyclopedia entries, he is the author of *Federal Law and Southern Order* (1987) and *Cold War Political Justice: The Smith Act, the Communist Party and American Civil Liberties* (1977). He has also edited two series, *Civil Rights: The White House and the Justice Department, 1945–1968* (1991) and *American Political Trials* (1981). His history of the American Judicature Society, entitled *To Promote the Effective Administration of Justice*, is currently in press.

Herman Belz is Professor of History at the University of Maryland, College Park. He is co-author of a widely used text, *The American Constitution*, now in its seventh edition, and author of *Emancipation and Equal Rights: Politics and Constitutionalism in the Civil War Era* (1978) and numerous articles and essays. He has recently written a study of modern civil rights policy entitled *Equality Transformed: A Quarter Century of Affirmative Action* (1991).

Laurence A. Benner is Professor of Law at California Western School of Law. He has written extensively on issues in criminal law, especially regarding right to counsel for the poor, and has served as a public defender and a member of the National Study Commission for Defense Services. He is co-author of *The Other Face of Justice* (1973), which evaluated the effectiveness of indigent defense systems throughout the United States.

David J. Bodenhamer is Professor of History and Director of the POLIS Research Center at Indiana University-Purdue University at Indianapolis. In addition to over thirty articles, chapters in books, and papers on legal and constitutional history, he is the author or editor of *Ambivalent Legacy: A Legal History of the South*, with James W. Ely, Jr. (1984), *The Pursuit of Justice: Crime and Law in Antebellum Indiana* (1986), and *Fair Trial: Rights of the Accused in American History* (1992).

Robert J. Cottrol is Professor of Law at Rutgers, Camden School of Law. He is the author of *The Afro-Yankees: Province's Black Community in the Antebellum Era* (1982). He is also the author of numerous articles examining legal and constitutional history.

Raymond T. Diamond is Professor of Law at Tulane University. He has written widely in the fields of constitutional history and race relations.

James W. Ely, Jr. is Professor of Law and History at Vanderbilt University. He is the author or editor of seven books, including *Ambivalent Legacy: A Legal History of the South*, with David J. Bodenhamer (1984), *An Uncertain Tradition: Constitutionalism and the History of the South*, with Kermit L. Hall (1989), and *The Guardian of Every*

Other Right: A Constitutional History of Property Rights (1992). He has also written numerous scholarly articles and papers on legal and constitutional history.

Kermit L. Hall is Dean of the Henry Kendall College of Arts and Sciences and Professor of History and Law at the University of Tulsa. His publications include *The Oxford Companion to the Supreme Court* (1992); *By and for the People: Constitutional Rights in American History* (1991); *The Magic Mirror: Law in American History* (1990); *The Politics of Justice* (1979); *A Comprehensive Bibliography of American Constitutional and Legal History* (1984, 1991); and, with James W. Ely, Jr., *An Uncertain Tradition: Constitutionalism and the History of the South* (1989). He is the author of more than fifty scholarly articles and essays in books. His most recent work is *"Heed Their Rising Voice": The Anatomy of New York Times v. Sullivan* (forthcoming, 1993).

Joseph L. Hoffmann is Professor of Law at Indiana University-Bloomington, where he joined the faculty in 1986 after serving a one-year clerkship with Justice William H. Rehnquist of the U.S. Supreme Court. His writings include articles and book chapters on the juvenile death penalty, federal habeas corpus law, and the principles of moral responsibility for crime. He is currently working on a National Science Foundation research project involving personal interviews with thousands of jurors who served in death penalty cases.

Gary L. McDowell is Bradley Visiting Scholar at Harvard Law School. He is the author or editor of numerous books, including *Taking the Constitution Seriously: Essays on the Constitution and Constitutional Law* (1981), *Equity and the Constitution: The Supreme Court, Equitable Relief, and Public Policy* (1982), and *Curbing the Courts: The Constitution and the Limits of Judicial Power* (1988). In addition, McDowell has authored numerous essays and papers dealing with aspects of American constitutional law.

Paul L. Murphy is Regents' Professor of American History at the University of Minnesota, and Distinguished Adjunct Professor of Legal History at the Hamline University School of Law. He is a former Guggenheim Fellow, Fellow of the National Humanities Center, and Senior Fulbright Lecturer at the University of Lagos, Nigeria. His many publications include *The Meaning of Freedom of Speech* (1972); *The Constitution in Crisis Times, 1918–1969* (1972) in the New American Nation Series; *World War I and the Origin of Civil Liberties in the United States* (1979); and *The Constitution in the Twentieth Century* (1987). He is also the editor of the series *Contributions in Legal Studies*.

Daniel T. Rodgers has taught at the University of Wisconsin and Princeton University, where he is currently Professor of History. He is the author of *Contested Truths: Keywords in American Politics since Independence* (1987) and *The Work Ethic in Industrial America, 1850–1920* (1978), which won the Frederick Jackson Turner Award of the Organization of American Historians. His major work focuses on the history of American ideas and culture.

Melvin I. Urofsky is Professor of History at Virginia Commonwealth University in Richmond, Virginia, and the author of several works on modern American constitutional history. His recent works include the widely used text *A March of Liberty* (1987), *A Conflict of Rights* (1991) about the Supreme Court and affirmative action, and a new biography of Justice Felix Frankfurter.

Table of Cases

Index

ABA. *See* American Bar Association
ACLU. *See* American Civil Liberties Union
Abortion rights, 3, 21, 190, 202
Adams, John, 5, 124, 125
Adolescent Family Life Act (1981), 70
Adultery, 21
Affirmative action, 230; and the burden on employers, 164–65, 166, 168; and the Civil Rights Act of 1964, 155–57; and Congress, 165–70; and preferential hiring, 158–61; and quotas, 159–63; and race norming, 169–70; and racial classification, 170–73. *See also* Title VII of the Civil Rights Act of 1964
American Bar Association (ABA), 11, 53–54
American Civil Liberties Union (ACLU), 12, 15, 50, 104, 201
American Family Association, 56
American Nazis, 42
American Revolution, 5–6, 9, 41, 75–76
Amish, 63, 69
Anti-Defamation League, 40
Anti-Federalists, vii, 26, 178
Aptitude tests, and affirmative action, 164
Arms. *See* Rights: to keep and bear arms
Art, 18, 39; flag desecration as, 51
Artisans, 8
Assembly, rights of, 7, 16
Assize of Arms of 1181, 73

Bail, excessive, 6, 215*n*1
Bail Reform Act of 1984, 114
Balancing test, for reasonable searches, 126
Beard, Charles, 12
Belief vs. action in religious expression, 61–62
Benson, Egbert, 125–26, 182
Berger, Raoul, 152, 182–83, 216*n*37, 231
Bible reading, 63, 199
Bickel, Alexander M., 30, 177
Bigamy, 21, 61
Bigotry, Minnesota law against, 39–41
Bill of Rights (U.S. Constitution), 14, 194, 201; application of, 26, 116, 194; Constitution as, 25; construction of, 3, 7–8, 223; intention of, 73; nationalization of through the Fourteenth Amendment, vii, 14, 20, 29, 83, 103–6, 121–22, 191, 195–97; origin of, 178–79; and property rights, 87; and right to privacy, 201; and the states, 26,

111, 194; as written document, 19. *See also* Rights; *specific amendments*; States: bills of rights in
Bingham, Jonathan, 79–80
Bird, Chief Justice Rose, 204
Black, Charles, 231
Black, Justice Hugo, 32, 105; on the Constitution, 14, 33–34; on emotive expression, 47; on the establishment of religion clause, 57, 58, 59, 64, 66, 67; on the Second Amendment, 83; on symbolic dress, 45, 52
Black codes, 79, 81
Blackmun, Justice Harry A., 117, 118; on affirmative action, 170; on cross-burning, 40–41; on the death penalty, 146; on emotive expression, 47; on the establishment of religion clause, 71; on property rights, 97
Blackstone, Sir William, 74
Booth, Sherman, 196
Bork, Robert, 21, 177, 179–80, 181, 189, 223–24
Boston Tea Party, 41
Brandeis, Justice Louis D., 41, 138
Brennan, Justice William J., Jr., 48, 102, 105, 147, 148, 203, 204; on affirmative action, 161, 162–63, 171; on the death penalty, 145, 153, 216*n*37; on the establishment of religion clause, 61, 67–68; on federalism, 192, 193, 205; on flag burning, 52–53, 54–55; on the free exercise of religion clause, 62–63; on the right to privacy, 130
Brooks, Jack, 54
Burger, Chief Justice Warren, 43, 102; on business necessity, 159; on cruel and unusual punishment, 142–43; on the death penalty, 146; and due process, 112–14; on emotive expression, 47; on the establishment of religion clause, 66, 67; on federalism, 193; and free exercise of religion clause, 69
Burger Court: and due process, 102, 112–14; and the religion clauses of the First Amendment, 63–64
Bush, George, 53, 54, 102; and affirmative action, 161, 167, 168; and federalism, 192, 193
Business necessity: and affirmative action, 159, 160, 164, 165–66, 168–69, 218*n*29

Cable television, 93
Cadena temporal, 144